Windows Server 2012: Up and Running

Samara Lynn

O'REILLY®

Beijing · Cambridge · Farnham · Köln · Sebastopol · Tokyo

Windows Server 2012: Up and Running

by Samara Lynn

Published by O'Reilly Media, Inc., 1005 Gravenstein Highway North, Sebastopol, CA 95472.

O'Reilly books may be purchased for educational, business, or sales promotional use. Online editions are also available for most titles (*http://my.safaribooksonline.com*). For more information, contact our corporate/institutional sales department: 800-998-9938 or *corporate@oreilly.com*.

Editor: Rachel Roumeliotis	**Proofreader:** Rebecca Freed
Production Editor: Holly Bauer	**Indexer:** Lucie Haskins
Copyeditor: Rachel Monaghan	**Cover Designer:** Randy Comer
	Interior Designer: David Futato
	Illustrator: Rebecca Demarest

December 2012:   First Edition

Revision History for the First Edition:

2012-11-09   First release

See *http://oreilly.com/catalog/errata.csp?isbn=9781449320751* for release details.

ISBN: 978-1-449-32075-1

[LSI]

Table of Contents

Preface

About This Book

Windows Server 2012 is not only the most significant update to the Windows Server operating system in recent years, but it is also all about cloud computing and the underlying technology for building clouds: virtualization.

Many features familiar to administrators of Server 2008 R2 and other legacy Windows Server versions have been updated in one way or another in Windows Server 2012, and this book introduces readers to the new features and capabilities.

There are two especially important concepts to keep in mind while reading this book. First, Server 2012 is all about the deployment, configuration, and management of cloud platforms—whether they are private, hybrid, or public clouds. Second, Server 2012 also centers on integrating workers' private mobile devices into the corporate network.

Audience

While it would probably suffice to say that this book is for any person interested in learning about the new capabilities of Windows Server 2012, this book does assume a certain level of experience in managing or deploying Windows networks, in particular with user accounts and permissions, Active Directory, DHCP (Dynamic Host Configuration Protocol), DNS (Domain Name System), and other major and fundamental Windows networking services and concepts. Anyone from novices to seasoned Windows system administrators can benefit from the small- to midsize-business test infrastructure deployment examples provided in the book.

Goals of This Book

This book focuses on the new features and capabilities that make Server 2012 an operating system tailored for the cloud. My goal is to get Windows system administrators acquainted with the new features by providing examples of deploying and configuring them.

New ways of managing virtual networks and storage, improved Unified Remote Access options, and advancements in storage with a new filesystem are some of the features you'll learn about that make Server 2012 "future forward." Step-by-step instructions—complete with screenshots—walk you through deploying and configuring what's new and what's been enhanced. All screenshots and instructions are based on actual deployment and configuration in a test environment as well as whitepaper documentation from Microsoft's TechNet.

Contents of This Book

Chapter 1 and Chapter 2 provide background on the development of Windows Server 2012, editions and licensing, requirements, and installation.

The subsequent chapters delve into specific features.

Chapter 3 and Chapter 4 cover new ways to manage Windows Server and new capabilities in Active Directory.

Chapter 5 introduces Dynamic Access Control and provides examples for deployment.

Chapter 6 and Chapter 7 detail advancements in and configuration of storage, clustering, and Hyper-V.

Chapter 8 focuses on new networking capabilities and outlines steps for deployment.

Chapter 9 covers Unified Remote Access.

Chapter 10 explores new ways to troubleshoot Windows Sever 2012 and additional management information.

Conventions Used in This Book

The following typographical conventions are used in this book:

Plain text

> Indicates menu titles, menu options, menu buttons, and keyboard accelerators (such as Alt and Ctrl).

Italic

> Indicates new terms, URLs, email addresses, filenames, file extensions, pathnames, directories, and Unix utilities.

`Constant width`

> Indicates commands, options, switches, variables, attributes, keys, functions, types, classes, namespaces, methods, modules, properties, parameters, values, objects, events, event handlers, XML tags, HTML tags, macros, the contents of files, or the output from commands.

`Constant width bold`

> Shows commands or other text that should be typed literally by the user.

`Constant width italic`

> Shows text that should be replaced with user-supplied values.

This icon signifies a tip, suggestion, or general note.

This icon indicates a warning or caution.

Using Code Examples

This book is here to help you get your job done. In general, you may use the code in this book in your programs and documentation. You do not need to contact us for permission unless you're reproducing a significant portion of the code. For example, writing a program that uses several chunks of code from this book does not require permission. Selling or distributing a CD-ROM of examples from O'Reilly books does require permission. Answering a question by citing this book and quoting example code does not require permission. Incorporating a significant amount of example code from this book into your product's documentation does require permission.

We appreciate, but do not require, attribution. An attribution usually includes the title, author, publisher, and ISBN. For example: "*Windows Server 2012: Up and Running*, by Samara Lynn (O'Reilly). Copyright 2013 Samara Lynn, 978-1-449-32075-1."

If you feel your use of code examples falls outside fair use or the permission given above, feel free to contact us at *permissions@oreilly.com*.

Comments and Questions

Please address comments and questions concerning this book to the publisher:

O'Reilly Media, Inc.
1005 Gravenstein Highway North
Sebastopol, CA 95472
(800) 998-9938 (in the United States or Canada)
(707) 829-0515 (international or local)
(707) 829-0104 (fax)

We have a web page for this book, where we list errata, examples, and any additional information. You can access this page at *http://oreil.ly/Win_Server_2012_UaR*.

To comment or ask technical questions about this book, send email to *bookques tions@oreilly.com*.

For more information about our books, courses, conferences, and news, see our website at *http://www.oreilly.com*.

Find us on Facebook: *http://facebook.com/oreilly*

Follow us on Twitter: *http://twitter.com/oreillymedia*

Watch us on YouTube: *http://www.youtube.com/oreillymedia*

Safari® Books Online

Safari Books Online (*www.safaribooksonline.com*) is an on-demand digital library that delivers expert content in both book and video form from the world's leading authors in technology and business.

Technology professionals, software developers, web designers, and business and creative professionals use Safari Books Online as their primary resource for research, problem solving, learning, and certification training.

Safari Books Online offers a range of product mixes and pricing programs for organizations, government agencies, and individuals. Subscribers have access to thousands of books, training videos, and prepublication manuscripts in one fully searchable database from publishers like O'Reilly Media, Prentice Hall Professional, Addison-Wesley Professional, Microsoft Press, Sams, Que, Peachpit Press, Focal Press, Cisco Press, John Wiley & Sons, Syngress, Morgan Kaufmann, IBM Redbooks, Packt, Adobe Press, FT Press, Apress, Manning, New Riders, McGraw-Hill, Jones & Bartlett, Course Technology, and dozens more. For more information about Safari Books Online, please visit us online.

Acknowledgments

A big thank you goes to Rachel Roumeliotis for her patience and guidance in this effort, to the O'Reilly editors, and to Rick Vanover for lending his technical expertise. Also, thank you to family and friends for their support. I would also like to thank Mary Jo Foley, an inspiration to me and other technology journalists—especially women in this field.

CHAPTER 1

Windows Server 2012: Overview

Introducing Windows Server 2012

The purpose of this book is to introduce and familiarize system administrators, or anyone who needs to get up and running with Windows Server 2012, with the platform's major new features and improvements and how to implement them. First, I'll offer a little background on the evolution of Microsoft's newest server operating system.

Three years after the launch of Windows Server 2008 R2, Microsoft unveiled Windows Server 2012, its latest server operating system. Server 2012 is the most significant server release since the update from Windows Server NT 3.51 to NT 4.0, which introduced the modern graphical interface to Windows Server.

Server 2012 is just as significant because, arguably, for the first time in a Windows Server release, it represents a server product based on the needs and wants of consumers rather than solely on the needs of the enterprise.

Server 2012 is designed for compatibility with and support for three major and current computing trends, all driven primarily by consumer demand: cloud computing, virtualization, and the continued "consumerization of IT," which is the surging demand from the workforce to use personal technology devices—in particular, mobile devices—in the work environment.

Microsoft has engineered Server 2012 to meet these three market trends with several upgrades and enhancements. Virtualization and cloud computing needs are met by new virtualization technologies baked into Hyper-V 3.0. Some of the capabilities include the ability to connect a datacenter to a public cloud, and features that allow system administrators to build hybrid and multitenant private clouds. Server hardware, storage, and networks can be virtualized, thereby reducing power costs, centralizing administration, and allowing for fast and efficient scalability as an infrastructure grows.

The consumerization of IT is a trend that has been of particular consternation to the field. As personal technology devices become more sophisticated and ubiquitous, people increasingly want to use their personal devices in the office. IT has to perform the delicate balancing act between maintaining control over the business networks that these devices access and delivering a rich user experience.

Server 2012 lends itself to navigating this balancing act with enhancements to Remote Desktop Services (RDS) and Virtual Desktop Infrastructure (VDI). Microsoft has made WAN-side improvements in VDI so that the remote desktop experience is as robust as connecting to apps and network resources within a LAN. Administration of Remote Desktop Services and remote clients is now centralized in an updated *Server Manager*, a one-stop shop that compiles all the primary tools a system administrator needs to manage a Windows infrastructure in a single interface.

Security improvements accommodate employees' personal devices to prevent data leakage, to retain strong access controls, and to adhere to compliance regulations such as Sarbanes-Oxley (SOX) and the Health Insurance Portability and Accountability Act (HIPAA). Overall, these are improvements with *Dynamic Access Control* (DAC)—the control over security and compliance in an organization in continuous and periodic intervals.

Server 2012 not only meets the changing technology needs of the workplace, but it also rolls out new capabilities and beefed-up legacy features. There is an abundance of new features and enhancements, some of them "under the hood" and not readily apparent to a user.

New Capabilities and Updated Features

Here's a quick, at-a-glance overview of some of those new features and enhancements.

Installation and Interface

Installation options for Server 2012 carry over from Server 2008 R2. As with Server 2008 R2, Server 2012 installs in two primary ways: Server Core or Server with a GUI (graphical user interface).

Server Core installation is the default option and reduces the amount of system resources needed to run a GUI install, optimizing server performance. A Server Core install reduces the amount of disk space needed as well as the servicing requirements and the server's potential attack surface.

Server with a GUI installation is the same as the Full Installation option in Server 2008 R2. The full graphical interface of Server 2012 is loaded, including the new Windows 8–like, modern UI–style interface and all the graphical tools needed to manage the server.

A new installation feature is the ability to switch between install options. For example, you may initially opt for the Server with a GUI install and use the graphical tools to configure the server. You can then switch to the Server Core installation and take advantage of its resource conservation and security.

This ability to switch between installation options creates an intermediary installation state called *Minimal Server Interface*. This interface is the result of starting with the Server with a GUI installation and then switching over to a Server Core install. With Minimal Server Interface, the Microsoft Management Console (MMC), Server Manager, and a subset of Control Panel are installed.

Whichever installation option you choose, you can remove any binary files for features and server roles you don't need. This is made possible by the new *Features on Demand* capability. Because you can cherry-pick features, you can still save disk space and reduce the server's attack surface after performing a Server with a GUI installation.

The new interface loaded after a Server with a GUI install is based on the tiled interface of the Windows 8 client. You can use this interface to perform common administrative tasks such as searching for and opening common management tools, creating shortcuts to frequently used programs, and running programs with elevated permissions. Programs like Internet Explorer are now Windows 8–style apps and work in very much the same way that mobile apps do; instead of being closed, apps are minimized in the background and become inactive.

Management

Server Manager, introduced in the first release of Windows Server 2008, provides server management based on server roles such as Active Directory Domain Services, Domain Name System (DNS), and Dynamic Host Configuration Protocol (DHCP). In Server 2012, Server Manager has a tile-based, modern interface. In addition to managing the local server, Server Manager now supports multiserver management.

Most administrative tasks can now be performed through the updated Server Manager utility. These tasks include deploying features and roles remotely to physical and virtual servers.

Server Manager now integrates other management tools such as RDS, IPAM (Internet protocol address management), Hyper-V, and file and storage management. Administrators can use the enhanced Server Manager dashboard as a centralized launching point for most server management tools.

Active Directory (AD) is also fundamental in managing a Windows environment, and improvements have been made in Active Directory Domain Services. `dcpromo`, the command used to promote domain controllers, is integrated within the Server Manager dashboard. The Active Directory installation wizard, built on PowerShell, is easier than ever to use, due to prerequisite checks and remediation actions in the case of installation issues—all part of the install process. An AD install can also be launched remotely with RSAT (Remote Server Administration Tools) installed on the Windows 8 client.

Management, as well as security, is strengthened with Dynamic Access Control. You can tag files and apply policies based on file classification. For instance, files can be tagged as "Human Resources only," and policies can be set to limit access only to the Human Resources groups. New support for expressions in access control lists (i.e., setting up permissions using an expression such as "User is member of <this group> AND/OR <that group>") gives granular access control management.

Central access policies and claims-based definitions also help manage security and verify user authentication across an organization. Access-denied remediation allows administrators to troubleshoot "access denied" messages users may receive when accessing files and folders, and allow administrators to give on-the-fly access if needed. File and folder classifications, such as classifying documents as "Internal only" or "Confidential" is done through the File System Resource Manager.

The familiar tool CHKDSK, used to check volumes for problems, has been enhanced. Microsoft claims that CHKDSK can check 300 million files in eight seconds while volumes are still online and running.

Windows PowerShell 3.0

Microsoft encourages system administrators to perform many server management tasks using enhanced PowerShell scripting with Server 2012. In the past, using PowerShell required learning the cmdlets (pronounced "commandlets") and syntax needed to manage a Windows environment. Many system administrators simply found using the graphical management tools easier.

PowerShell 3.0 eases that learning curve in several ways. First, PowerShell 3.0 uses a simplified language syntax that is closer to natural language. Also, improved cmdlet discovery plus automatic module loading makes finding and running cmdlets easier than ever. The Windows PowerShell Integrated Scripting Environment (ISE) 3.0 helps PowerShell beginners with scripting and gives advanced editing support.

 Server 2012 includes over 140 new PowerShell cmdlets for managing networking features and Hyper-V.

Storage

ReFS (Resilient File System) is a new local filesystem introduced in Server 2012. ReFS is designed to work with extremely large storage capacity, up into the petabytes. ReFS is tailored to use in conjunction with Storage Spaces (explained next). With ReFS, mirrored Storage Spaces can detect and automatically repair corruption.

The *Storage Spaces* feature allows virtualizing storage in Server 2012. In Storage Spaces, storage pools are created and a storage space is allocated from a storage pool. Windows sees this storage space as a virtual disk. Because this storage is virtualized, organizations do not need to invest in additional hardware for storage, so there are some savings associated with the feature as well as flexibility in expanding storage when the need arises.

Data deduplication—the automated find and removal of duplicate data, particularly in backup jobs—is an inherent feature in Server 2012. Data dedupe allows for more storage with less space.

File and storage management can be administered through Server Manager's File and Storage Services and Storage Service. Both are available in Server Manager, but can also be launched and configured with PowerShell.

Remote Access

Remote access has been enhanced and Server 2012 engineered to provide *unified remote access*, the concept of managing remote access across an organization from a single console within Server Manager.

Under the umbrella of unified remote access are two improved features: DirectAccess and BranchCache. DirectAccess allows end users to connect to corporate resources seamlessly, and its deployment has been improved in Server 2012 from Server 2008 R2. BranchCache allows storing data in remote (or branch) offices, and in Server 2012, remote access to that data is more efficient.

In addition to managing remote access from the GUI with Server Manager, Server 2012 allows user to deploy remote access through PowerShell commands.

On the client side, remote desktops now have the option of the Windows 8–style interface with its tiles and mobile operating system capabilities. Remote clients also have a rich user experience through enhanced RemoteFX, which provides 3D graphics and Voice over IP (VoIP) to remote users.

Networking

A significant new networking feature is network interface card (NIC) teaming, which allows you to join multiple network cards into a single, logical NIC. NIC teaming provides network connection failover or link aggregation, increasing network speeds. Prior to Server 2012, NIC teaming was achievable in Windows servers only through third-party solutions and only with the appropriate hardware. NIC teaming is now a native capability in Server 2012 and in Hyper-V 3.0.

Internet protocol address management is another new networking feature. With IPAM, administrators can perform IP address discovery, import IP address information into spreadsheets for asset management, monitor DHCP and DNS, track IP address changes (as well as monitor suspicious addresses), and more.

The Domain Name System Security Extensions (DNSSEC) feature helps protect DNS traffic from threats. In Server 2012, DNSSEC has been made simpler to deploy and integrates with Active Directory.

Several networking features have been boosted in Server 2012's virtualization technology, Hyper-V. These include network QoS and network metering.

Hyper-V 3.0

A large number of major updates and new features can be found within Server 2012's virtualization platform, Hyper-V. Hyper-V has been enhanced in such a large way that technology pundits are making the case that Microsoft's virtualization capabilities are now on a level with established competitors in the virtualization space like Citrix and VMware.

Because there are so many new capabilities and enhancements in Hyper-V 3.0, it's easiest to break them down by category:

Multitenancy and isolation have been improved with:

- Private virtual local area networks (PVLANs) that provide isolation between two virtual machines on the same LAN.
- Virtual port access control lists (port ACLs) provide a method of controlling which network traffic passes to virtual machines, based on IP and MAC addresses.
- The Hyper-V extensible switch allows third parties to write software that extends the management of Hyper-V. Potential applications include traffic monitoring, firewall filters, and ways to detect network intruders.

Multitenancy occurs when an organization hosts several different virtual infrastructures in one physical environment. Companies that host services for multiple customers on one platform have multitenant environments. One customer's data has to be kept from another customer's, even if that data resides on the same physical hardware. Isolation is keeping control over who has access to specific virtualized resources.

Flexibility and scalability:

- Enhanced live migration means online and running virtual machines can be migrated from one host to another without downtime.
- With a new import wizard, administrators can import virtual machines from one host to another. The import wizard also detects and assists in problem remediation.
- Live merge allows merging virtual machine snapshots back into a virtual machine while it's still online and running.

Performance:

- Resource metering gives the power to track how much CPU, memory, storage, and network resources are used by a virtual machine.
- Virtual Hard Disk Format (VHDX) aids in boosting performance on large-sector disks. VHDX supports up to 16 TB of storage and has mechanisms to guard against corruption as well as performance degradation.
- Support for 4 KB disk sectors is a new feature for supporting large disk sectors to keep up with storage innovations. The data storage industry is transitioning the physical format of hard disk drives from 512-byte sectors to 4,096-byte sectors (also known as 4 K or 4 KB sectors). This transition is driven by several factors, including increases in storage density and reliability.

  However, most of the software industry has depended on disk sectors of 512 bytes in length. A change in sector size introduces compatibility issues in many applications. The storage industry is introducing 4 KB physical-format drives to provide increased capacity.
- QoS (quality of service) minimum bandwidth is a new feature that allows virtual machines and services to be assigned a minimum level of bandwidth and prioritization. QoS is important because it gives administrators the ability to specify which virtual machines should be given bandwidth priority and provides a means of predicting network performance. For organizations that host services for customers, QoS allows them to adhere to customers' service-level agreements (SLAs), which guarantee those customers a minimum amount of bandwidth for accessing a hosted service.

High availability:

- The new Hyper-V supports incremental backup of virtual hard disks while the virtual machine is running.
- Improved Hyper-V clustering provides protection against application and service failure, and system and hardware failure.

Storage:

- Unlimited live storage migration gives users the ability to perform multiple live simultaneous migrations. Clustered environments can use higher network bandwidths (up to 10 GB).
- Cluster Shared Volumes can integrate with storage arrays for replication and hardware snapshots.
- Virtual Fibre Channel allows for connecting virtual operating systems to storage arrays, integrating virtual machines with storage array networks (SANs).

You can perform many more Hyper-V administration and management tasks through PowerShell. PowerShell cmdlets are also available for configuring and managing storage and networking for both VMs and the hosts within Hyper-V.

In addition to these new features and improvements, Hyper-V hosts now support up to 320 logical processes and up to 4 TB of memory. Virtual machines support up to 64 virtual processors and up to 1 TB of memory.

IIS 8

Server 2012 introduces the new Internet Information Services 8 (IIS 8) and ASP.NET 4.5. New features in IIS include more robust security: IIS protects websites from external threats such as brute-force web and FTP attacks, and offers defense against DoS (denial of service) attacks.

IIS can now use a large number of processor cores more efficiently, keeping up with advances in server hardware. Centralized SSL (Secure Sockets Layer) certificate support enables you to store SSL certificates in a central location and automatically bind them to web applications.

IIS CPU throttling is a new feature administrators can use to increase a web application's processor time to ratchet up performance as needed, and it can be used to scale down processor time when that app's usage returns to normal levels.

Security

Data security is provided by new features that we've already addressed, such as Dynamic Access Control, which provides data governance and tight control over user authentication and verification of user identity across an organization. In Hyper-V, inherent security provides the ability to isolate virtualized networks in multitenant environments.

IIS 8 also has security mechanisms such as FTP logon restrictions, which aid in preventing brute-force attacks against an FTP server.

In addition to security already available in these features, *BitLocker*, a data protection feature introduced in Windows Vista, has also undergone upgrading in Server 2012. BitLocker is a security method that can be enabled on both the server end and on the Windows 8 client side. For extra security, BitLocker can be deployed on machines that support *Trusted Platform Module* (TPM), a hardware component available in newer computers that helps protect user data and guard against any tampering with a system while that system is offline.

In Server 2012 (and in Windows 8 client), BitLocker has some enhancements. Server 2012 and Windows 8 client are both now deployable to an encrypted state during install.

BitLocker now offers two encryption options: Full Volume Encryption, and Used Disk Space Only, where only used blocks on a targeted volume are encrypted, allowing for quicker encryption.

BitLocker passwords on data volumes can be changed as well as PIN numbers and passwords on client machines.

On a trusted wired network, BitLocker systems can be enabled to automatically unlock the operating system volume during boot.

Finally, Server 2012 includes BitLocker support for Windows Failover Cluster Shared Volumes on Windows Server "8" Beta running the Windows Failover Cluster feature.

Clustering

Clustering is grouping separate servers into one group to act as a single system. It provides high availability in case a server goes down. In Server 2012, advancements have been made in clustering both physical and virtual servers.

A failover cluster now supports up to 64 nodes. Improvements to the validation wizard and the migration wizard in failover clustering make it easier to set up clustered file servers as well as migrate existing clustered servers to new clusters.

In Hyper-V 3.0, failover clustering supports up to 4,000 virtual machines. An improved Cluster Shared Volume feature eases the configuration and operation of clustered virtual machines.

Cluster-Aware Updating (CAU) is a role that allows administrators to schedule automatic updates to clustered servers with no downtime during the update process.

Requirements

Server 2012's hardware requirements include a minimum 1.4 GHz 64-bit processor, 512 MB RAM, and 32 GB of free disk space.

Upgrades from Server 2008 R2 are supported.

Summary

Almost every feature and capability present in Server 2008 R2 has been upgraded or enhanced in Server 2012. These enhancements, along with the new features, make for a very extensive feature set in Server 2012. A vast number of these new and improved features are native within the operating system and require no user interaction. These features and improvements are ones commonly deployed in an organization, from small to midsize businesses to enterprises.

In the following chapters, I'll take you step by step through deploying and configuring the new capabilities and improvements in Server 2012.

CHAPTER 2

Windows Server 2012 Requirements and Installation

In this chapter, you will learn about the available editions of Server 2012 and which version is right for your organization. In addition, you will discover the hardware requirements for installing Server 2012 as well as what's required for deploying Hyper-V.

This chapter also outlines which upgrade paths from legacy Microsoft server products are supported and details step-by-step procedures for each installation option: Server Core and Server with a GUI. Also, I'll give instructions on how to convert from one Server 2012 interface to another—and explain why an administrator would want to do so—as well as explain how to deploy the Minimal Server Interface and customize the server features using Features on Demand.

Server 2012 Editions

Windows Server 2012 is currently available in four editions, also known as *SKUs* (an acronym for "stock keeping units"). As with the last server release—Server 2008 R2— all SKUs are available only in 64-bit; no 32-bit SKUs are available. Microsoft has done away with the Enterprise SKU of Server 2008 R2 in an attempt to streamline versioning and licensing. The four currently available editions are Windows Server 2012 Datacenter, Windows Server 2012 Standard, Windows Server 2012 Essentials, and Windows Server 2012 Foundation.

Pricing for each edition can vary, of course, based on the number of servers as well as every user or device accessing the server directly or indirectly. Each user and device requires its own CAL (client access license).

To give you a general idea of pricing, here is the cost of each edition for an open, no-level estimated retail price:

Datacenter
>   Processor and CAL: $4,809

Standard
>   Processor and CAL: $882

Essentials
>   Server (and up to 25 users): $425

Foundation
>   Server (and up to 15 users): OEM (original equipment manufacturer) only (i.e., has to be preinstalled with server hardware)

Server 2012 Datacenter

The Datacenter edition is the beefiest offering of Server 2012 and is designed for enterprises. If your organization is heavily dependent on virtualization and cloud deployments, then the Datacenter edition is the best option.

High availability is a key advantage with Datacenter because you can *hot-add* and *hot-replace* processors as well as hot-replace memory. "Hot" in this context refers to the ability to replace and add these components without needing to shut down the server.

Datacenter supports an unlimited number of virtual machines (VMs) running on up to two processors. In addition, Datacenter supports unlimited network and remote access connections; the number of connections is limited only by available network bandwidth and any hardware constraints. This is the edition to go with if your network needs enterprise-class virtualization and high scalability, because you can quickly expand the server to meet the demands of an organization that adds lots of users and resources such as data and devices.

Datacenter customers will typically purchase volume licenses. Volume licenses can also be purchased through Microsoft's Software Assurance program (*http://www.micro soft.com/licensing/about-licensing/how-volume-licensing-works.aspx*). Licensing costs are based on the size of the business and number of PCs and devices that need to connect to the server. If your organization will use many virtual machines, needs a cloud-ready platform, and has hundreds of clients, your best option is the Datacenter edition.

Server 2012 Standard

The Standard edition of Server 2012 is suited for midsize organizations without heavy virtualization demands and those that run most business applications and systems on-site. Enterprise offers the same features as Datacenter, except you can run only up to two VMs on two processors.

Server 2012 Essentials

Server 2012 Essentials is the server edition suited for smaller organizations (fewer than 25 PCs, devices, and/or end users). This edition does not offer Hyper-V, provides a limited-application server role, and offers no Windows Server Update Services (WSUS). Essentials can run on a server with up to two processors.

Server 2012 Foundation

Foundation is a small-business edition that comes preinstalled only on servers targeted for the SMB (small to midsize business) market. It's ideal for small businesses with no more than 15 users. Foundation does not include Hyper-V or Windows Server Update Services. It has partial or limited file services, network policy and access services, and limited remote desktop services.

If your organization has existing server licenses and CALs in place for legacy Windows Server, some of that licensing may be honored and applied to a Windows Server 2012 upgrade. Consult Microsoft's Windows Server 2012 licensing FAQ (*http://bit.ly/ RnPa1I*) to determine which licensing model your organization should go with.

Server 2012 Requirements

Server 2012 has specific hardware requirements for installation, despite the edition you are installing. Minimum requirements are:

- 1.4 GHz x64 processor (only 64-bit server architecture is supported)
- 512 MB of RAM
- 32 GB of free disk space
- DVD-ROM
- Super VGA (800 × 600) or higher resolution monitor
- Keyboard
- Mouse or compatible pointing device

Keep in mind, if you are installing Server 2012 on a system with more than 12 GB of RAM, you will need more than 32 GB of disk space for paging, hibernation, and dump files. You also will need more memory if you're installing over a network.

Also, remember these are minimum requirements with no roles added to the installation. For the optimal installation experience, use the best hardware possible, and if you have to bump up any specification and are working within a limited hardware budget, splurge on the most memory you can. Currently, most servers—especially ones targeted to small to midsize businesses—ship by default with at least 2 GB of RAM.

Hyper-V 3.0 Requirements

Adding the Hyper-V role to Server 2012 requires some particular server specifications. If you plan to add the Hyper-V role to Server 2012, you need to increase the minimum hardware requirements for Hyper-V.

Deploying Hyper-V in Server 2012 requires:

- A 64-bit AMD-V or Intel-VT virtualization-capable processor.
- At minimum, 4 GB of RAM to run up to four virtual machines. Take note, this memory requirement differs from the minimum memory requirement needed to install only Server 2012. If you plan to run five or more virtual machines, plan on more memory.

Installing Server 2012

In this section, I give detailed instructions for installing Server 2012 in the two offered installation options: Server Core and Server with a GUI (graphical user interface). Before you install either server option, Microsoft recommends a few best practices; these are helpful to follow, although in my experiences, one of the must-do server installation preparation tasks is to research any possible compatibility issues with drivers and any applications that must run on a server. If you have a mission-critical business app, you don't want to install or upgrade to Server 2012 only to "break" that app—meaning rendering it completely useless. If the server has drivers and apps that are not compatible with Server 2012, you can still run into problems after install or upgrade, even after following Microsoft's best practices to the letter.

 Savvy server administrators will perform a new server upgrade or install on a test server not connected to the production environment. While budget limitations don't always allow IT to purchase backup server hardware identical to production hardware, it's a good idea to have an older server available that you can deploy Hyper-V on to set up virtual machines. This way, you can test a Server 2012 install or upgrade and then install any business-critical apps to ensure everything runs well together.

In addition to heading off any compatibility issues, follow these best practices to help make for a smooth install:

1. **Disconnect uninterruptible power supply (UPS) devices.** These and other UPS equipment are typically installed through a serial connection to a server. Since their connections can cause issues with the detection process during the server install, it's best to disconnect any UPS hardware before installing Server 2012.

2. **Back up servers.** Performing a backup job before installing or upgrading to Server 2012 is critical. Backups of not just data, but also server configuration and key infrastructure components such as DHCP, are recommended. In addition, you want to back up boot and system partitions and the system state data. Another way to back up configuration information is to create a backup set for Automated System Recovery.

3. **Disable antivirus and antimalware software.** Security software running during install or upgrade can interfere with both.

4. **If updgrading from Server 2008 R2, run Windows Memory Diagnostic.** Test for any potential memory issues during an upgrade by running Windows Memory Diagnostic in Server 2008 R2's Administrative Tools.

5. **Load third-party mass storage devices.** Sometimes, problems recognizing devices you are trying to install from, such as DVD drives or USB flash drives, crop up during installation. To prevent such problems, if the device's manufacturer has supplied a separate driver file, save the file in either the root directory of the media or, for AMD-based systems, into the *amd6* folder. To provide the driver during setup, on the disk selection page, click Load Driver (or press F6). You can browse to locate the driver or have Setup search the media.

6. **Configure Windows Firewall.** After an upgrade or install, server applications that must receive unsolicited inbound connections may fail until you create inbound firewall rules to allow them. Check with your application vendor to determine which ports and protocols are necessary for the application to run correctly.

 There is only one supported upgrade path to Server 2012 that will keep preexisting data and compatible programs intact. That path is an upgrade from Server 2008 R2. It is up to you, as a server administrator, to ensure that any programs installed on a Server 2008 R2 machine will not "break"—that is, be rendered inaccessible or unable to execute after upgrading to Server 2012.You can check which software is certified as compatible or will be made compatible with Windows Server 2012 by accessing this catalog on Microsoft's website (*http://www.windowsservercatalog.com/*). Upgrading any server running legacy Microsoft operating systems, including Server 2003 or Server 2008 non-R2, will require backing up all data residing on that server, performing a clean install of Server 2012, and then reinstalling applications.

Next, I'll detail step-by-step procedures for performing a Server Core installation and a Server with a GUI installation of Windows 2012.

Server Core Install

Starting with Server 2012, Microsoft recommends using the Server Core installation method. This is because Server Core's interface reduces the amount of space needed for installation as well as the potential attack surface of the server. No graphical shell means less of an entryway for malware and threats. Unless you need the additional graphical management tools and interface that come with a full installation, consider going with Server Core if you feel you are ready for that in a production capacity. Of course, if deploying Server Core, you are managing the server using Windows PowerShell. While PowerShell is easier to use in Server 2012 than in previous server versions—thanks to the now over 2,300 cmdlets as well as an enhanced Integrated System Environment that lets you easily search for the cmdlets you need to perform administrative tasks—for many administrators, using PowerShell still requires quite a learning curve.

 If you are not comfortable with your PowerShell skills and lack of a UI for troubleshooting, this is one reason to avoid Server Core.

PowerShell in Server 2012 remains context-sensitive. If you place, for example, a space between the wrong set of characters or switches within a command line, you will end up with the command not executing and, often, puzzling error messages upon running the command.

Some server tasks are simply easier to do within the GUI if you are not very familiar with using PowerShell. Server administration often means getting tasks done in a timely manner. Thus, it just makes sense that if a server task requires either having to search through and correctly enter the proper PowerShell commands or simply right-clicking somewhere in the server's interface, many administrators will still opt to do the latter.

Still, learning PowerShell for performing some administration shouldn't be dismissed. PowerShell offers advantages over GUI-based management when it comes to automating routine tasks. The new snippets feature, when enabled, will remember the syntax of your most commonly used PowerShell commands—an absolute time saver for server duties that have to be performed routinely. Many companies require regular security reports on who has access to what data on the network. You can use PowerShell to set up an automated script to run on a regular basis that will pull access control lists (ACLs) against files and folders on the network.

Although you have the choice to deploy Server 2012 as a Server Core or Server with a GUI install, a big advantage of Server 2012 is that it's easier than ever to use both the command line and the GUI for server administration. One of the biggest deployment advancements Server 2012 has over Server 2008 R2 is the ability to switch from Server Core to the Server with a GUI mode. Some applications require the GUI to install, so this flexibility comes in handy at those times when you absolutely need the full interface. We'll take a look later in the chapter at how to convert Server Core install into Server with a GUI.

In Server Core mode, you perform server management tasks using the command line, through Windows PowerShell, or remotely. These management tasks include adding, configuring, and uninstalling server roles such as DHCP.

By default, there are 13 server roles available when Server 2012 is installed in Server Core mode:

Active Directory Certificate Services
> AD CS allows for managing and installing public key certificates. Certificates provide extra security within a network because the identity of a user, device, or service is bound to a corresponding private key.

Active Directory Domain Services
> AD DS is a directory that stores and manages data used for communication between users and domains. AD DS controls user logins, authentication, and directory services. AD DS is central in Windows networks.

Dynamic Host Configuration Protocol service
> The DHCP service dynamically assigns IP addresses to devices on a network.

Domain Name System service
> The DNS service is used to resolve network host names and services by IP address on a network and/or for resolving Internet host names from IP addresses.

File Services
> File Services lets you centrally manage and provide access to files and directories on a network. File Server Resource Manager (FSRM), a suite of tools you can use to manage server resources on local or remote servers, is installed along with File Services.

Active Directory Lightweight Directory Services
> AD LDS provides directory services in much the same way that AD DS does, without the need to deploy domains and domain controllers.

Hyper-V
> Hyper-V 3.0 is Windows Server 2012's virtualization technology.

Print and Document Services

> Print and Document Services allows for sharing printers and scanners on a network and also provides centralized print server and network printer management. It also enables migrating print servers and deploying printer connections using Group Policy.

Streaming Media Services

> With Streaming Media Services, clients on a network can receive streamed multi-media content.

Web Server

> The Web Server role installs IIS (Internet Information Services) 8.0, allowing for website creation and hosting as well as deploying web applications in an organization.

Windows Server Update Services

> WSUS provides a centralized way to distribute Windows Updates to clients throughout a network.

Active Directory Rights Management Server

> AD RMS is a data protection technology that works with AD RMS–enabled applications to help safeguard digital information from unauthorized use. With it, you can define who can open, modify, print, forward, or take other actions with the information.

Routing and Remote Access Server

> RRAS provides remote users access to resources on a network.

A Server Core installation does not provide the graphical shell of Windows Server. There is no desktop experience available. In addition, Server Core does not provide the Microsoft Management Console (MMC). Administrative tasks you would perform in the MMC are done though the command prompt or PowerShell.

Of course, just because you go with a Server Core installation of Server 2012 does not mean you can't add management tools and features. Thanks to the new Features on Demand capability, you can add and remove components and management tools. Adding and removing features will be covered later in this chapter. For now, let's look at a step-by-step Server Core installation of Server 2012.

Server Core installation procedures

After you've inserted the installation media into the CD-ROM, DVD, or USB flash drive, or executed an install from the network, the install wizard begins. The first screen prompts you to click "Install now" to get the install process up and running (see Figure 2-1).

Figure 2-1. First screen of a Server 2012 installation

The install wizard then prompts you to select installation preferences such as language, time and currency format, and keyboard or other input device settings, as shown in Figure 2-2.

Figure 2-2. Installation preferences

Next, select the installation mode. For a Server Core install, the selection option is Windows Server 2012 Enterprise (Server Core Installation), as shown in Figure 2-3. Click Next to continue.

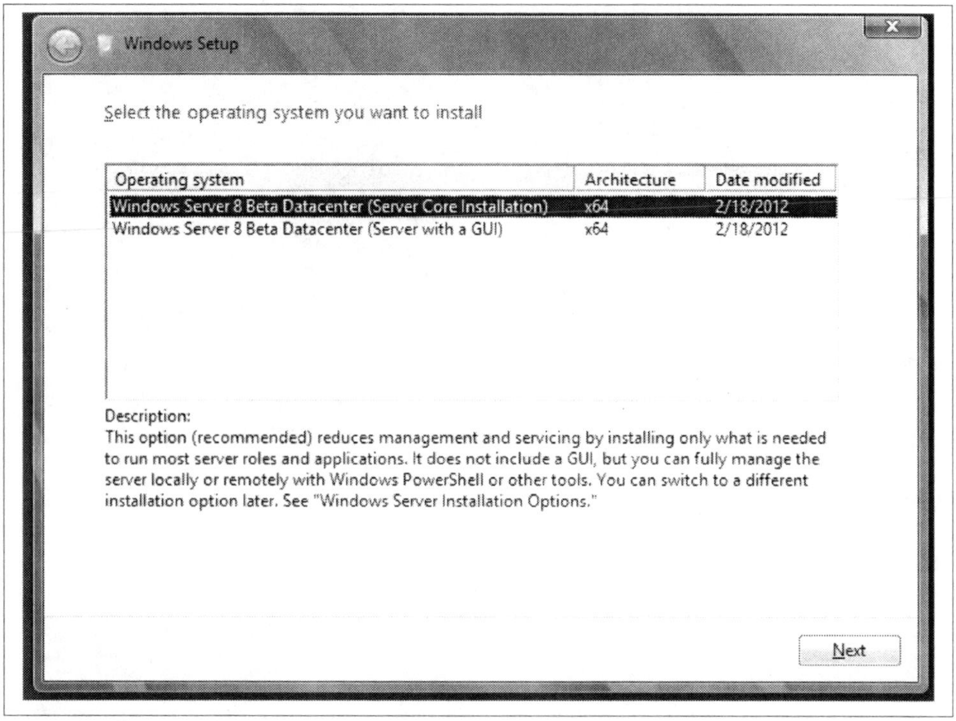

Figure 2-3. Server installation mode options

You are then asked to check a box to agree to the license terms. You cannot continue with installation if you don't check the box (see Figure 2-4). Once you do, click Next.

You'll then select the option to perform a fresh install of Server 2012 or an upgrade from Server 2008 R2 (see Figure 2-5). Select "Custom: Install Windows only (advanced)" for a new install, or "Upgrade: Install Windows and keep files, settings, and apps" for an upgrade.

Now, select how you want to partition drives and the location to install Server 2012, as shown in Figure 2-6. Typically, most server administrators will create a system partition for loading the server operating system. You can create another partition for the rest of the space on the hard drive(s) and then allocate it into volumes after install, depending on your storage needs.

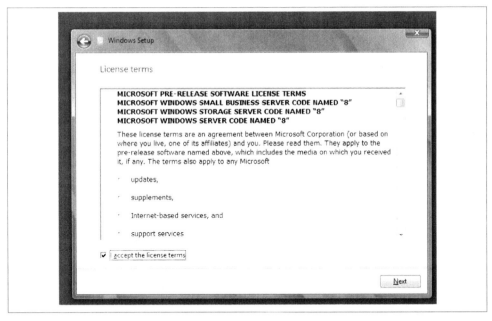

Figure 2-4. License terms agreement

Figure 2-5. Select the installation type: Custom for a new install, or Upgrade for upgrading from Server 2008 R2

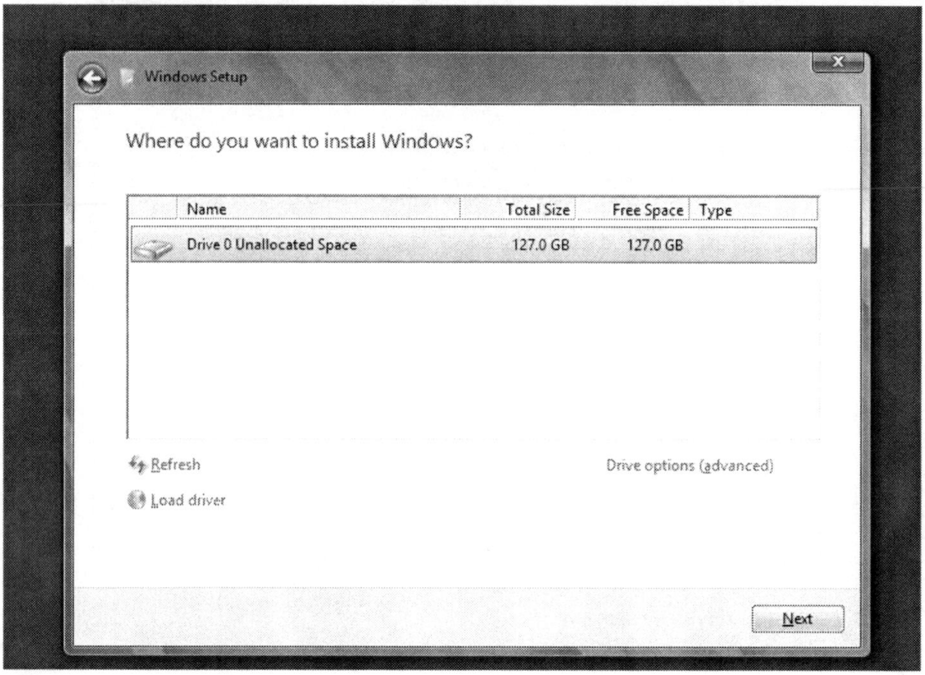

Figure 2-6. Setting up drive partitions

I do recommend installing the operating system—in this case, Server 2012—on its own system partition and then creating separate partitions to store data. The partition and volumes containing the server data are what is usually included in regularly scheduled backup jobs. This way, if the server gets damaged or corrupted, you can reinstall the OS if you have to and then can restore data from backup. This is good practice on small desktop servers with one or two drives, or larger rack-mounts with up to eight drives. Configurations will vary depending on any RAID (Redundant Array of Inexpensive Disks) configurations deployed, but it's best to keep the server install on a separate partition from data.

In this screen, you can also load third-party drivers that may be needed for Windows 2012 to recognize connected devices.

Windows then copies the server files to the hard disk, and after they're installed, Server Core installation is complete. The next screen you will see is the Administrator login window (see Figure 2-7). Windows will prompt you to create a local Administrator's password.

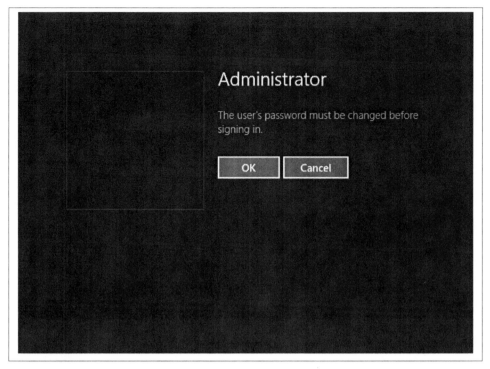

Figure 2-7. Initial local Administrator login

If you've worked with Windows Servers before, you'll notice that the interface changes in Server 2012's login screen from previous versions of Windows Server. One of the new interface features is an eyeball icon in the password field (see Figure 2-8). Clicking it and holding down the left mouse button after entering a password will change the password characters from asterisks to the actual values.

After you log into a Server Core install of Server 2012, all you will see is a command prompt screen—no desktop icons, no Start button, and no Windows Explorer (see Figure 2-9). Any tasks you perform after install must be done through the command line.

Figure 2-8. The eyeball icon changes asterisks to text

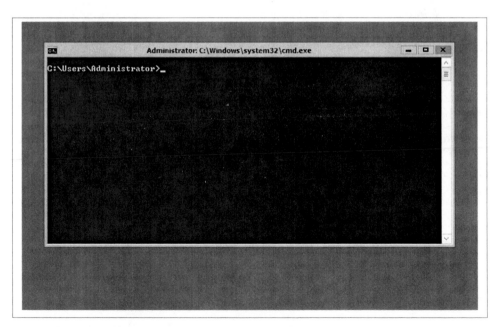

Figure 2-9. The Server Core install interface

Although the interface of Server Core is sparse, you can still perform almost any tasks from the command prompt. For example, install PowerShell by running the command **sconfig** at the command prompt (see Figure 2-10). You can also perform administrative duties from the command line—such as joining the server to a domain or workgroup, renaming the server, or configuring networking settings—and other tasks with the Sconfig utility.

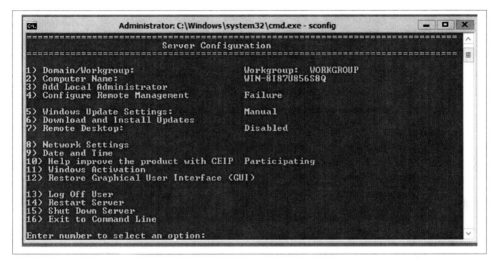

Figure 2-10. Running the Sconfig utility from the command prompt

Server with a GUI Install

The Server with a GUI installation option is equivalent to the Full Installation mode in Server 2008 R2. This option installs the full Windows Server standard interface and all of the management tools.

The Server 2012 interface includes the modern UI–style appearance of the Windows 8 client. However, support for Windows 8–style apps is not enabled by default. To enable it, you must install the Desktop Experience feature. Desktop Experience is installed through Server Manager or Windows PowerShell and is covered in Chapter 3.

Server with a GUI deployment requires about 4 GB more space than a Server Core installation. As with the Server Core installation mode, you are not stuck with the GUI interface if you choose to initially set up your server in Server with a GUI mode. Options for converting from a full installation are covered later in this chapter.

Many server administrators still feel more comfortable managing a server with the full graphical interface; however, as mentioned, there are advantages to using PowerShell to automate routine management tasks. If you have a relatively small network (fewer than 250 users and devices) to manage, and don't have a lot of experience with PowerShell, you may just want to get acquainted with Server 2012 through the GUI. You can always access and learn PowerShell later.

The beginning steps for performing a Server with a GUI install are similar to the Server Core installation process.

Server with a GUI installation procedures

In all likelihood, the Server with a GUI option is the install mode most server administrators will go with, especially when installing or upgrading Server 2012 for the first time.

Microsoft cites good reasons for its recommendation to install Server Core mode rather than the full GUI, such as security, saving on system resources, and even automating some tasks. However, I prefer having a full GUI. With GUI mode, you can always launch PowerShell. My preference is to have all management tools available. If you are a PowerShell guru who can script in your sleep, there are definite benefits, as stated, with a Server Core install. If you aren't proficient in PowerShell, a full GUI is the way to go—at least while you get acquainted with Server 2012.

The initial steps for a Server with a GUI install are the same as a Server Core install: insert your installation media into the server to boot into the install wizard, where you'll select install preferences and launch the install. The only difference is that the "Server with a GUI" option is selected instead of the "Server Core" option.

As with a Server Core install, you accept license terms, set up your partitions and drive configuration, and simply follow the install wizard.

After the GUI mode install finishes, you'll see the Ctrl-Alt-Delete page, which pulls up the login screen (see Figure 2-11). This page is the first introduction to the new Windows 8–style look in Server 2012.

Press Ctrl-Alt-Delete to bring up the local Administrator login screen, as shown in Figure 2-12.

Figure 2-11. Windows 8–style login

Figure 2-12. Administrator login screen

After login, Windows Services loads, personalized settings are established, and you are brought to the Server 2012 desktop. The Server Manager dashboard opens by default (see Figure 2-13). Server Manager has a tile-based interface refreshed from Server 2008 R2. Server Manager and other components of the full desktop interface are explored in more depth in Chapter 3.

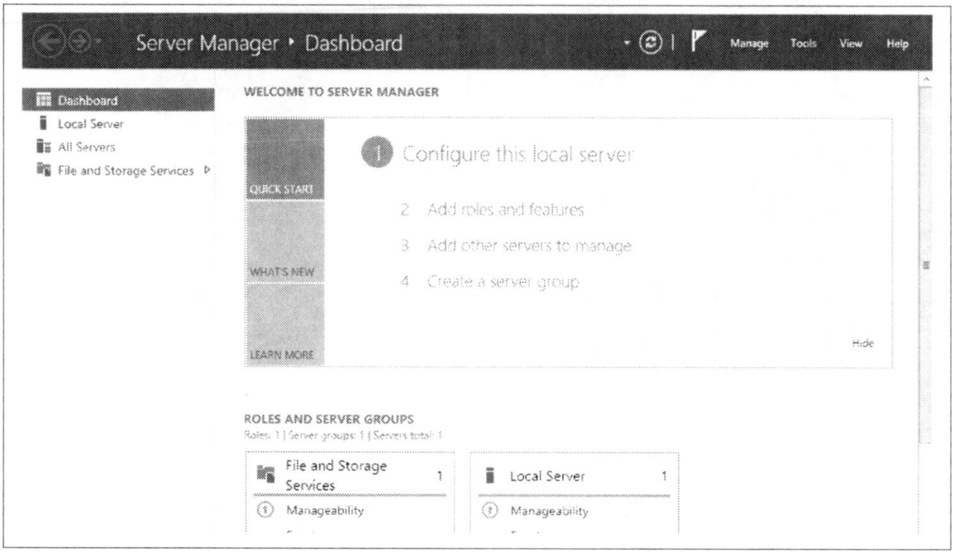

Figure 2-13. The new Server Manager dashboard

Switching Between Install Modes

No matter which installation option you chose, thanks to the flexibility of Server 2012, you can switch install modes after installation without losing existing configurations.

What are the benefits of switching from the full interface to a Server Core install or a Server Core install to the full interface? One reason could be the full install is consuming too many server resources. Maybe you want to reduce the threat attack surface that comes with a full installation. Or, perhaps you have become comfortable enough administering the server through PowerShell that you can afford to streamline the server and get rid of the full interface.

Whatever your reason, you have a couple of options to convert from the full install mode. You can convert through a simple PowerShell command, or you can remove the graphical shell of a full install to trim down to a core install.

Converting Server Core to Server with a GUI

To convert a Server Core install into a Server with a GUI install, you will need to create a folder to mount a Windows Imaging File (WIM). WIM files are images of the operating system and reside on the installation media, in the *sources* folder. The image file that gets mounted is the *install.wim* file, which is located inside the *sources* folder.

To get started, first run the command **mkdir** from the command prompt to create a directory named *mountdir*. The syntax is mkdir c:\mountdir. (See Figure 2-14.)

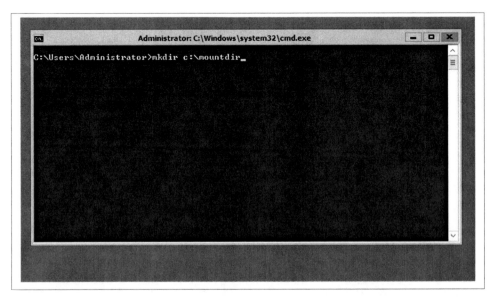

Figure 2-14. Creating a directory named mountdir for mounting the WIM file

After you run the mkdir command, the *mountdir* folder is listed under the root of the *C:* drive (see Figure 2-15).

Next, you need to find the index number associated with the Server with a GUI image you want to install. For example, I am converting from Server Core with the Datacenter edition of Windows Server 2012. I want to find the Server with a GUI image located on my installation media and the index number that references that image. To do so, use the Dism command at an elevated command prompt. The proper syntax is runas / user:administrator to elevate permissions within the command prompt. Click Enter, and you will be prompted to enter the administrator password.

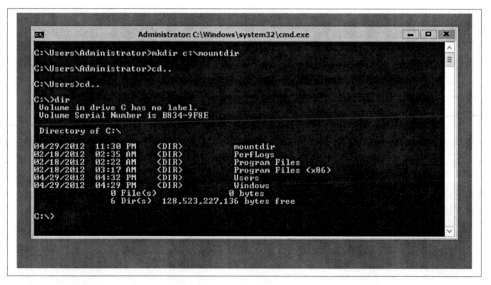

Figure 2-15. Newly created mountdir directory

Then run the following to get the correct index number (also shown in Figure 2-16):

```
Dism /get-wiminfo  /wimfile:drive where installation media
is located:\sources\install.wim
```

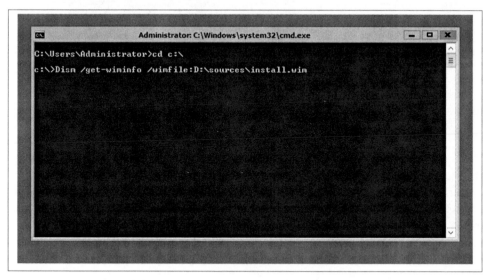

Figure 2-16. Command to locate the index number of the appropriate Server with a GUI image

Upon successfully running the command, you'll see the Deployment Image Servicing and Management tool load. Find the index number of the Server with a GUI image you want to install (see Figure 2-17).

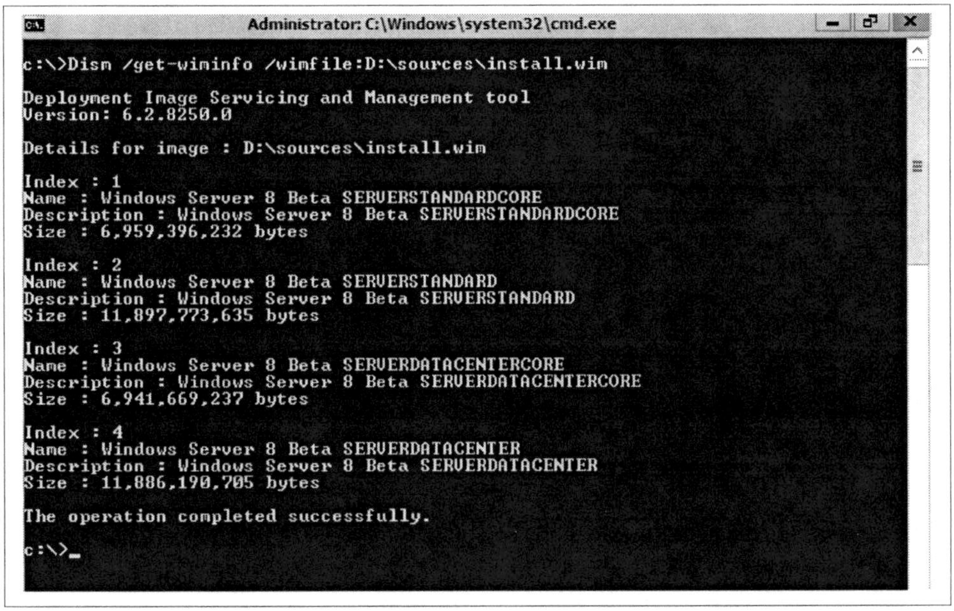

Figure 2-17. List of image files and associated index numbers

Mount the appropriate image file with the following command (also shown in Figure 2-18):

```
Dism /mount-wim /WimFile:drive where installation media is
located:\sources\install.wim  /Index:#_from_step_2 /MountDir:c:\mountdir/readonly
```

This again launches the Deployment Image Servicing and Management tool. The Server with a GUI image is mounted.

After the message "The operation completed successfully" appears on screen, the image mount is complete. The final step requires installing the GUI from the mounted image with PowerShell. Launch PowerShell by simply typing **powershell** at the command line. Again, you must run PowerShell with the administrator account's elevated permissions for the installation to work.

Run the cmdlet:

```
Install-WindowsFeature Server-Gui-Mgmt-Infra,Server-Gui-Shell -Restart -Source
c:\mountdir\windows\winsxs
```

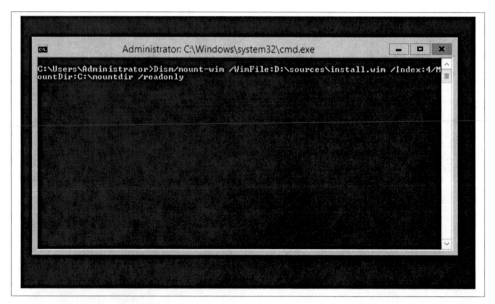

Figure 2-18. Mounting the image file

If the cmdlet is successfully executed, you will see the GUI installation start within
PowerShell (see Figure 2-19).

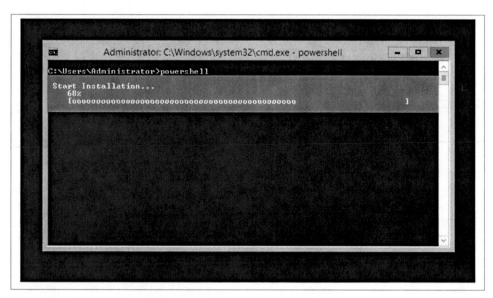

Figure 2-19. The GUI installation process within PowerShell

After install, the server reboots. When the server comes back up, the Ctrl-Alt-Delete screen is displayed. Login and the Server Core interface are now replaced with the full Windows 2012 Server shell.

You can also use Windows Update as the source, instead of a WIM file, by using this Windows PowerShell cmdlet (make sure you have an Internet connection):

```
Install-WindowsFeature Server-Gui-Mgmt-Infra,Server-Gui-Shell –Restart
```

Converting Server with a GUI to Server Core

To convert from Server with a GUI to a Server Core installation with Windows Power-Shell, run the following cmdlet:

```
Uninstall-WindowsFeature Server-Gui-Mgmt-Infra -restart
```

Successful execution of the preceding cmdlet starts the removal process of the server shell (see Figure 2-20).

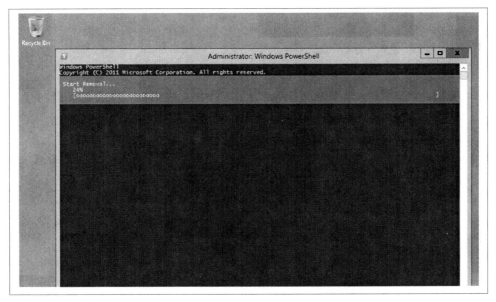

Figure 2-20. Converting Server with a GUI to a Server Core install

The server reboots once the graphical interface is removed. When the server comes back up, after login, the core interface is loaded.

If you initially install with the Server with a GUI option and then use the preceding command to convert to a Server Core installation, you can later revert to a Server with a GUI installation without specifying a source. This is because the necessary files remain stored on the disk, even though they are no longer installed. For more information, and for instructions on how to completely remove the Server with a GUI files from disk, see the section "Customizing the Interface with Features on Demand" (page 35).

If you convert to a Server Core installation, Windows features, server roles, and GUI management tools that require a Server with a GUI installation will be uninstalled automatically. You can specify the `-WhatIf` option in PowerShell to see exactly which features will be affected by the conversion.

Deploying Minimal Server Interface

Windows Server 2012 also offers an interface that is between Server with a GUI and Server Core: the Minimal Server Interface. With an initial Server with a GUI install, you can convert to the Minimal Server Interface through Server Manager. Minimal Server Interface removes components of the Server Graphical Shell, including Internet Explorer 10, Windows Explorer, the desktop, and the Start screen. The Microsoft Management Console (MMC), Server Manager, and a subset of Control Panel are retained.

To convert Server with a GUI to a Minimal Server Interface, from Server Manager launch the Remove Roles and Features Wizard. Select from the features list Graphical Management Tools and Infrastructure (see Figure 2-21).

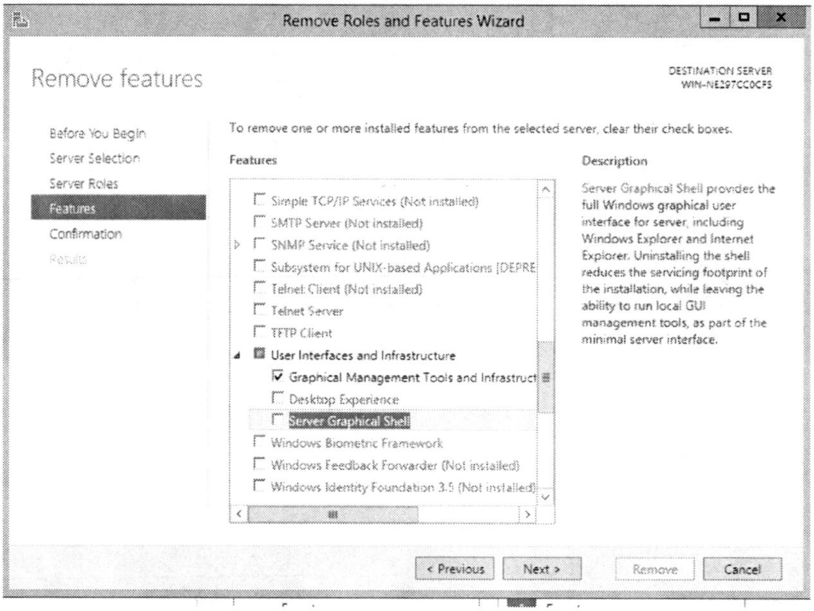

Figure 2-21. Converting Server with a GUI to Minimal Server Interface

Click Next. Check the box next to "Restart the destination server automatically if required." Click Remove. When prompted, allow automatic restarts. (See Figure 2-22.)

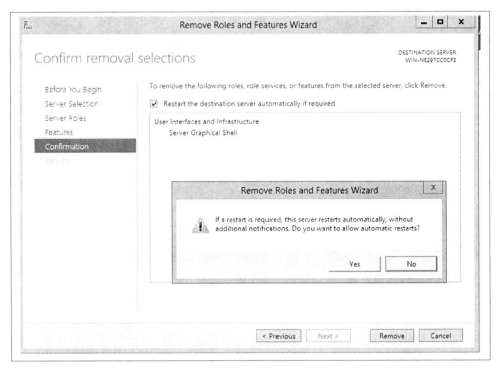

Figure 2-22. Allowing automatic restarts

The result is an interface that is a Server Core UI with graphical components, such as Server Manager (see Figure 2-23).

Customizing the Interface with Features on Demand

Features on Demand can be used to remove specific roles and features. By cherry-picking which components reside on your server, you can save disk space. In Hyper-V virtual machines, Features on Demand reduces the footprint of a virtual machine—in some instances, removing particular roles and features can reduce the size of a virtual machine by more than one gigabyte.

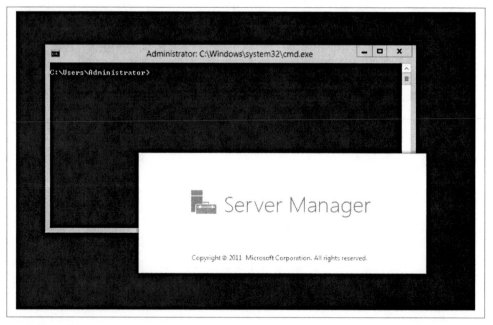

Figure 2-23. Minimal Server Interface

This is one of my favorite features in Server 2012. I'm not quite sure why Microsoft isn't singing the praises of Features on Demand and hitting administrators over the head repeatedly about how great it is, instead of going on about Server Core install recommendations. Minimal Server Interface is a far better and more flexible option than simply going with a Server Core install if you don't want the full GUI; it's a customized GUI that you pretty much design based on your management needs.

Another big advantage in Server 2012 over previous server versions is that in prior versions of Windows servers, you could disable server roles and features, but the binary files for them remained on the server. With Server 2012, however, these files are fully removable. Uninstalling files associated with server roles and features is a state called "disabled with payload removed."

To remove these roles and features, you can use a PowerShell cmdlet. For instance, to remove Windows Explorer, Internet Explorer, and all dependent components, you can run the command:

```
Uninstall -WindowsFeatures Server-Gui-Shell -remove
```

Once you remove a role or disabled a feature with payload removed, you can reinstall it. Reinstalling requires access to an installation source (typically on the installation media). Use the PowerShell command `Install-Windows Feature` with the `-Source` parameter. If you don't specify a source, Windows will attempt to download the needed files using Windows Update.

Summary

Before deploying Server 2012, planning is critical. Determining the edition of Server 2012 that's best suited for your organization's needs can be a discovery operation. Considering factors such as cost, features, and whether or not virtualization will be leveraged can help you select the most appropriate edition of Windows Server. Small infrastructures with light virtualization and cloud deployment needs can opt for the Standard edition. Smaller organizations without high data demands can look into Essentials, or even Foundation editions, depending on the services needed and number of users that have to be supported. Larger organizations with heavy virtualized workloads and cloud infrastructures currently deployed (or planned to deploy) will want to consider the Datacenter edition. Also, it's critical to ensure that the appropriate system requirements are met prior to installation. Remember, Hyper-V has its own requirements for deployment, so make sure those are met as well if you plan to install the Hyper-V role.

Take care of preinstallation housekeeping tasks, such as backing up data, before installing Server 2012. Decide if a Server Core install or the full Server with a GUI install is best suited for your administrative tasks, and whether or not you can support it. If a lightweight, resource-conserving installation is a good fit for your server hardware, then Server Core is the way to go, especially if you can manage many common tasks with PowerShell. If you prefer the full GUI and have the hardware resources, consider the Server with a GUI install mode, or the Minimal Server Interface option for a hybrid of GUI and PowerShell. Or, if you really want a customized management environment, explore the Features on Demand capability, which will allow you to pick the graphical tools you want to use within the core interface.

Server 2012 is remarkably flexible in installation and setup options, more so than in legacy versions. Use that flexibility to your advantage to maximize management efficiency!

CHAPTER 3

Managing Server 2012

Some of the most exciting advancements in Server 2012 are with server management. You have an enhanced Server Manager interface as well as a more robust PowerShell environment. Server management tools can also run on remote client machines; you don't have to manage servers locally. With Server 2012, it's easier than ever to manage multiple servers from a single Server Manager console.

Server Manager has a refreshed, tile-based interface, yet the look remains familiar enough for those who have used Server Manager in previous Windows Server versions. Server Manager provides a centralized console for performing management tasks. The important term here is *centralized*; you can do many key server tasks (such as adding server roles and features), set security policies, configure remote desktops, and much more, all from the central Server Manager dashboard.

Most Windows infrastructures, even in smaller organizations, have multiple servers. One of the challenges of server administration in previous Windows Server versions was efficiently managing multiple servers. Server Manager now gives administrators the ability to add multiple servers into the dashboard for quickly viewing and managing servers deployed throughout an organization. This is a key enhancement, because having the ability to manage all of your servers from one interface cuts down on administration types and lets you consistently administer servers whether they are onsite, remote, or virtualized. Server Manager's multiserver management capabilities are also in line with the continuing shift to "the cloud"—the trend of moving critical business services and applications as well as storage to hosted, online servers and out of the datacenter. More efficient management of multiple servers means added flexibility in managing and scaling up cloud-deployed servers, applications, and services.

PowerShell offers even more management control over a Windows environment, especially for automating tasks. New cmdlets and improvements have been made to make PowerShell more enticing for server administrators to use.

However, many admins, especially those managing small to midsize infrastructures, can't let go of using the GUI for server administration. While good administrators take the time to learn at least the basics of PowerShell commands, let's face it: sometimes it's just easier to point and click to do a task. Configuring network settings is one example.

Therefore, in this chapter I detail how to perform common server management tasks primarily using Server Manager and other GUI components such as the Microsoft Management Console (MMC). However, throughout this book I'll also outline ways of performing some of these tasks through PowerShell.

In addition, this chapter familiarizes administrators with the Server 2012 GUI, how to manage multiple and legacy Windows servers, using apps, and finally, how to install GUI management tools on a client to remotely administer Server 2012.

Server 2012's Interface

After you log into the Server with a GUI interface, the first window that opens automatically is the Server Manager dashboard. Although Server Manager is where you would perform most administrative tasks, what if you want to get to the desktop and Start button?

Server 2012's GUI omits the Start button from previous Windows operating systems. By default, the Recycle Bin is the only icon displayed on the desktop (see Figure 3-1).

Only the taskbar remains from the Server 2008 interface in the initial desktop view. In Server 2012, the taskbar has three pinned shortcuts: Server Manager, PowerShell, and Windows Explorer.

Be forewarned: if you are used to managing Server 2008 R2 and legacy Windows Servers, you may find the interface changes frustrating. I was quite disoriented at first when in Server 2012's desktop screen—I didn't even know where to click to shut the system down! After working with Server 2012 for about a week or so, I discovered that none of the tools or menus we're used to working with in Windows Server is missing. They've just been rearranged somewhat. The Start menu, for instance, is now its own screen independent from the desktop. It's actually easier in some ways to find programs and tools in Server 2012 than in past versions. The rest of this chapter shows you how.

You'll see a small square tile directly to the left of the Server Manager icon on the taskbar. Hovering over this square with the mouse cursor brings up the Start screen shown in Figure 3-2.

Figure 3-1. Server with a GUI desktop

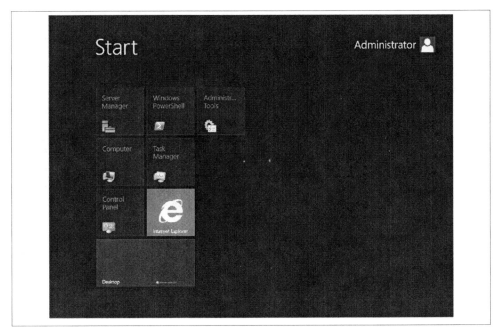

Figure 3-2. Server 2012 Start screen

Navigating the Tiled Interface

The Start screen has the same tile-based interface as the Windows 8 client, only with fewer tiles and a more uniform color. Tiles in Server 2012 are so named because that's what they look like: the aligned squares used to adorn floors and bathroom or kitchen walls. Tiles are to Server 2012 what icons are in Server 2008; click a tile, and the associated program opens.

In the Start screen, administrators will find all of the additional Server applications that appear to be missing in the desktop view. Seven tiles are displayed by default in a streamlined Start menu: Server Manager, Windows PowerShell, Computer, Task Manager, Control Panel, Internet Explorer, and Desktop. At the upper-right corner of the screen is the name of the user account logged into the server.

On the far righthand side of the taskbar is a small square containing an icon of a magnifying glass and four tiles. Hovering over this square, shown in Figure 3-3, pulls up the Charms menu.

 Clicking the small square's magnifying glass reduces the size of the Start menu.

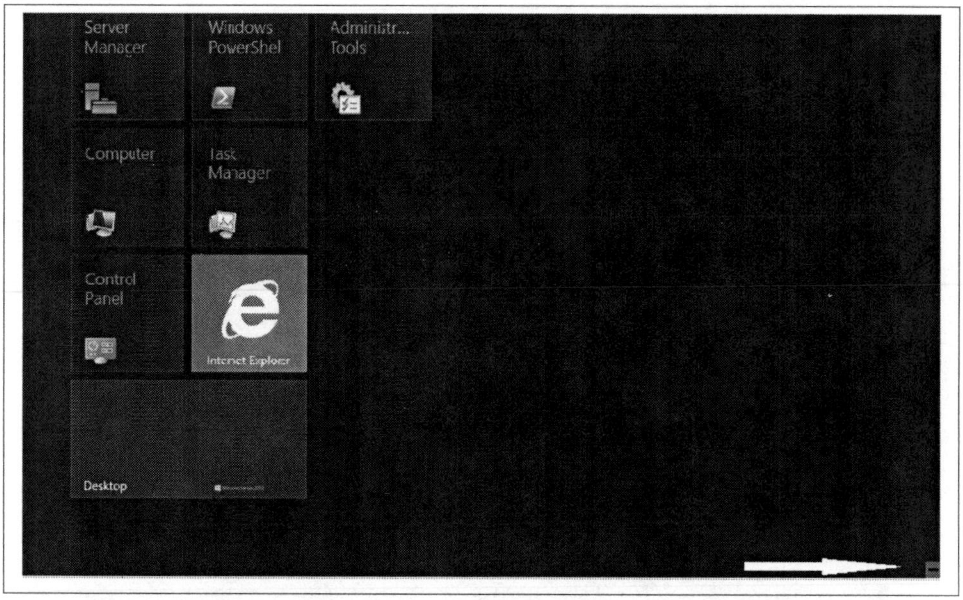

Figure 3-3. The arrow points to the square used to open the Charms menu

The Charms menu floats on the right side of the screen when activated. As shown in Figure 3-4, the icons or "charms" it displays are Search, Start, and Settings. A window displaying date and time—as well as network connectivity—also appears on screen with the Charms menu. Having the date and time prominently displayed on a server screen may seem odd, but it is handy since the Start screen does not have the System Tray as in Server 2008, which displayed the date and time in the bottom-right corner.

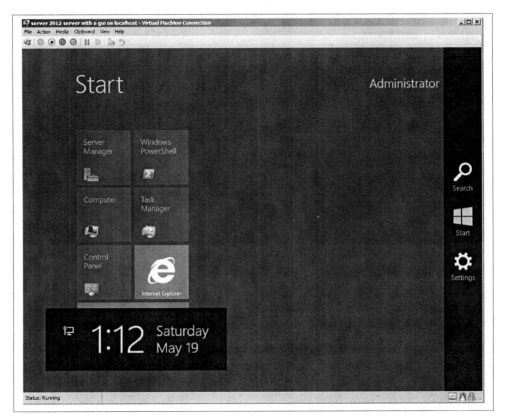

Figure 3-4. The Charms menu

A right-click on the Start menu screen pulls up another menu featuring the option to open "All apps," as shown in Figure 3-5.

 In a technology world that has moved from PC-centric to mobile-centric, programs and applications are increasingly referred to as *apps* even those programs installed on servers and desktops.

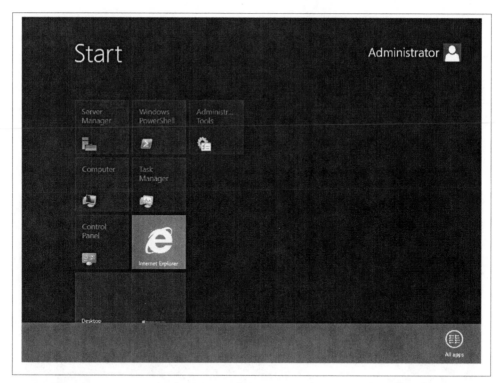

Figure 3-5. "All apps" option

When clicked, the "All apps" screen displays all applications installed on Server 2012, including Performance Monitor, Notepad, Paint, Windows Server Backup, and more.

Because the new interface was initially designed to accommodate touchscreen mobile devices, the layout of tiles sweeps across the screen to facilitate touch gestures. You can use the scroll buttons on the bottom of the screen to move through the tiles, but it's easiest to just use the arrow keys.

Microsoft's decision to include the tile-based interface of the Windows 8 client in Server 2012 has generated a lot of controversy and outright bewilderment among many beta testers in the tech community. Remember, though, you don't have to work within the GUI interface. You can opt to install Server 2012 in the lightweight, command-line-based Server Core mode, or you can use the Minimal Server Interface and select only the shell components you want to install.

Don't confuse the desktop and Start menu. In Server 2012, the two are in separate screens whereas in Server 2008 R2 the Start menu is within the desktop. In Server 2012, you can switch from the desktop to the Start menu and vice versa. The quickest way to switch back and forth between the two is to use the Windows logo key on the keyboard.

Accessing and Running Management Tools

Since there are two main screens in Server 2012 with a GUI—the Start screen and desktop—there are a few ways to access the main management utilities. This section lays out how to quickly get to the most commonly used management apps, run apps as an administrator, and launch the Microsoft Management Console.

Finding management apps

Here's where you'll find the most commonly used management apps:

Control Panel
> The Control Panel tile is part of the default Start menu that appears once you've installed Server 2012 with a GUI. Control Panel is also accessible in the "All apps" screen.

Windows PowerShell
> As with Control Panel, you will find Windows PowerShell's tile on the Start menu or by going into "All apps." Additionally, upon installation of Server 2012 with a GUI, this tile is pinned to the taskbar in the desktop view by default.

Command Prompt
> The Command Prompt icon is found under "All apps."

 There's a difference between Command Prompt and PowerShell. Command Prompt is used to execute DOS-based commands and for creating batch files. PowerShell is a full scripting environment for administering Windows and higher-level tasks like managing permissions.

Running as an administrator

To run programs as an administrator from the GUI, right-click on the app's tile to select it with a checkmark, and then from the window that appears on the bottom of the screen, click "Run as administrator."

Launching the Microsoft Management Console

To open the MMC, from the Start screen type **MMC** and select the MMC icon from the search results.

The MMC interface has been refreshed since Server 2008 R2, although 2012's MMC console includes a Local Backup snap-in and there is no Server Manager snap-in. (See Figure 3-6.)

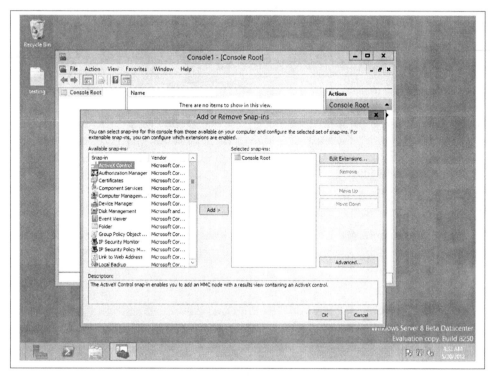

Figure 3-6. The MMC

You can also customize the GUI's desktop and Start menu to your needs and add short-cuts to find these apps even faster. The next section details how to tailor both.

Customizing the Interface

There are quite a few options for customizing the desktop and Start menu.

Customizing the desktop

The desktop can be customized in very much the same way as in Server 2008 R2 or any other recent Windows operating systems. Right-click any empty space on the desktop to pull up a submenu from which you select "Screen resolution."

From the Screen Resolution window (shown in Figure 3-7), you can adjust the display settings. Clicking the "Make text and other items larger or smaller" link brings up the Display window (Figure 3-8).

Figure 3-7. Screen resolution

If you have ever tweaked the display settings in Windows, this screen will be familiar. You can change the desktop background, window colors, the screen saver, and more to customize the desktop. One desktop option you don't have in Server 2012 is the Aero theme. You can give Server 2012's desktop more of a Windows 8–style look by installing the Desktop Experience feature. To do so, from Server Manager's "Add Roles and Features" wizard, select the checkbox next to Desktop Experience underneath the "User Interfaces and Infrastructure" feature.

You can place apps from the full Start menu onto the desktop by adding them as shortcuts. For example, if you want to add a shortcut to Control Panel, you can right-click anywhere on the desktop, click New, and then click Shortcut. In the Create Shortcut window you then simply type **Control Panel**, but you could also choose to browse to the program's location by clicking Browse. You then click Next, name your shortcut Control Panel, and then click Finish. You now have a shortcut to Control Panel on the desktop.

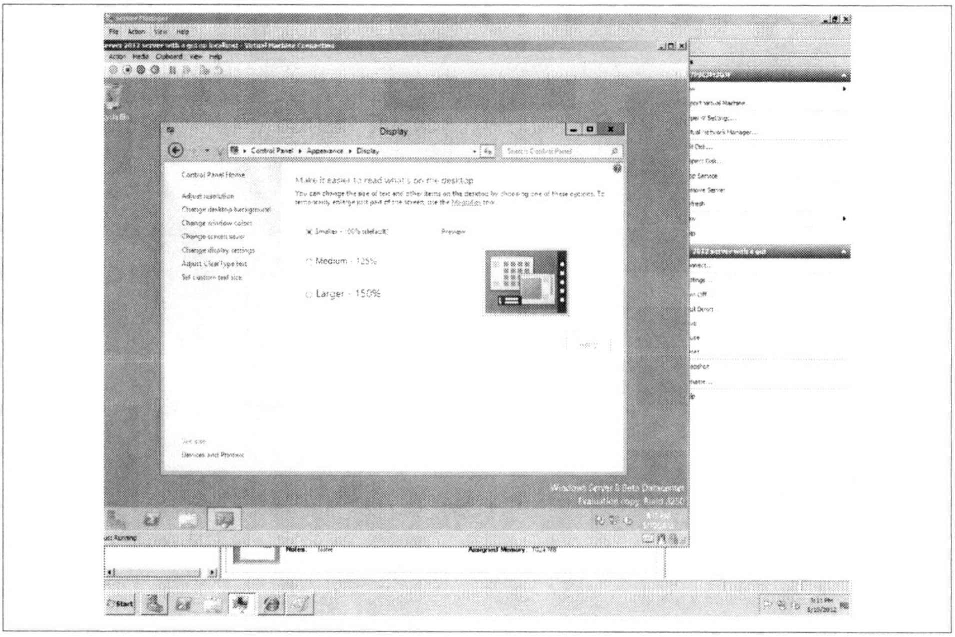

Figure 3-8. Display window

You can also pin apps to the taskbar. Switch into the Start menu view and open "All apps." Right-click the app you want to pin, and the tile gets highlighted with a checkmark. At the bottom of the screen, several clickable options appear once a tile is checked: "Pin to Start," "Pin to taskbar," "Open new window," "Run as administrator," and "Open file location." Clicking "Pin to taskbar" places the tile's associated program as a shortcut on the taskbar on the desktop. In Figure 3-9, the Performance Monitor tile is checked.

In Figure 3-10, the Performance Monitor shortcut is pinned to the taskbar. There isn't a set limit on the number of shortcuts you can pin to the taskbar. When the number of items pinned exceeds the length of the taskbar, up and down arrows are shown at the far right of the taskbar. These arrows allow you to scroll through all the pinned items. Pinning too many items causes the taskbar to get crowded, however. Scrolling through many shortcuts defeats the purpose of quickly accessing and opening an app, so reserve pinning for apps you use frequently.

Unpin the shortcut by right-clicking it from the taskbar and selecting "Unpin this program from taskbar."

When an app is pinned to the taskbar in desktop view, its tile remains in the full Start menu. You can also unpin shortcuts from the taskbar from the Start menu.

Figure 3-9. Checked Performance Monitor tile

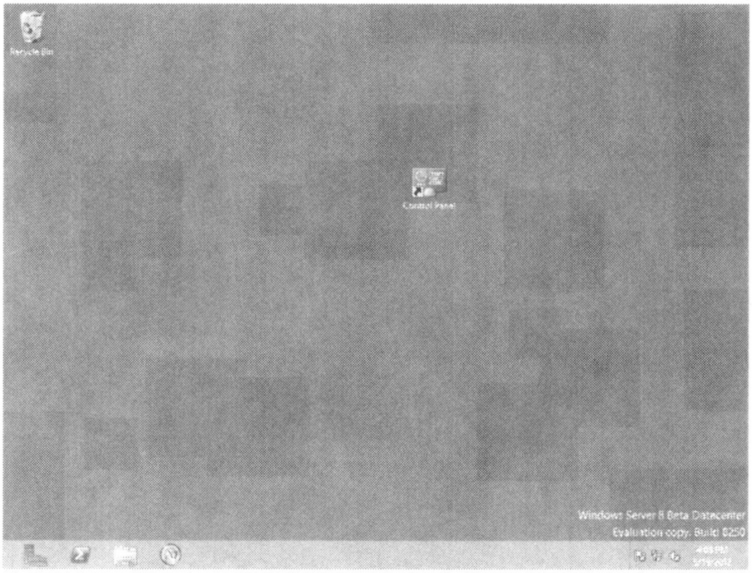

Figure 3-10. Performance Monitor shortcut pinned to the taskbar

Customizing the Start menu

The Start menu view is also customizable. Although by default the Start menu has only seven tiles, you can add more. To add another app tile to the Start menu, right-click anywhere on the screen in the Start menu view to pull up "All apps."

Adding tiles follows the same steps as pinning items to the taskbar. Right-click the app to check it and select "Pin to Start" from the bottom menu that appears.

You can also choose to hide administrative tools, which is useful if you manage the server remotely and don't want anyone accessing them on the local machine. To do so, bring up the Charms menu. Click Settings. In the resulting window, click Settings again. To hide the tools, toggle to No under the "Show administrative tools" option. (See Figure 3-11.)

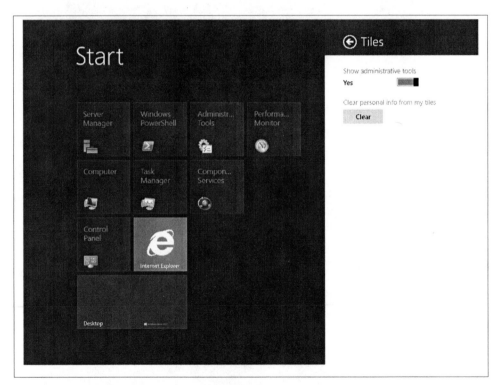

Figure 3-11. Show or hide administrative tools

Logging Off, Restarting, and Shutting Down

The lack of a Start button has made the simple tasks of logging off, restarting, or shutting down Server 2012 rather unintuitive. You perform all of these actions differently than you did in Server 2008 R2.

To log off and log in as another user, click the current user's name in the upper-right corner of the Start screen. From there, click "Sign out." You can also choose to lock the screen. When the screen is locked, the option to "Switch user" is displayed—which is another way to log off and on again with a different account.

To shut down or restart, bring up the Charms menu and click Settings. At the bottom of the Start submenu that appears, there are six icons, one of which is Power. Clicking this icon gives you the choice to either shut down or restart the server.

Performing Searches

One of the most powerful features within the Server 2012 GUI is search. To search for an app, from the Start screen, just start typing. The search results screen will display a list of relevant matches. Figure 3-12 shows the search results displayed when you type **task**.

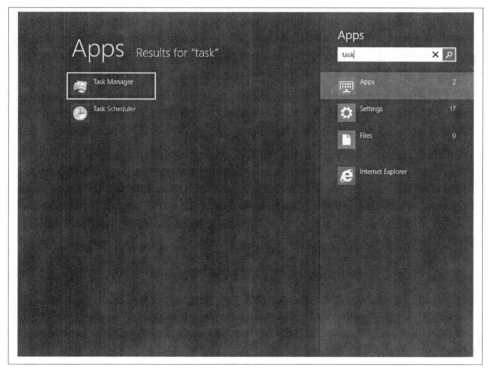

Figure 3-12. Search results for "task"

You can pull up the Search screen by clicking Search from the Charms menu. From there you can search for apps or files and even do web searches.

Within the desktop, you can perform searches as in Server 2008 R2 by opening the Windows Explorer icon pinned to the taskbar and typing in the Search field.

Server Manager

Server Manager has been at the forefront of Windows Server administration since the first release of Windows Server 2008. Server Manager is the central hub for performing many administrative tasks in the graphical shell.

The interface has been updated in Server 2012 and many new capabilities added. Multiserver management, including the ability to create and manage server groups, is one major enhancement. While you can remotely connect to other servers to manage in Server 2008 R2, you can actually add remote servers into the local console in Server 2012. This capability makes server management far more seamless and efficient.

Server 2012's Server Manager allows you to do more management tasks than in Server 2008 R2 and provides greater control over a Windows infrastructure. The console gives you real-time status of deployed servers and server roles. You can perform actions on servers from within the console with just a click. Because you can see server and role status at a glance and take action from within the console, you can reduce the turnaround time for any server problems that may arise.

IPAM (Internet protocol address management) is a new feature within Server Manager that allows you to manage the IP address space of your network. We'll delve further into IPAM in Chapter 8, which covers networking.

Server Manager is such a critical part of configuring and managing Windows Server 2012 that it is also covered in part of the deployment scenario in the following chapters of this book. For now, however, our focus is simply on launching Server Manager and performing preliminary server tasks, such as deploying server roles and features, using the updated BPA (Best Practices Analyzer), adding multiple servers, and creating server groups.

Launching and Working with Server Manager

After you log into Server 2012's Server with a GUI mode, Server Manager loads automatically. You can also fire up Server Manager from the desktop (where you'll find a shortcut to it pinned to the taskbar), or from the Start screen (which has the Server Manager tile on the Start menu).

Server Manager's tile-based new look is shown in Figure 3-13. The large tile at the top center features quick-start wizards that allow you to configure the local server.

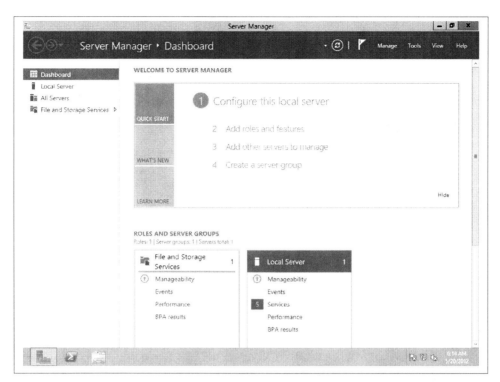

Figure 3-13. Server Manager

Adding server roles and features

Server roles are dedicated functions a server provides. Common roles include DHCP, DNS, File Services, and IIS. In Server 2012, there are 19 server roles you can deploy. Features enhance server roles and are often required for deploying roles.

To add a server role, open Server Manager and click "Add roles and features" under "Configure this local server." The "Add Roles and Features" wizard opens (Figure 3-14).

Click Next and then select the installation type. Here you can choose to install roles or features or set up a Remote Desktop Services scenario-based installation for deploying a Remote Desktop Session Host server. For now, we'll focus on adding a single server role. I've selected "Role-based or feature-based installation" in Figure 3-15.

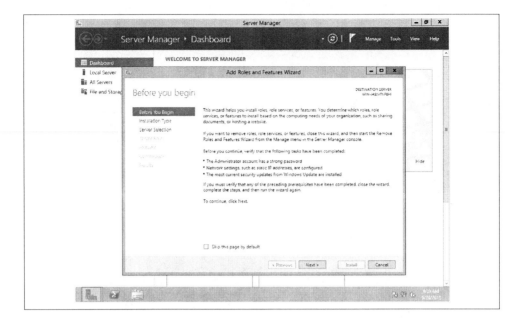

Figure 3-14. Add roles and features

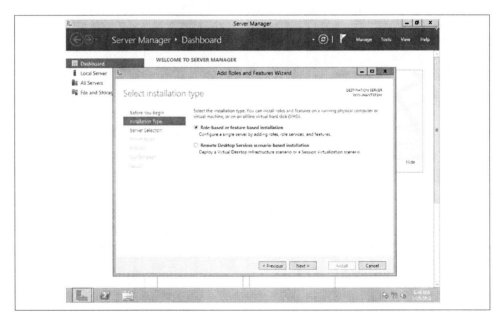

Figure 3-15. Installing a role

The wizard then prompts you to select the destination server. Roles and features can be added to the local server, a remote server, or a virtualized server. In Figure 3-16, the local server is selected as the destination.

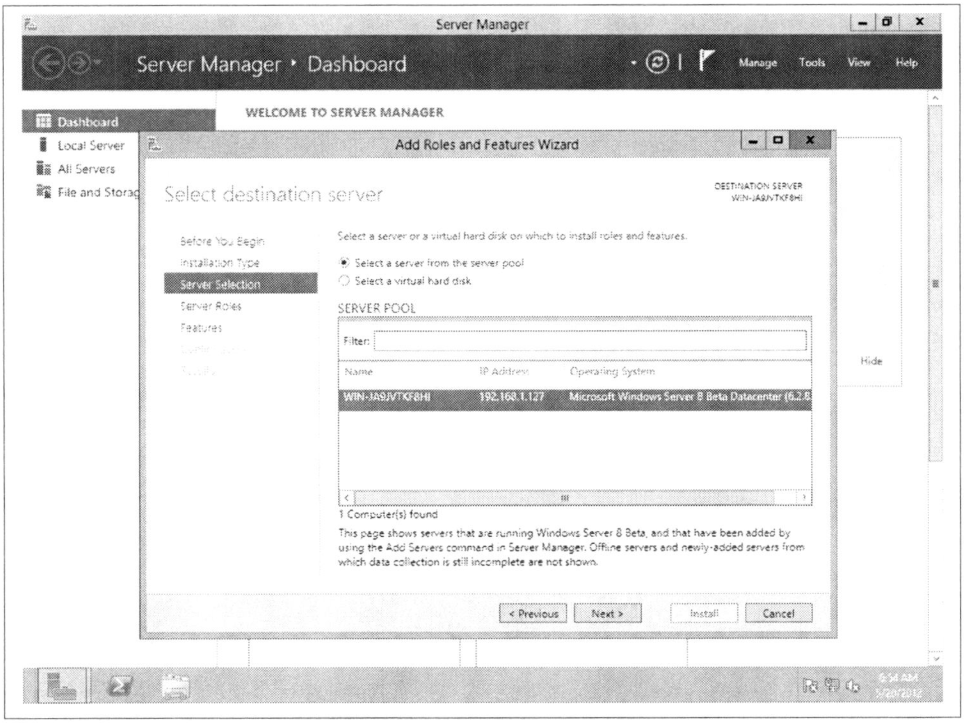

Figure 3-16. Role will be installed on the selected local server

The next step is to select the role or feature you want to install. In Figure 3-17, I've selected the Windows Server Update Services (WSUS) role to install on the local server.

Required components needed to deploy a role or feature are automatically displayed during the installation of that specific role or feature. For example, to install the IIS role as part of creating a WSUS server, you must install the .NET 4.5 Framework component. Windows will display and provide the option of installing all the components needed to install a role (Figure 3-18).

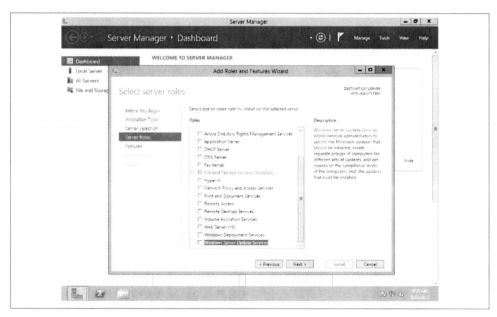

Figure 3-17. Selecting the WSUS role

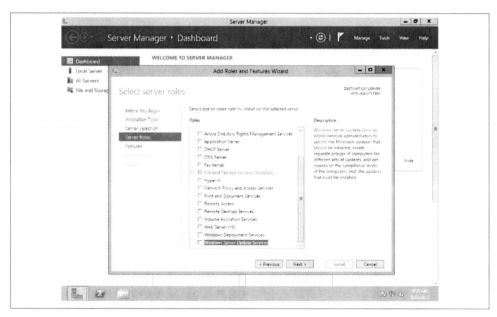

Figure 3-18. Required features for installing the WSUS role

The wizard displays any information administrators need to know about installing the service. For example, as I am adding the WSUS server roles, the wizard offers useful information advising that at least one WSUS server in the network needs to be able to download Microsoft updates from the Internet and that WSUS server-to-server and server-to-client communications should be set up to use SSL (Secure Sockets Layer). The last step of the WSUS role installation asks me to select where either locally or remotely downloaded updates should be saved (Figure 3-19).

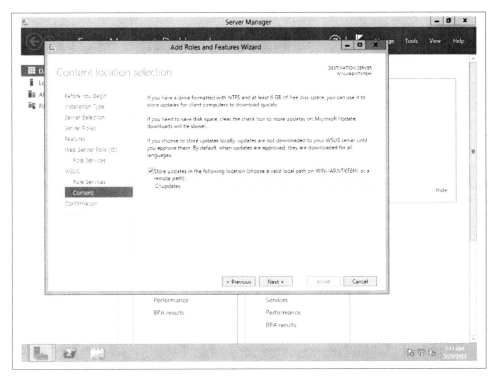

Figure 3-19. Final step of WSUS role installation

As shown in Figure 3-20, the wizard will confirm all software being installed and ask if you want to restart the destination server automatically if required.

Click Install to begin the role installation process. (See Figure 3-21.)

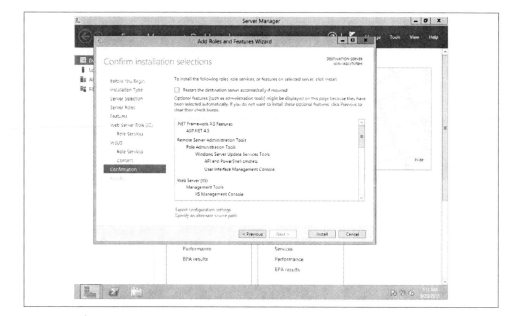

Figure 3-20. Confirmation

Figure 3-21. Start of role install

In the Server Manager console, I now have two additional items in the left pane of the Server Manager dashboard: IIS and Windows Server Update Services (Figure 3-22).

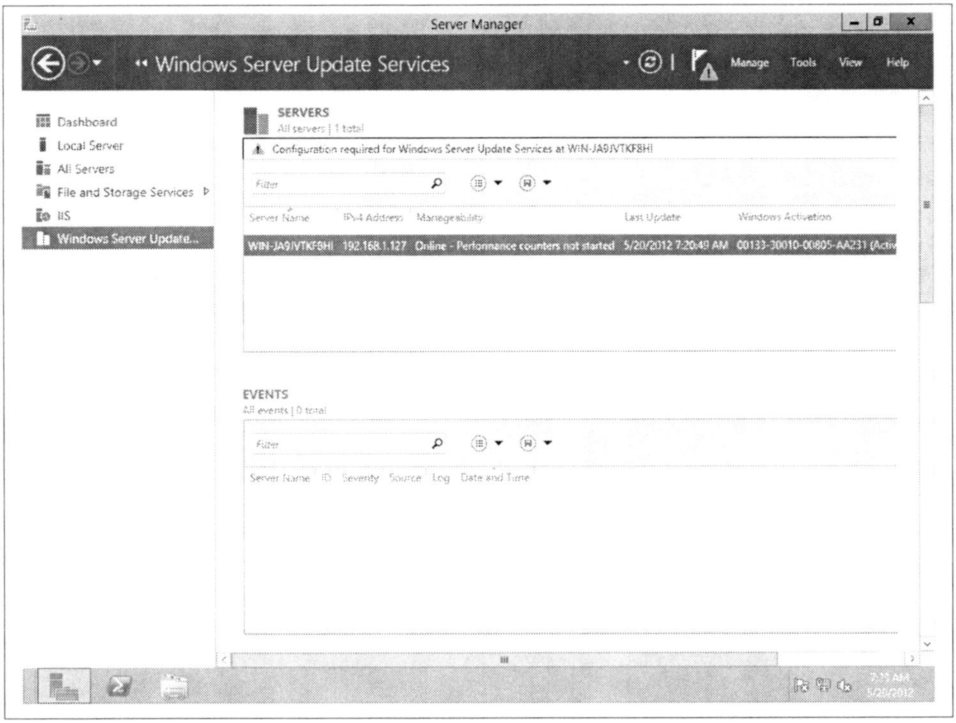

Figure 3-22. The WSUS role and required components are installed

What's very helpful in Server 2012's Server Manager is that you aren't left to your own devices to figure out how to configure a newly installed role. Notice in Figure 3-22 the yellow triangle with the exclamation point. This is a notification indicating that you need to take some additional action after installing the WSUS role. Clicking the triangle displays more information. In the case of the WSUS role I installed, I need to do some post-deployment configuration to get the role to work properly. The notification features a "Launch post-deployment tasks" link that's useful in configuring newly added roles.

Installed roles are added as tiles to the Start menu for quick access outside of Server Manager.

Multiserver management and groups

One of the more challenging management feats in past Windows Server versions was managing both a local server and remote servers—such as those in a branch office or virtualized—efficiently from one console. Multiple server management is a highlight of Server Manager in Server 2012.

To add other servers in the Server Manager dashboard, from the "Configure this local server" link, click "Add other servers to manage." The Add Servers wizard displays, as shown in Figure 3-23.

Figure 3-23. Add Servers wizard

You can add a computer by performing an Active Directory search, through DNS by adding the server's computer name or IP address, or by importing a *.txt* file that contains servers by name or IP address.

In Figure 3-24, a remote Server 2012 virtual machine has been added through a DNS search of the virtual server's IP address. Once the server is discovered, click the right-pointing arrow to add it to the Selected computer list. Click OK.

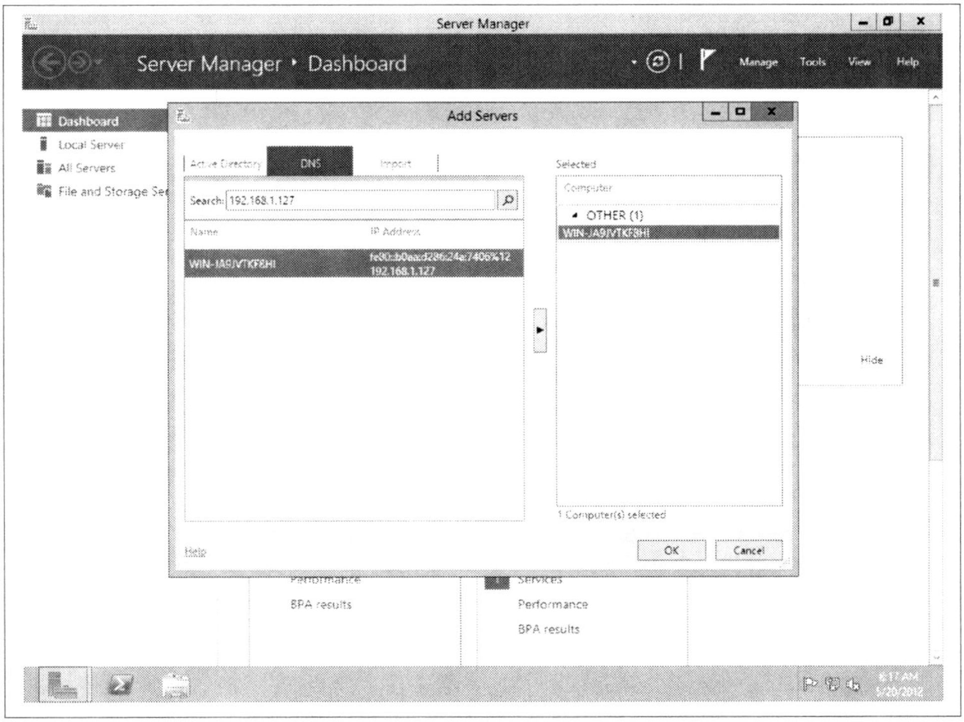

Figure 3-24. Adding a Server 2012 member server

Adding legacy servers to Server Manager

Legacy servers can also be managed with Server 2012's Server Manager. Server 2003, 2008, and 2008 R2 servers are added into the Server Manager console in the same way as a Server 2012 machine. The older operating systems don't have all the same task options as Server 2012 in Server Manager, but this makes managing a mixed environment easier by having a unified console.

Managing Server 2012 Remotely

You can certainly run Server Manager locally from a domain controller, but best practices dictate running graphical tools from a remote client machine. Running ADAC, Server Manager, and other tools remotely reduces the overhead on a server.

RSAT (Remote Server Administration Tools) includes Server Manager, MMC snap-ins, consoles, Windows PowerShell cmdlets, and command-line tools for managing roles and features that run on Server 2012.

You can use RSAT on Windows 8 to manage Server 2008 R2 or Server 2008, but—according to Microsoft—only in "limited cases." To save yourself problems, run the proper RSAT version for the proper server on separate clients.

Installing RSAT

RSAT for the Windows 8 client is available from Microsoft's Download Center (*http:// www.microsoft.com/en-us/download/details.aspx?id=28972*). Both 32-bit and 64-bit editions are available.

Before installing RSAT, make sure any older versions of the Administration Tools Pack or RSAT are removed from the client machine, if previously installed.

Download and install the *Windows6.2-KB958830-x64.msu* file for 64-bit, or *Windows6.2-KB958830-x86.msu* for 32-bit.

After install, go to the Start screen in the Windows 8 client and open Administrative Tools (Figure 3-25).

Figure 3-25. Administrative Tools tile (far upper-right)

Within the *Administrative Tools* folder are the graphical utilities needed to run Windows Servers, including Active Directory Administrative Center, DNS Manager, DHCP, and Server Manager. (See Figure 3-26.)

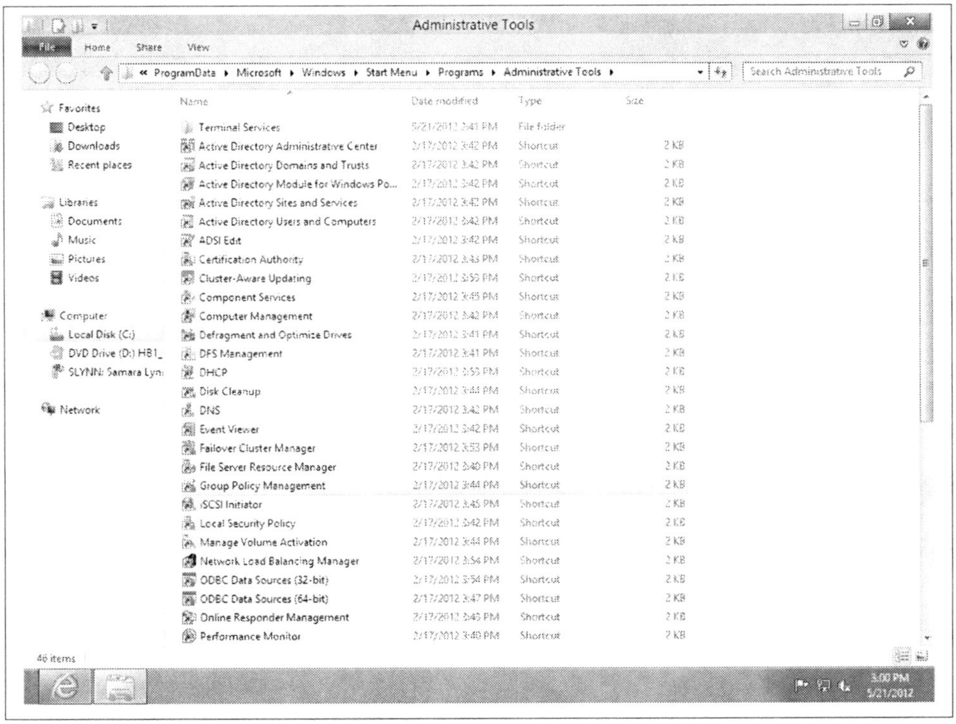

Figure 3-26. The Administrative Tools folder

In Figure 3-27, Server Manager is opened on a Windows 8 client joined to the same domain as a Server 2012 system. Click Manage at the top-right corner of the Server Manager menu, then click Add Servers, to bring the servers you want to manage into the console.

You can search for servers via Active Directory, via DNS, or by importing the servers' information in a file. Figure 3-28 shows a search for all servers in the domain.

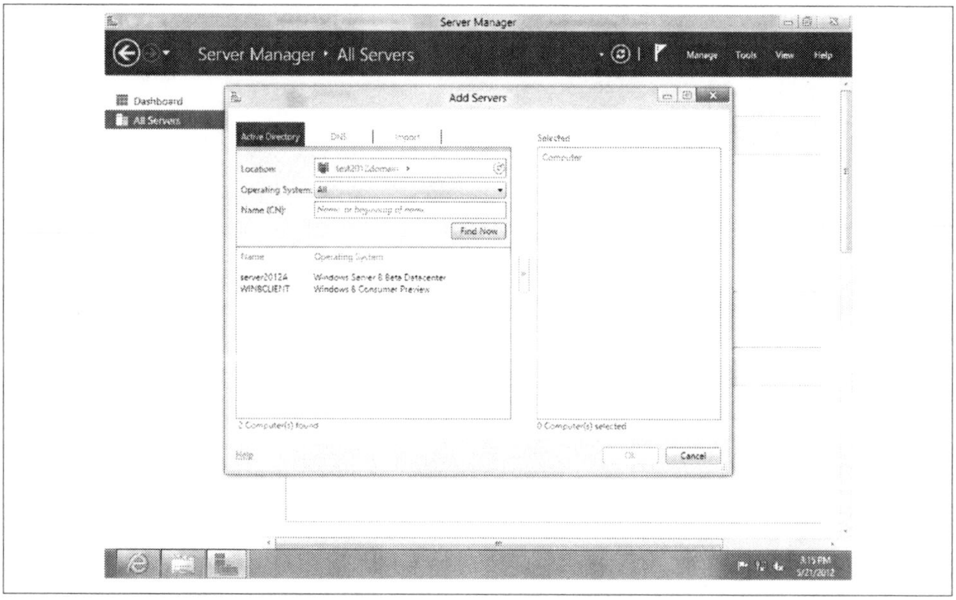

Figure 3-27. Server Manager running on a Windows 8 client

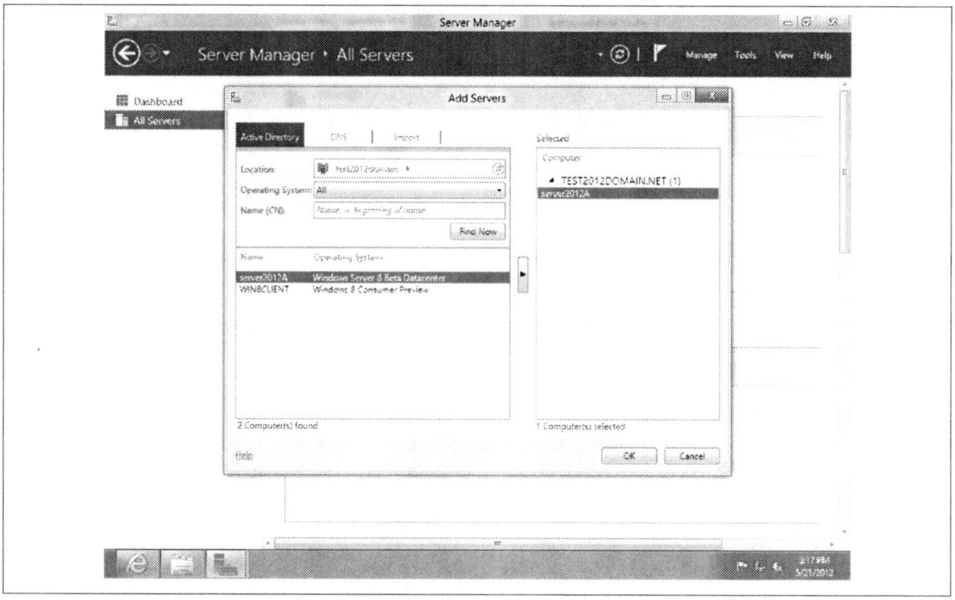

Figure 3-28. Server search

Click the arrow to the right of the server listing to add the server(s) into the console.

Once you add a server, all the roles and features installed on the server are displayed in the client's Server Manager console, just as if you were using Server Manager on the local server.

Summary

Server Manager is the heart of managing Windows Server 2012. With a clean, modern interface, Server Manager is not only more pleasant to work in, but it also gives you more management capabilities, offering you control over an entire Windows infrastructure.

Because you can add Server 2012 into legacy domains as well as monitor legacy servers from Server 2012 Server Manager, Microsoft's latest operating system truly fits into the realistic, mixed Windows machine environment found in the IT infrastructures of most businesses and organizations.

Management apps built for Server 2012 help to extend management features. Finally, you can easily manage Server 2012 through GUI tools on Windows client machines using RSAT.

CHAPTER 4

Active Directory

Perhaps no aspect of a Windows environment can cause as many headaches, frustrations, and consumption of valuable IT time as Active Directory (AD). Active Directory was first introduced into Windows Server with the release of Server 2000 and has steadily evolved in subsequent Windows Server versions. Server 2012 includes the most polished Active Directory services offering to date. One major reason why this is the best AD yet is that an Active Directory Domain Services (AD DS) deployment now integrates all the steps required to deploy new domain controllers into a single interface with the new Active Directory Domain Services Configuration Wizard.

AD DS is also easier to manage in Server 2012 due to an enhanced wizard built on PowerShell that integrates with Server Manager. Preinstallation checks with the Adprep.exe tool and prerequisite validation are part of the install process, helping to lessen the chance of errors with an AD DS install.

Do these enhancements mean deploying and managing AD is flawless in Server 2012? Not by any means. While deploying Server 2012 AD for the first time, I ran into some errors and cautions warning me that certain services or features had to be added or configured a certain way for a successful AD install.

Yet I got those warnings and errors automatically, not by having to hunt through Event Viewer for AD-related warnings, as I would normally have to do in Server 2008 R2 and older Windows Server versions. Warnings, errors, and suggestions for getting the server in shape to run AD are all displayed as easy-to-read, comprehensible alerts within the updated Server Manager. The entire AD install deployment centralized in Server Manager makes AD deployment more efficient and easier to troubleshoot.

This chapter introduces the new Active Directory Administrative Center (ADAC) interface. I'll also cover deploying and managing AD DS, as well as how to join Server 2012 to an existing domain and, conversely, join a member Server 2012 machine to a Server 2008 R2 domain.

The chapter also outlines using new and updated features in AD, such as using the AD Recycle Bin to restore deleted objects, performing AD searches, deploying AD with PowerShell, and remotely managing Server 2012.

Deploying Active Directory Domain Services

With both Server Manager and Active Directory refreshed with updated management interfaces in Server 2012, the install process may be not as familiar even to those who have installed AD DS before. Before installing Active Directory Domain Services, ensure that DNS Server is running on the network; otherwise, you will be prompted to install DNS after the AD install.

Installing Active Directory

To deploy Active Directory Domain Services on a local Server 2012 machine, launch Server Manager and select "Add roles and features" in the "Configure this local server" area of the dashboard.

Select "Role-based or feature-based installation," and click Next. Then select the local server (or the server to which you want to deploy AD DS) as the destination server. Choose Active Directory Domain Services. (See Figure 4-1.)

There are several features and tools that you are required to install along with AD DS. These features are listed, and you are given the option to install them as well. To do so, click "Add features," then click Next.

You can opt to install additional features, or just click Next once again to begin the installation process (Figure 4-2).

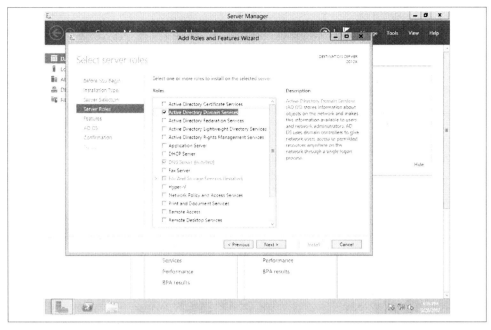

Figure 4-1. Selecting Active Directory Domain Services

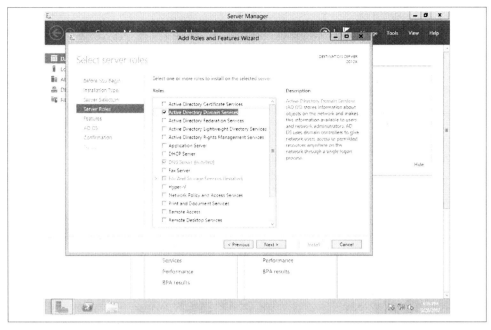

Figure 4-2. Start of the AD DS install

After a successful install, Server Manager's notification prompts you to "Promote this server to a domain controller," as shown in Figure 4-3.

 Of course, you don't want to just start adding servers as domain controllers (DCs) in a network. Most readers will probably already have DCs deployed. You can certainly add Server 2012 as a physical or virtual DC, or as a read-only DC for security purposes. Before promoting any new Server 2012 deployments to DCs, consider your existing infrastructure and what role Server 2012 should play.

Figure 4-3. Notification to promote to domain controller

You have several options to promote to a DC. You can use the GUI or PowerShell. There's some confusion about whether or not Microsoft has eliminated the Dcpromo command system that administrators have long used to promote servers to DCs.

Dcpromo can still be executed in Server 2012. You run the command by pointing to an answer file, using the `dcpromo.exe` command in the command prompt. The answer file is a text file you create with specific fields that will customize an unattended DC promotion based on the configuration needed for your particular organization.

Promoting DCs using Dcpromo and an answer file is necessary only if an organization already has in-place automation for creating DCs or for infrastructures that need to deploy large numbers of DCs. For smaller organizations, using the DC install and promotion capabilities within Server Manager is easier and more efficient because you have less chance of syntax errors than with creating answer files. For those comfortable with scripting, PowerShell also provides a good alternative for creating and promoting servers as DCs.

The Active Directory Administrative Center allows you to add a DC to an existing domain, add a new domain to an existing forest, or add a new forest. To set up an entirely new domain without an existing forest, select "Add a new forest," as shown in Figure 4-4. You must specify a root domain name, in the form of *<domainname>.com* or *<domainname>.net*, for example, or whatever top-level domain (TLD) ending is designated for your organization.

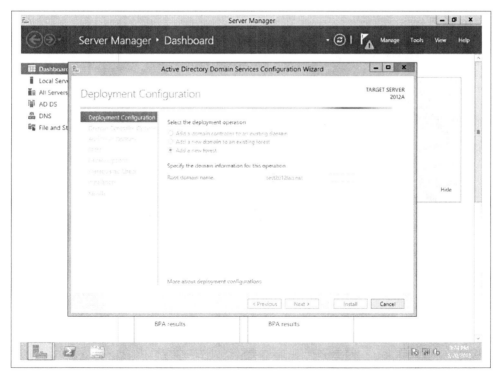

Figure 4-4. Adding a new forest

Next, you have to select the forest and domain's functional level. The functional level you select depends on whether you have an existing AD domain or forest and which servers you are running. For instance, if your infrastructure has Server 2003 servers, you may keep the forest or domain level set at Windows 2003 until all DCs are upgraded to Server 2008 or 2008 R2.

Server 2012 can be set to Server 2012 AD, Server 2008 R2, Server 2008, or Server 2003 functional levels. If the DC is going to also function as a global catalog server, or as a read-only DC, you can select those capabilities in this step as well. It is important to ensure that adding a new DC does not execute an unplanned upgrade of the functional level of the domain, so read all of the wizard text closely when joining an existing domain.

Finally, in the next screen (Figure 4-5), you can also set the Directory Services Restore Mode (DSRM) password.

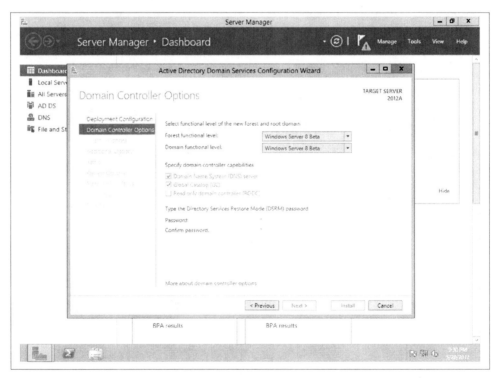

Figure 4-5. Setting the functional level of the domain

Before final installation, a prerequisites check is automatically run to ensure that there are no issues with the AD install (Figure 4-6).

After a successful install, AD DS is listed in the dashboard, as shown in Figure 4-7.

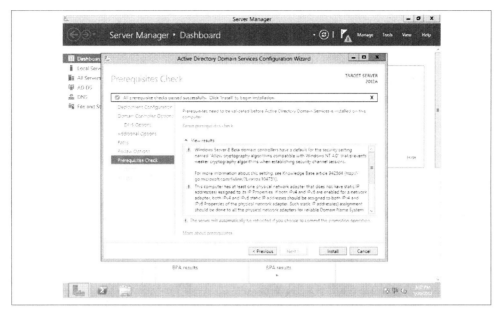

Figure 4-6. Prerequisites check

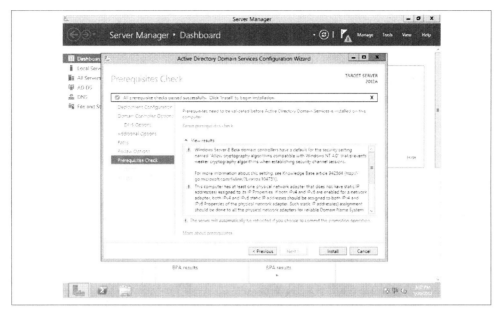

Figure 4-7. Successful install of AD DS

Adding Machines to a Server 2012 Domain

Traditionally, IT professionals will upgrade servers before upgrading client machines or just replace dated user machines with new ones preinstalled with the latest Windows client operating system. It's conceivable that there will be organizations that will want to join not only Windows 8 clients, but Windows 7 (and in some cases, Windows XP) machines, to Server 2012 domains.

Client machines and servers can be joined to domains in large organizations and enterprises via automated methods such as scripting and batch files. This section focuses on client-side installation through the GUI, the method typically employed in smaller networks. These steps will also work for virtual machines.

Joining Windows 7 to a Server 2012–Level Domain

From System Properties in the Windows 7 client's Control Panel, click the Computer Name tab and click Change, as shown in Figure 4-8.

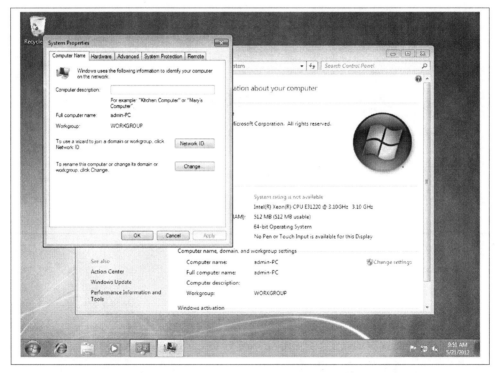

Figure 4-8. Windows 7 System Properties

Enter the domain name under "Member of" in the Domain field (Figure 4-9).

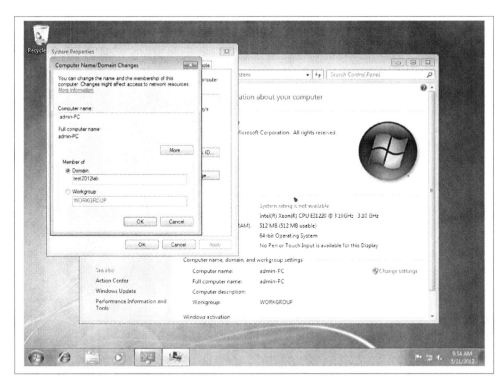

Figure 4-9. Entering the domain name

Enter user account credentials with permission to join computers to the domain. A confirmation message pops up when the machine is successfully joined (Figure 4-10).

Once the client machine is joined to the domain, you can find the machine in the Computers container in the ADAC, as shown in Figure 4-11.

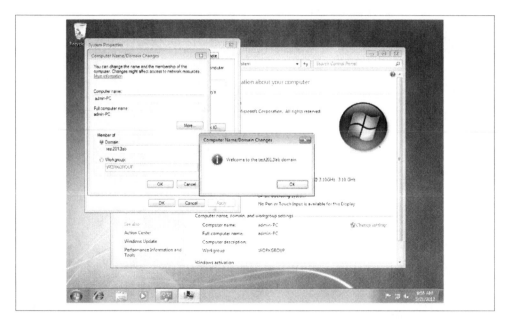

Figure 4-10. Successfully joining the domain

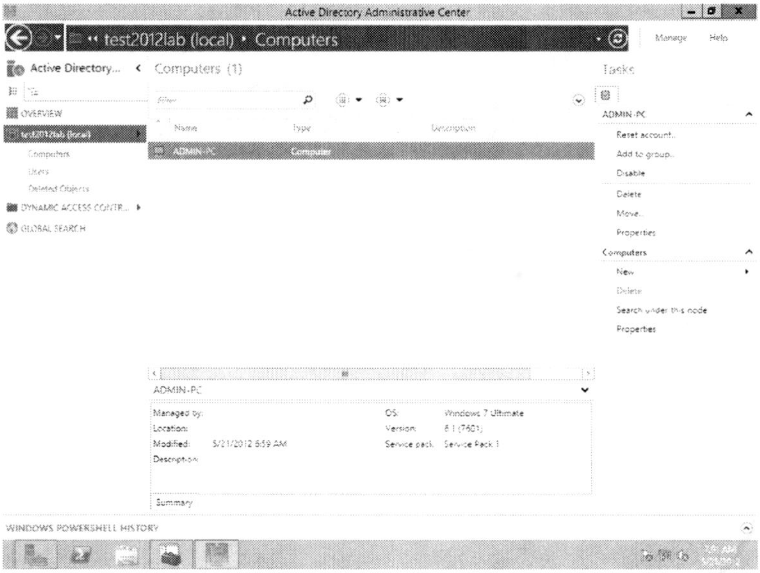

Figure 4-11. Machine joined to domain, now listed in the ADAC

Joining Windows 8 to a Server 2012–Level Domain

Since Windows 8 was released in Consumer Preview version, there has been lots of controversy surrounding the Windows 8 client and criticisms that the operating system is designed more as a consumer mobile operating platform with less emphasis on the enterprise. However, it's inevitable that Windows 8 will find its way into business infrastructures, if only for its novelty at first. I remember my days as a Windows Server administrator, having to fit the latest client OS into the domain infrastructure simply because some C-level executive wanted to test-drive the latest operating system!

There's good news and bad news about joining Windows 8 to corporate domains. Windows 8 systems installed on ARM-based mobile devices—called Windows RT—can't officially join a Windows domain. That does not mean you can't introduce Windows RT mobile devices into your organization's infrastructure; there are native Windows capabilities and plenty of third-party utilities for mobile device management (MDM).

You can, however, join computers with Windows 8 installed to a domain, as well as Windows 8 virtual machines. To install Windows 8 clients to a Server 2012–level domain, you follow the same procedures as for joining a Windows 7 client. Launch the Control Panel and click "System and Security." Click System and then "Advanced system settings."

Click the Computer Name tab and click Change. Type the domain name into the Domain field. Once joined, the computer is added in ADAC in the Computers container.

The procedures for joining Server 2003, 2008, and 2008 R2 as member servers to a Server 2012 domain follow the same steps as joining Windows clients.

The refreshed Server Manager interface in Server 2012 allows you to quickly add a Server 2012 to a domain. To do so, open Server Manager. Click "Configure this local server." Under Properties, click Workgroup, as shown in Figure 4-12.

The Workgroup link brings up the System Properties window, from which you can add the server to a domain (Figure 4-13).

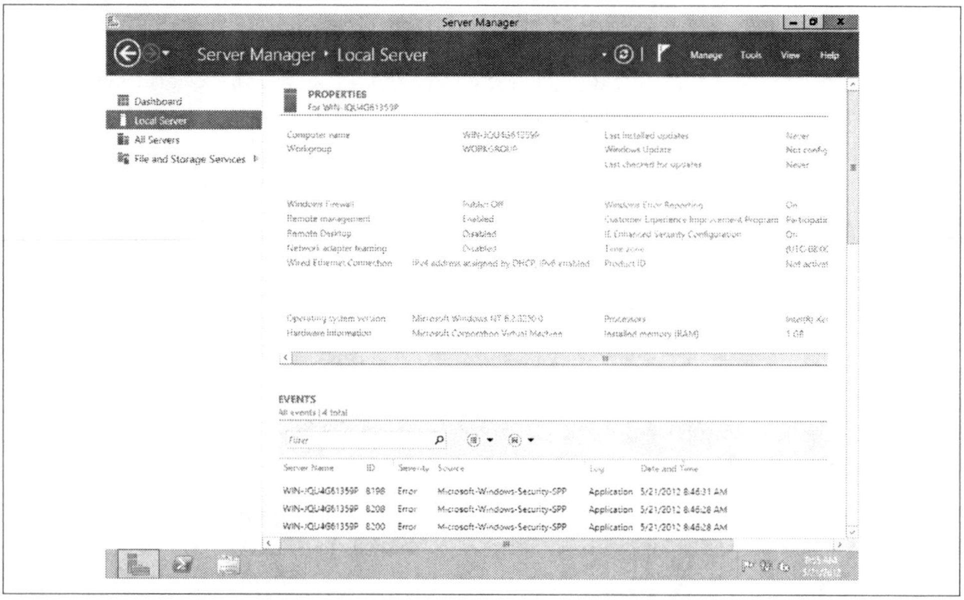

Figure 4-12. Clicking Workgroup to join Server 2012 to a domain

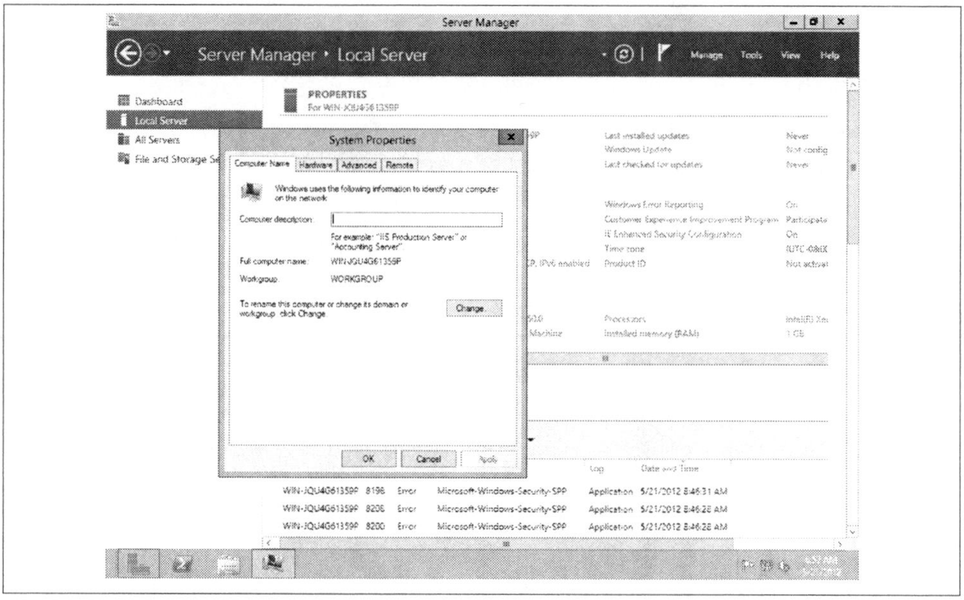

Figure 4-13. Clicking Change to add to the domain

Joining Server 2012 to a Server 2008 R2–Level Domain

You can add Server 2012 machines to other functional levels of Active Directory domains, although such a mixed environment won't have the benefits of a Server 2012 domain.

To add a Server 2012 machine to a Server 2008 R2 domain, for example, open Server Manager. Click "Configure this local server." Under Properties, click Workgroup. Under System Properties, add the server to the 2008 R2 domain. (See Figure 4-14.)

Once added, the Server 2012 machine is listed in the Computers container in the Server 2008 R2.

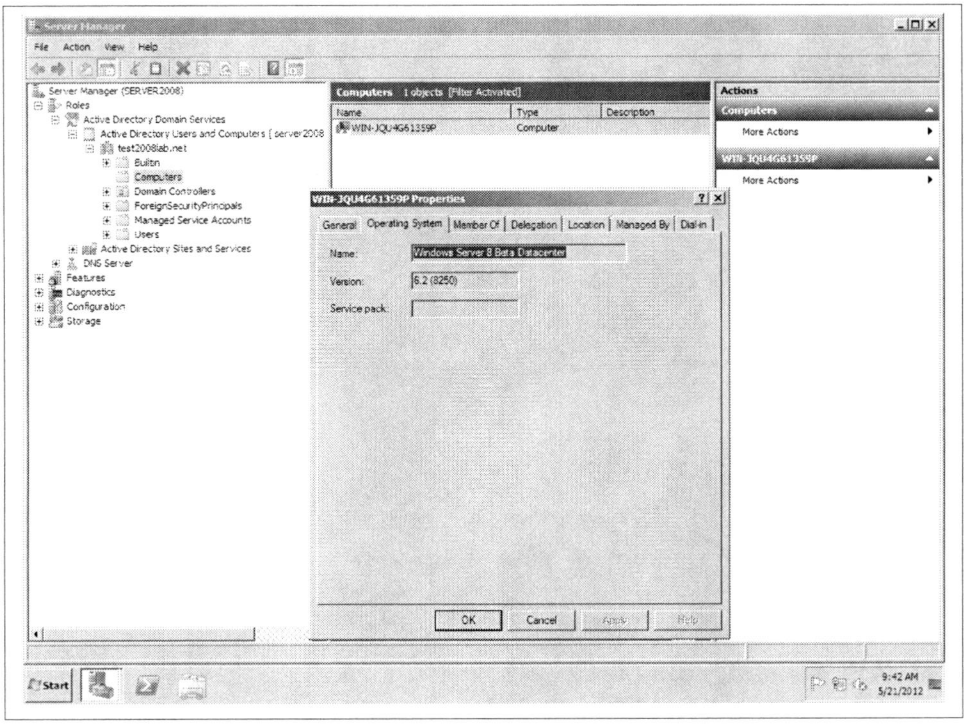

Figure 4-14. Adding Server 2012 to a Server 2008 R2 domain

Managing Active Directory

The Active Directory Administrative Center is the console used to manage AD. You launch the console from Server Manager by clicking Tools.

Navigating ADAC

ADAC has the same tiled interface as Server Manager. The interface provides a nice overview that offers useful links and help documentation on AD, as well as detailed deployment of Dynamic Access Control (covered in Chapter 5).

Figure 4-15 shows the initial ADAC screen. From here, you can reset the domain administrator's password and perform a global search against AD. On the left side of the screen, you can select the DC you want to manage.

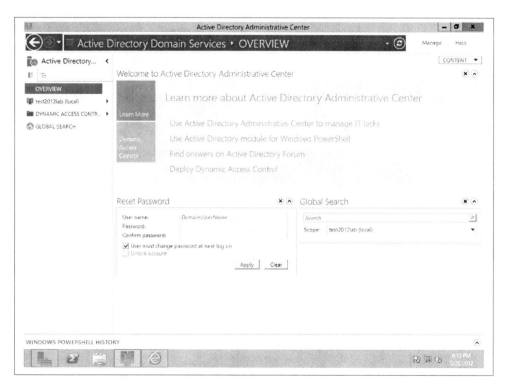

Figure 4-15. The ADAC initial screen

When you select the DC, a listing of all the AD objects, including containers and organizations units (OUs), is displayed. On the right of the screen is a menu for performing various AD-associated tasks, such as adding new objects, deleting objects, searching, and viewing properties of containers (permissions, for example).

The layout for creating objects in AD has gone through some changes. First we will walk through creating a new group.

To begin creating a new group, open Server Manager. In the dashboard, from the left menu, click "AD DS." Right-click the local server (or the server on which you've installed AD) and select Active Directory Administrative Center, as shown in Figure 4-16.

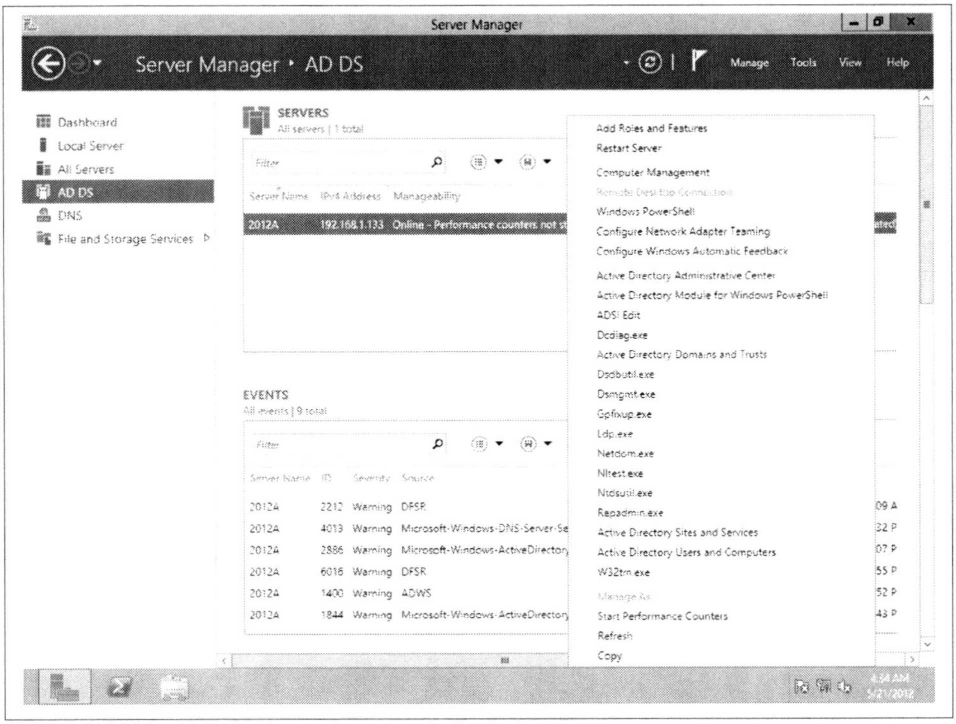

Figure 4-16. Selecting Active Directory Administrative Center

From the left menu in ADAC, click on "AD DS." All AD container objects are displayed. From the righthand Tasks menu, under Program Data, click New and then Group (Figure 4-17).

The Create Group screen opens. Fields with red asterisks are required. In Figure 4-18, I name my group *Human Resources NY*. As you type the group name, the field directly under the "Group name" field, Group (SamAccountName), is automatically populated.

> Group(SamAccountName) is used as an alternate logon for legacy pre-AD clients and servers such as Windows 95.

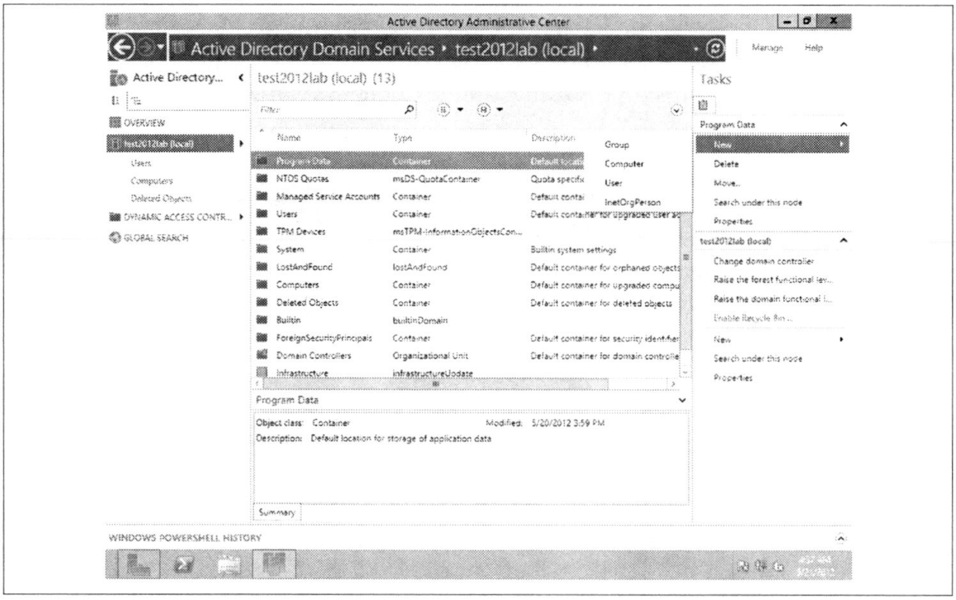

Figure 4-17. Tasks menu options

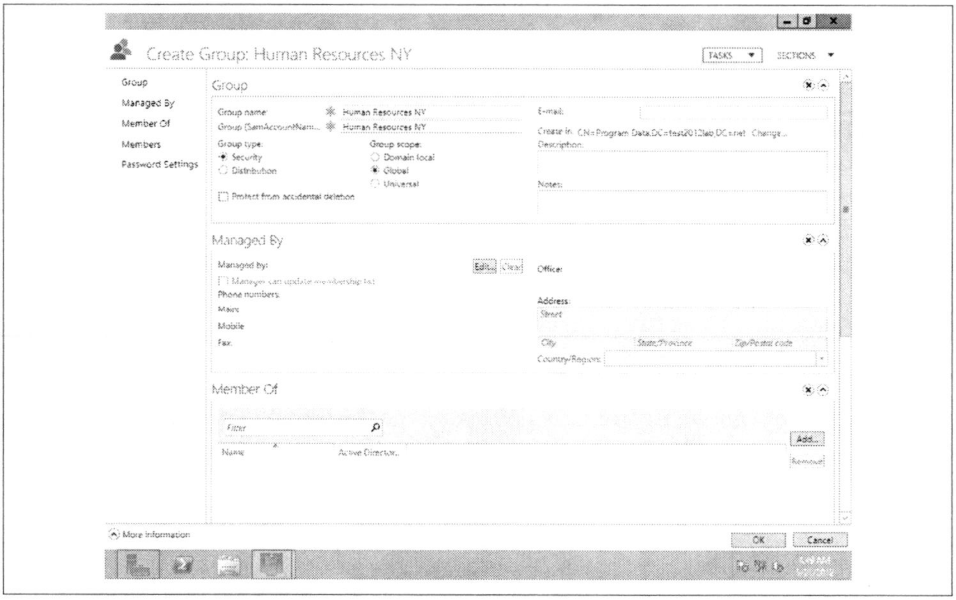

Figure 4-18. Creating groups

Next, select the group type; by default, this is set to Security, but you can set it as an email distribution list as well. Then choose the group scope. The default scope is Global, but we can set it to only the local domain or to universal (i.e., permissions and accessibility across multiple Active Directory forests).

You can add a member to the group or make the group a member of a parent group under the "Members" and "Member of" sections, respectively. The rest of the fields are optional, such as adding information about who manages the group, a description, notes about the group, and so on.

If you don't need to see all that information in the Create Group screen, you can hide sections. For example, a small organization with few IT staff members may not need to specify who manages a group. To customize this interface, click the Sections drop-down button at the top right of the Create Group screen. As shown in Figure 4-19, checked sections are displayed. To hide a section, simply uncheck it.

Figure 4-19. Adding and removing sections

You can also close a section by clicking the X button directly above and to the far right of each section.

If you use a specific section at times, you may just want to collapse it when you don't need it instead of closing it. To collapse a section, click on the arrow next to the X button directly above and to the far right of each section.

The interface is consistent for creating any kind of AD object in ADAC, although fields may change depending on the object (such as a new computer or user). Creating and managing users is detailed more thoroughly in Chapter 5.

ADAC also allows you to perform domain-wide duties, such as changing the domain controller or raising the forest or domain functional level.

AD Recycle Bin

The Active Directory Recycle Bin is a way to restore deleted AD objects without losing any of those objects' attributes. For example, if you delete a user account and restore it using the AD Recycle Bin, that account retains its permissions and group memberships.

 When creating a new AD object, you can set it to never get accidentally deleted by checking "Protect from accidental deletion" in the Create screen.

ADAC in Server 2012 provides an easy way to enable the AD Recycle Bin. From the right side of the ADAC window, under Tasks, click Enable Recycle Bin (Figure 4-20).

Click OK in the pop-up message to confirm enabling the Recycle Bin (Figure 4-21). Refresh the screen and a new container, Deleted Objects, is listed.

To restore a deleted object, open Deleted Objects and either right-click the container and select Restore to restore the object to its original location, or click Restore To to specify a location (Figure 4-22). You can also access the same commands under the Tasks menu.

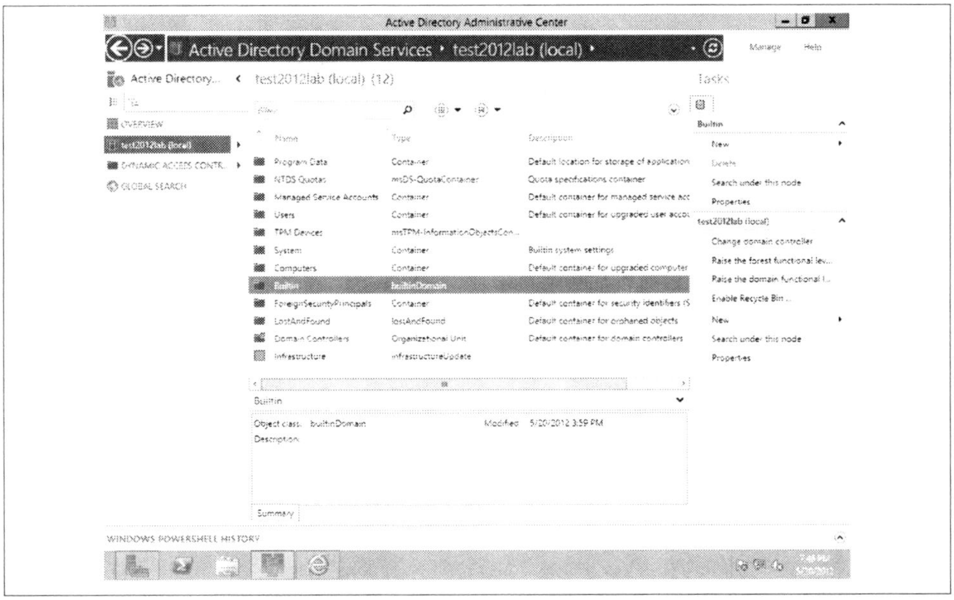

Figure 4-20. Enabling the Recycle Bin

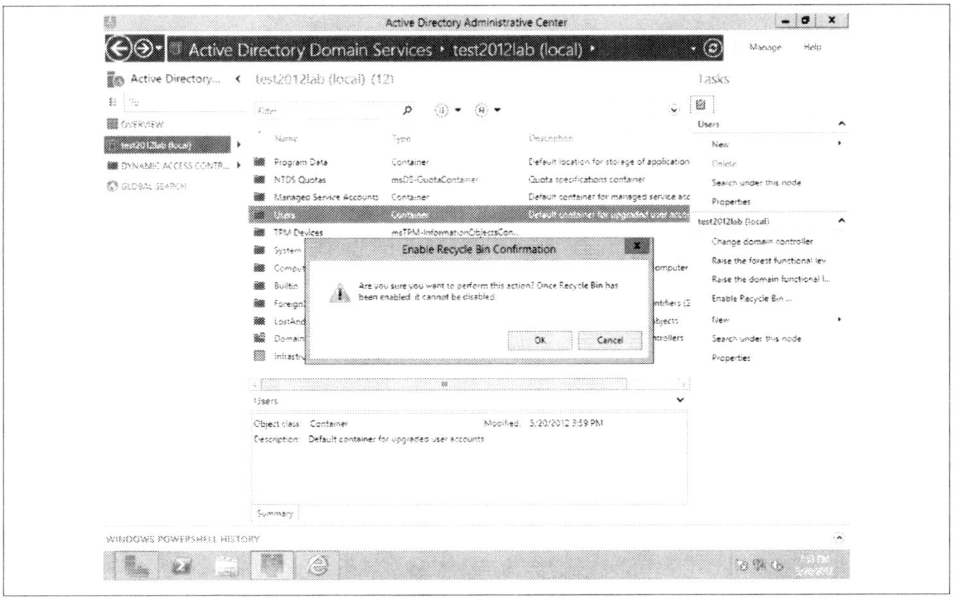

Figure 4-21. Confirming to enable the Recycle Bin

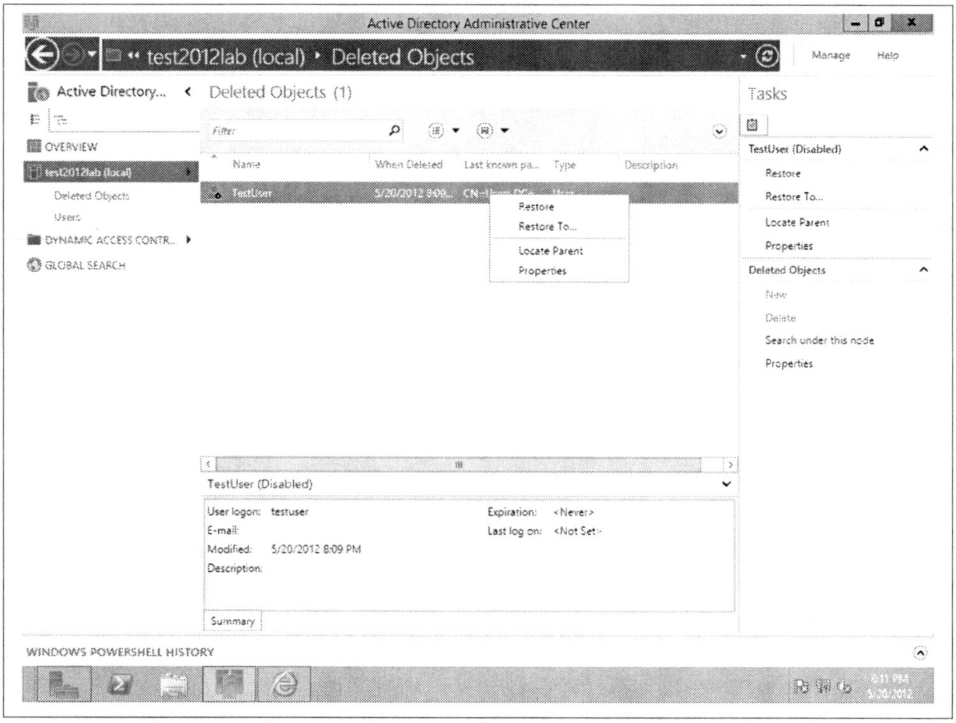

Figure 4-22. Restoring deleted objects

Performing Searches in ADAC

Sometimes you need to perform an action on a specific object within AD. Perhaps you have to disable a user account for a user who no longer is part of your organization. It can be tedious to scroll through Active Directory looking for that user account, especially in large organizations that may have many AD objects.

That's where ADAC's search capabilities come in very handy. You can perform global searches in the ADAC against the local AD or throughout an entire AD infrastructure.

To search, click Global Search on the left menu of ADAC. You can type a term directly, or you can build a search query for more complex searches.

To start building a query, click the arrow to the far right of the search field to display the "+Add criteria" drop-down menu (Figure 4-23).

The drop-down list contains the fields you can search against to build your query. Figure 4-24 shows a query built with the Name, City, and State fields.

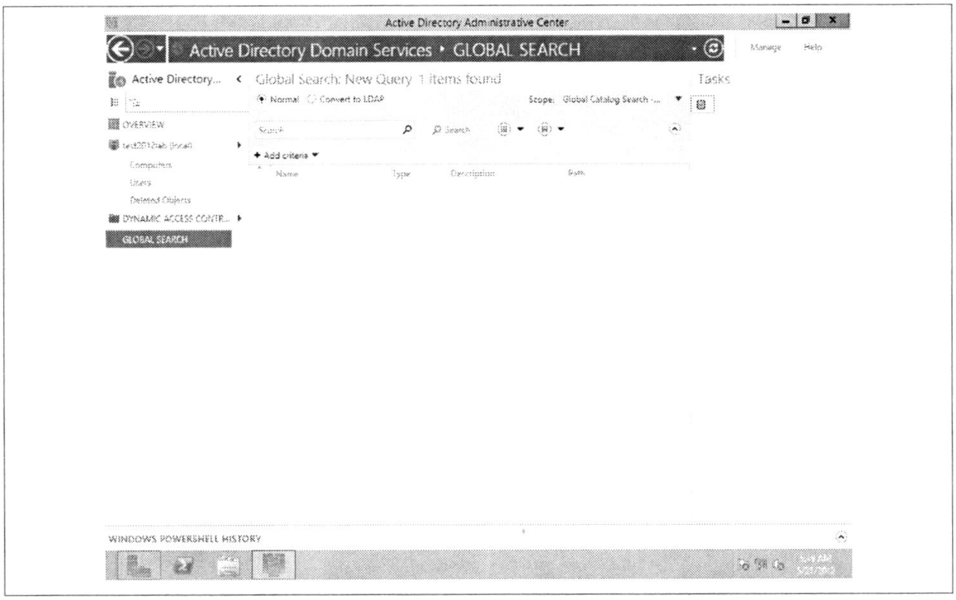

Figure 4-23. Adding criteria for a query

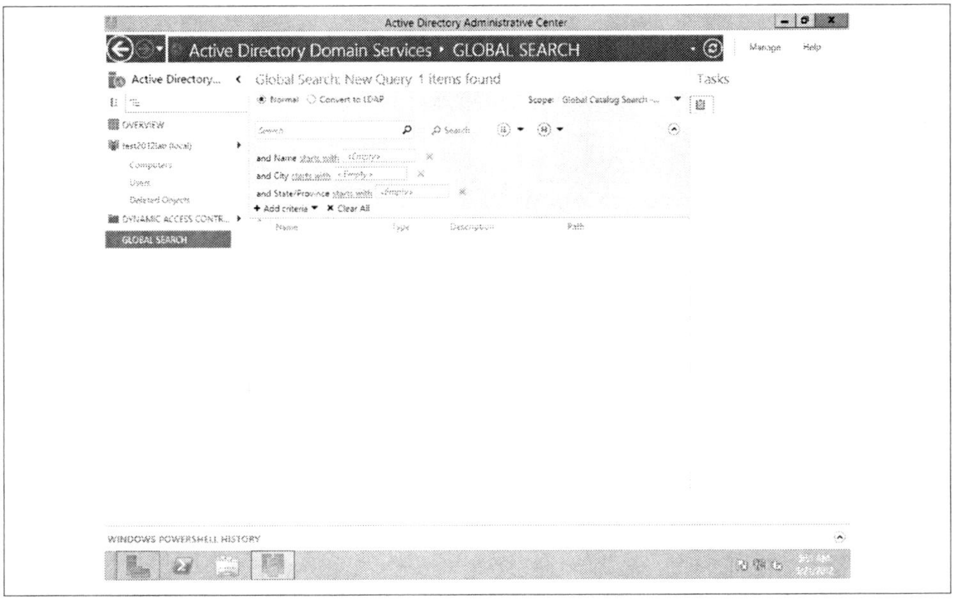

Figure 4-24. Building a query

Press Enter or click the magnifying glass to execute the query.

You can save queries by clicking the disk icon to the right of the search field (Figure 4-25).

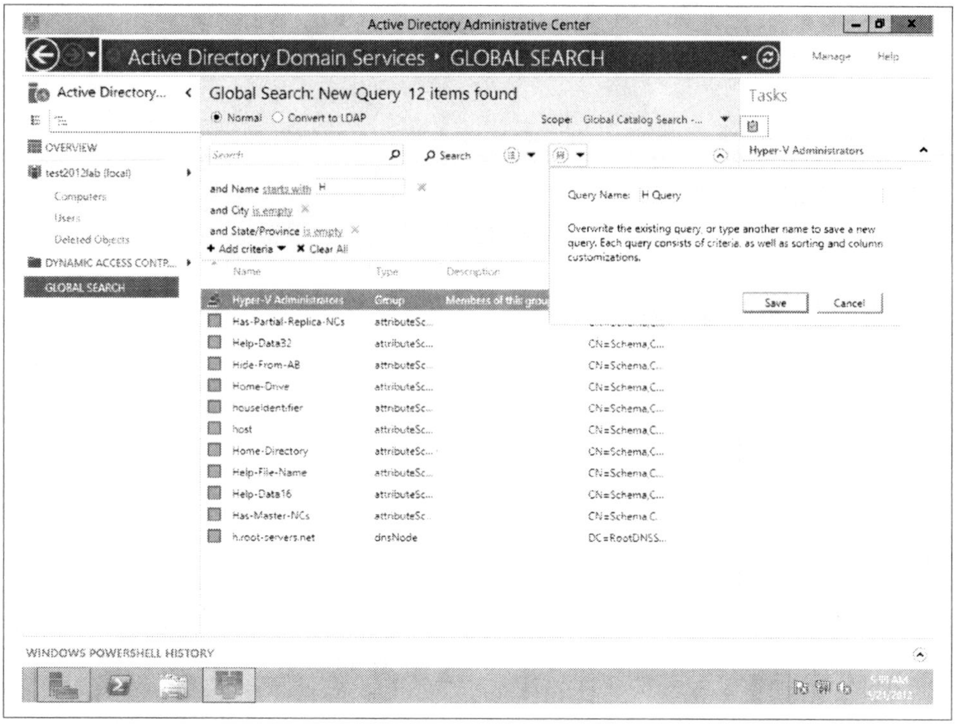

Figure 4-25. Saving a query

Once you've saved a query, you can quickly access it by clicking the query list icon (Figure 4-26).

Windows PowerShell History

At the bottom of the ADAC interface is Windows PowerShell History, a section that is collapsed by default. By clicking on the up arrow all the way to the right of the section, you can expand the area.

Displayed here are all the PowerShell commands associated with the tasks you perform in the ADAC GUI. It's a great way to become acquainted with PowerShell syntax. The Copy option will copy selected syntax to the clipboard for you to save for later use.

Take the time to learn how the routine tasks are iterated with PowerShell. Microsoft could not have made it easier with Server 2012 for you to see how much more efficiently you can do some of your normal tasks with PowerShell. So, when you need to get many things done, you have a scripted way to avoid spending incredible amounts of interactive time in the GUI.

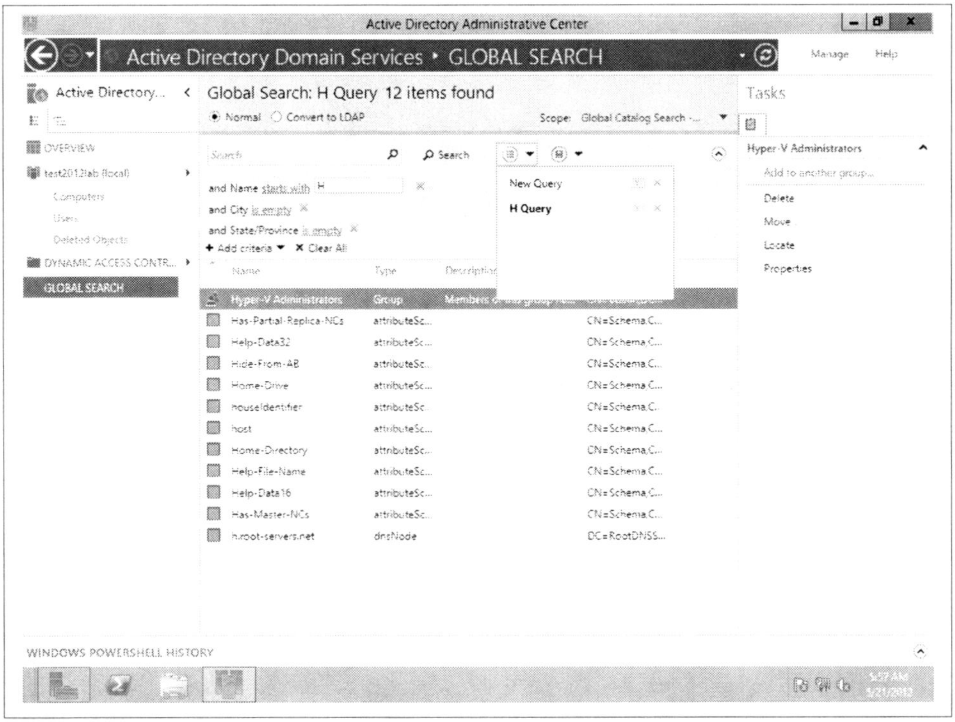

Figure 4-26. Accessing the query list

Using PowerShell to Deploy Active Directory

The administrative tasks performed in the ADAC can also be handled in PowerShell. While the focus of this book is not to teach PowerShell, it's a good idea to become familiar with PowerShell to do major management tasks such as deploying AD.

To deploy AD via PowerShell, type the following in the PowerShell console (Figure 4-27):

```
Install-windowsfeature -name AD-Domain-Services -IncludeManagement Tools
```

Upon successful execution, the installation begins, as shown in Figure 4-28.

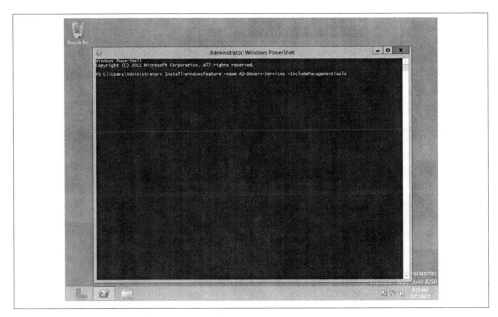

Figure 4-27. Deploying AD with PowerShell

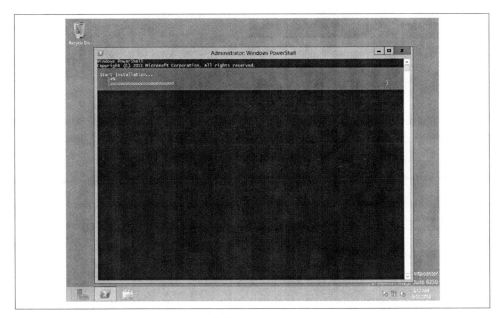

Figure 4-28. Installing AD in PowerShell

After AD is deployed, a confirmation is displayed, as well as any follow-up action needed for a successful AD deployment.

 Just about any task that can be performed in the ADAC GUI can be done in PowerShell. For example, to enable the ADAC Recycle Bin, you can use this cmdlet:

```
Enable-ADOptionalFeature -Identity'CN=RecycleBinFeature,
CN=OptionalFeatures,CN=DirectoryService,CN=WindowsNT,
CN=Service,CN=Configuratio,DC=xyz,
DC=local'ScopeForestofConfiguratioSet-Target 'xyzlocal'
```

Summary

Active Directory Domain Services is more efficient to manage in Server 2012. It offers more centralized administration with preinstallation checks, and integrated Adprep.exe with the install process means a more hassle-free deployment experience.

Having AD DS configured easily and correctly is a critical step to ensure the effectiveness of a directory service for amenities such as user identity management, security and authorization management, and device management.

Although the Active Directory Administrative Center has capabilities that have been included in previous Windows servers, such as search and the Recycle Bin, the interface has changed enough that it's important to familiarize yourself with where to find features and how to use them. The interface also offers customization functionality, such as the ability to collapse or hide sections when creating new AD objects.

Server 2012 Active Directory can run at the Server 2012 functional level, or it can be incorporated into older functional levels of Active Directory domains, although some functionality may be sacrificed.

While it may seem like a bother to use PowerShell to execute commands that you can perform with just a click in the GUI, it's worth getting acquainted with various Power-Shell commands—in particular, ones related to Active Directory tasks—in order to manage AD quickly and efficiently. The best way to grasp PowerShell's potential is to imagine needing to apply a slight change to every user object in Active Directory—a process that would take forever with the GUI. Investing a little time in learning Power-Shell can make accomplishing such seemingly daunting tasks quick and easy, and this is a central theme of Server 2012.

CHAPTER 5

Managing Users and Data with Dynamic Access Control

Without question, the one major new capability that you will have to get to know at some time or another—and no matter how big or small the infrastructure—is Dynamic Access Control (DAC).

DAC provides rich, centralized control over data and user permissions through various mechanisms, including expression-based access conditions (i.e., if *x* condition is met, then access is granted), centralized access policies, and centralized auditing.

The reason DAC is so significant is because it reduces many of the pain points that arise when you're trying to deploy, manage, and keep the reins on permissions throughout a Windows forest or domain. Managing Windows permissions, as many of us know, can easily spiral out of control.

Permissions, in general, have been managed through NTFS, Active Directory, and the use of groups. In many cases, a user who is not a member of a particular group needs access to a file in a shared folder belonging to that group. What often ends up happening in such cases is that unnecessary groups are created. NTFS permissions get sloppy in parent and child folders, and keeping track of which users have access to what data becomes an auditing nightmare. Not only do you face group membership bloat when access permission management gets out of control, but you also encounter the issue of security token overload. As a company grows and more users (employees) are added, very often the number of groups increases. Group and user increases invariably lead to an increase in Kerberos security tokens. These tokens are created for users and contain all the groups to which a user belongs. With Kerberos bloat, users can experience a slow login process and myriad login errors. Inherent properties of DAC help to reduce both group complexity and token bloat.

Being able to audit user access and changes to data is a good practice in any infrastructure, but it becomes crucial in organizations that are mandated to follow compliance regulations such as Sarbanes-Oxley (SOX) and the Health Insurance Portability and Accountability Act (HIPAA). These are federal regulations that dictate a set of requirements for digital data in the finance and healthcare industries, respectively. These requirements include robust auditing and accountability mandates for IT staff, executives, and privacy officers so they know who is accessing what data and are able to supply reports on such activity.

Access policies and auditing aren't new features in Windows Server, but Dynamic Access Control is. DAC allows for complex, natural-language statements on which to base access and auditing policies.

In addition, DAC introduces enhanced data classification. Documents can be automatically classified based on their content. This means, as a server administrator, you can create a rule that will classify any file that contains parameters you specify—for instance, any file containing the words "company confidential" can be classified as "sensitive" and automatically encrypted using RMS (Rights Management Services).

Even with the new and improved permissions management DAC delivers, there are still times when users may need access to a file or folder share for which they do not have explicit permissions. There also may be issues when existing NTFS permissions do not align with the newly deployed DAC. For these scenarios, Microsoft has included a feature in DAC called Access Denied Remediation. Users can request access to data that they don't have permissions for from the data content owner or IT department. While not truly automated remediation (because the user has to send a request via email, and then IT staff or the data content owner has to configure the data appropriately), Access Denied Remediation can help reduce calls to the IT helpdesk from users seeking access to restricted content.

The Building Blocks of DAC

There are two fundamental components of Dynamic Access Control: claims and resource properties.

If I state, "I live in New York," I am making a *claim*. Claims have been integrated into Kerberos authentication in Server 2012. With claims, you can identify and configure permissions for users and devices based not only on the security groups to which they belong, but also on claims you configure, such as, "This user's security clearance is High."

A *resource property* is a customizable label that you can apply to data to classify it. You can create resource properties that identify a file or folder as Sensitive, Confidential, Human Resources Group Only, or any other properties you may need to keep data safe in your organization.

Claims and resource properties are the building blocks of DAC and the components upon which central access policies and auditing are built. You can get very complex and detailed with DAC, but keep in mind that successfully deploying it begins with proper setup of claims and resource properties. In the next sections, I'll detail the step-by-step configuration of DAC to get you up and running with this major new capability in Server 2012.

Requirements and Predeployment Pointers

Before testing and deploying DAC, you need to keep a few pointers in mind. While Microsoft touts DAC as the saving grace for many IT woes, there are problems that can still crop up with deploying DAC.

The biggest caveat is that DAC works only on Server 2012, Windows 8, and Windows RT (the tablet OEM version of Windows 8) clients. Of course, most Windows shops already have servers, Active Directory, NTFS permissions, and their entire Windows ecosystem in place. So what to do?

The expectation is that most infrastructures will add in perhaps a Windows Server 2012 domain controller and some Server 2012 file servers. This will enable use of user claims and other components of DAC within a current Windows environment. These server boxes don't even have to be physical servers; DAC can be deployed on virtual machines.

Microsoft is also offering the Data Classification Toolkit (*http://www.microsoft.com/en-us/download/details.aspx?id=27123*) to help deploy DAC across multiple servers in an organization. The toolkit can implement some aspects of DAC to Server 2008 R2.

Your biggest concern as a server administrator might be potential conflicts between existing NTFS permissions and DAC. Even if you bring over data from, let's say, a Server 2008 R2 file server onto a new Server 2012 box, that data is inheriting NTFS permissions already in place. So which takes precedence: NTFS or the DAC controls?

There is one good rule of thumb to remember when you're deploying DAC into existing Windows networks: NTFS permissions won't give more access than a claims-based rule allows, and a claims-based rule won't give more permission than NTFS allows. That may look convoluted on paper, but when DAC is deployed and configured with NTFS permissions, it becomes easier to see that rule in action.

I would also recommend deploying DAC in a test environment with a replication of your file servers. Again, these can be virtualized machines. Allow time for testing how and if DAC impacts your current security settings. When the time comes to deploy DAC, start with less critical data. The idea of DAC is to incorporate it gradually into existing infrastructures.

Finally, DAC can be complicated to set up. There are lots of steps and new concepts for legacy Windows server administrators to get used to. The following setup instructions detail fairly simple DAC deployments, but the idea is to get you familiarized with terms and the deployment process. Keep in mind that DAC can be used for very complex and sophisticated access control expressions and configurations.

Deploying DAC

There is a basic workflow in deploying DAC. The key component of DAC is a central access policy. The workflow for creating a central access policy begins with configuring claims; as mentioned previously, these are properties used to compare user accounts and files to determine if a user has the requirements needed to access a file. These properties, or claims, are added to a resource property list.

The next steps involve the actual creation of the central access policy. The resource property list is applied to this policy. The policy is then published throughout the domain.

We can then deploy DAC to file servers, and the central access policy is pushed out to folder shares.

The last step is to validate DAC. The process is summed up in the chart in Figure 5-1.

Preparing Claims

When configuring claim types for users, you are adding existing Active Directory attributes to the list of attributes used to evaluate who gets access to what.

In this example deployment, we'll use the Payroll user department as part of the calculation to determine whether a user has access to files in the Payroll folder share.

From Server Manager, open Tools and then Active Directory Administrative Center, and click Dynamic Access Control. Click Claim Type→New→Claim Type.

Under Source Attribute in the resulting window, scroll to look for Department; then, click that attribute and make Value Type equal String. Here, we are basing the existing Department attribute on the new claim type we will create.

Under Display Name, type **Department** and click OK. (See Figure 5-2.)

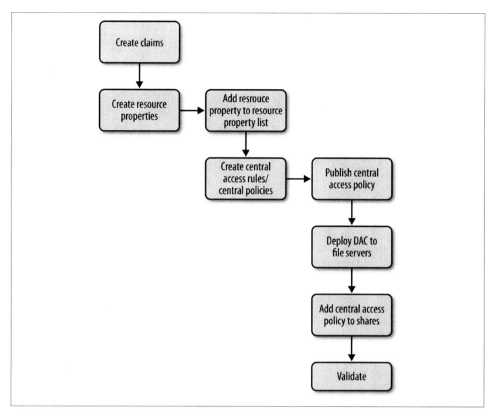

Figure 5-1. DAC basic deployment workflow

In the Active Directory Administrative Center, you will now see a new claim type.

 In Figure 5-2, you can see the option "Protect from accidental deletion." This protection is enabled by default for objects created in DAC. If you want to delete an object, you must uncheck this option.

Configuring Resource Property for Files

Next, you must add a resource property to match the claim we've created. Resource properties are used by file servers to classify data. There are several predefined resource properties, but you can create new ones.

To create a new resource property, from the ADAC click Resource Properties, New, and then Resource Property.

Under Display Name, add Department Payroll and make Value equal Payroll, then click OK twice. Now the resource property, Department Payroll, is listed. (See Figure 5-3.)

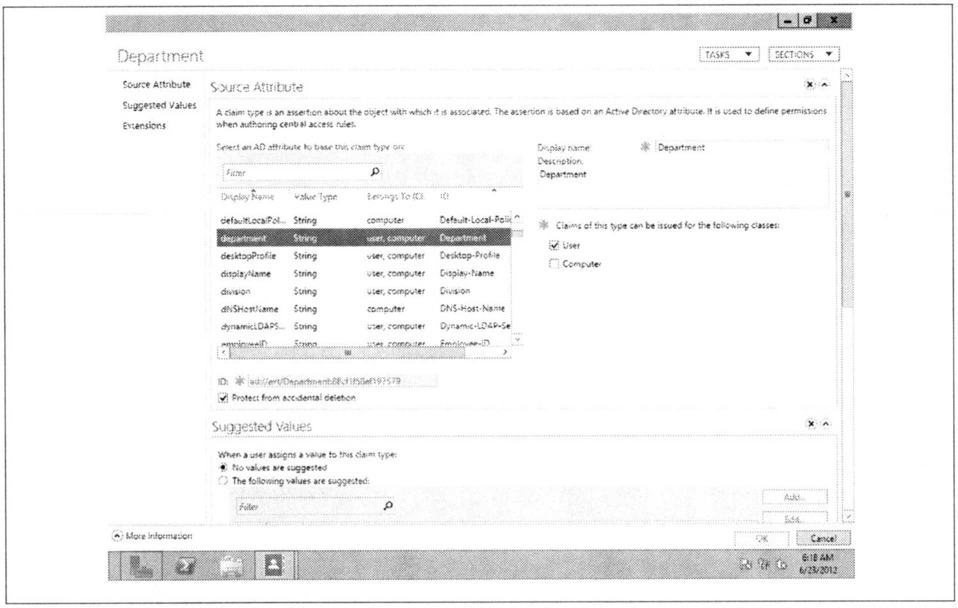

Figure 5-2. Configuring a new claim type

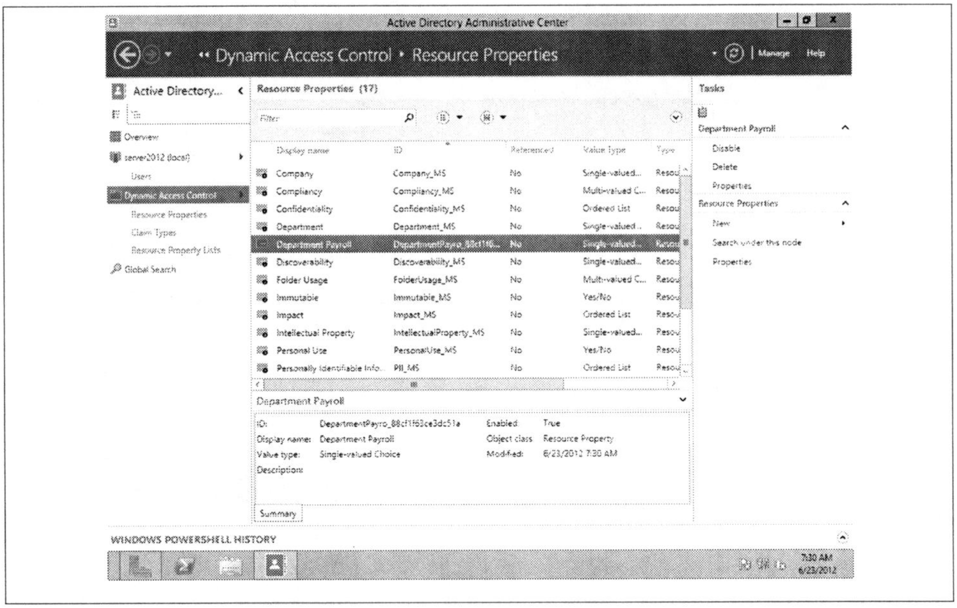

Figure 5-3. Configuring a new resource property

Adding a Resource Property to the Global Resource Property List

Every resource property has to be added to a resource property list. These lists make the resource property available to file servers. DAC resources can have individual lists target specific file servers, but for our purposes here, we are going to add the resource property to the Global Resource Property List.

From the ADAC, click Dynamic Access Control, Resource Property List, and then Add Resource Property. Click the Department Payroll resource we created before; next, click the right arrows and then OK.

Now, you should have the Department Payroll resource listed as a member of the Global Resource Property List. (See Figure 5-4.)

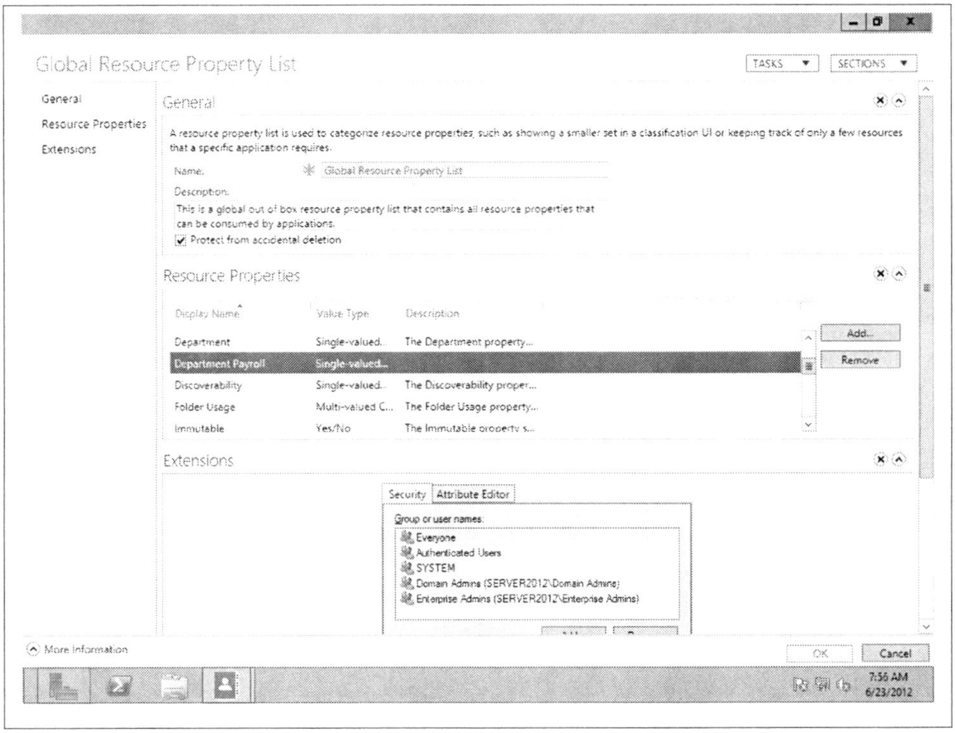

Figure 5-4. Adding a resource property to the Global Resource Property List

Creating a New Central Access Rule

A central access rule is similar to an access control list (ACL). With such a rule, you can set conditions for user access to data—for example, you can set up a rule such as "If x condition is met, then access is granted."

In this example, we'll require that a user's department attribute match the value of a folder share's department attribute.

Open up ADAC, and click Dynamic Access Control, Central Access Rules, New, and then Central Access Rules.

Under Name, type `Department-Payroll-Match-Required`. You can name your rule anything; just make sure you can easily identify what the rule is supposed to do. Under Target Resources, click Edit and then "Add a condition."

Now add two conditions: Resource Department Payroll Exists and Resource Department Payroll Equals Value Payroll, and then click OK. (See Figure 5-5.)

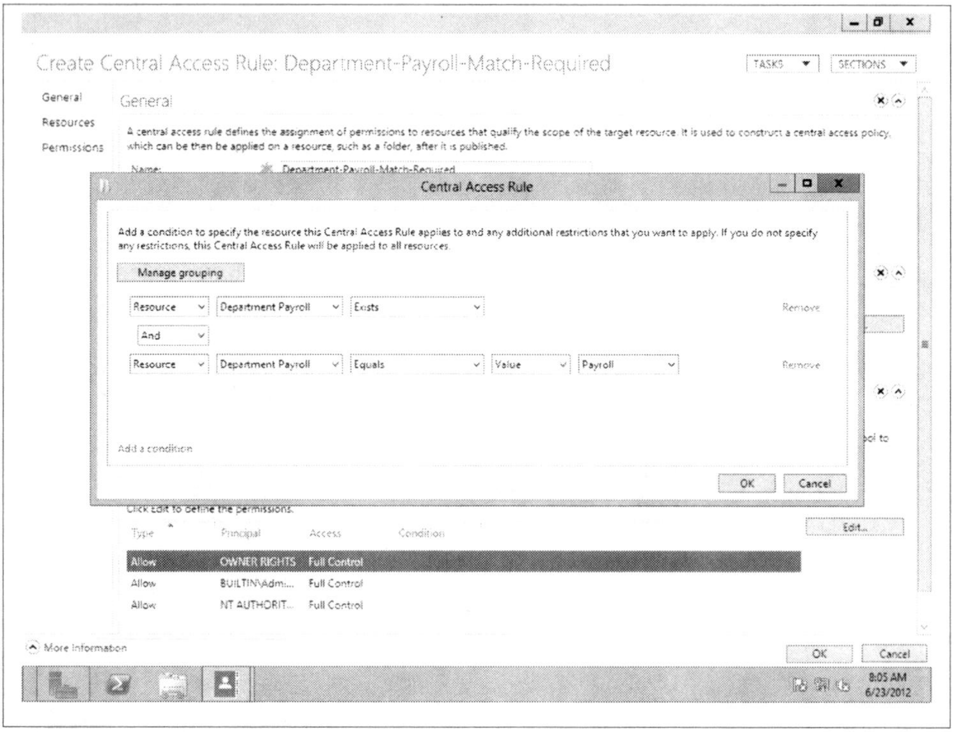

Figure 5-5. Creating a central access rule

Under Permissions, select "Use following permissions as current permissions" and click Edit to define permissions. For example, you can choose to give the Payroll Department Full Control to any data this rule is applied to. To test permissions without actually putting them into effect, select "Use following permissions as proposed permissions."

Creating a Central Access Policy

Now we need to add the new central access rule to a central access policy. With DAC, there is one central access policy per file or folder.

From ADAC, click Dynamic Access Control, Central Access Policies, New, and then Central Access Policy.

Name your policy Domain File Server Policy, and then click Add. The Department-Payroll-Match-Required rule is available to add to the policy. Now, click the right arrows to add, and click OK.

Publishing a Central Access Policy

Once you've created the central access policy, you need to push it out to file servers using *group policy objects* (GPOs).

From Server Manager, click Tools and then Group Policy Management. Right-click the domain name and click "Create a GPO in this domain and Link it here."

Let's name the GPO "Dynamic Access Control Policy," click OK, and then click "New policy." At this point, remove the default group that's granted access, "Authenticated users," because we don't want all authenticated users to have access to the payroll data.

On this screen, select Object Type to choose the file server(s) to which to apply the policy. Ensure that Computers is checked as the Object Type.

Next, right-click the policy you named Dynamic Access Control Policy and then click Edit. Then navigate to Computer Configuration→Policies→Windows Settings→Security Settings→File System and right-click Central Access Policies. Now select Manage Central Access Policy. Here, select the policy you created, then click OK and exit the Group Policy Management Editor.

To complete publishing, there are two more tasks to perform: enable Kerberos armoring and update Group Policy.

Kerberos armoring addresses security concerns that dogged Kerberos authentication, such as vulnerability to brute force attacks and spoofing. With Kerberos armoring, a secured tunnel is created between a domain client and a domain controller.

Kerberos armoring is easy to enable. From Group Policy Management, navigate to Computer Configuration→Policies→Administrative Templates→System→KDC. Enable "KDC support for claims, compound authentication and Kerberos armoring."

To perform a group policy update, simply launch Windows PowerShell and run the command: **GPUPDATE /FORCE**.

Configuring the File Server

The steps outlined thus far detail the necessary configuration for DAC on the domain controller side. We will perform the next steps on the file server where we want to apply the created claims-based access rule.

Launch that file server's Server Manager. From the Dashboard, click "Add roles and features," and keep clicking Next until server roles are selectable. Add the File Server Resource Manager Feature as part of the already-installed File and Storage Services.

Once that's complete, go to the folder share on which you want to perform access controls. In our case, this is the Payroll share for which we set up claims-based conditions at the beginning of the example. Right-click the folder, go into its properties, and click the Classification tab. You should see the resource property we created earlier listed here —a good indication that your DAC configuration is going well.

 If you don't see the resource property or properties you created in the Classification tab, the domain may be taking a little long to replicate changes. You can force an update by running the command **Update-FSRMClassificationpropertyDefinition** from Windows PowerShell.

Adding the Central Access Policy to the Folder

Before adding the central access policy to the Payroll share, you should perform another forced Group Policy update to make sure the central policy defined by the Dynamic Access Control Policy GPO is applied to the file servers.

Next, go into the properties of the folder share; click the Security tab and then Advanced. Click Central Policy and then Change. From the drop-down menu, select your central access policy (the one you named Domain File Server Policy), click Apply, and then click OK. (See Figure 5-6.)

Validating the Configuration

After completing all these steps and configuration requirements, you'll want to test to see if what you set up works. A really handy capability in DAC is the ability to view a user's effective permissions once you have configured some aspect of DAC. Let's view the effective permissions of two domain users for the Payroll network folder. The user Betty Test is a member of the Executives security group, but not a member of the Payroll group. Henry Pym is a domain user with membership only to the Payroll group.

If DAC is configured correctly, Betty should have no access to the Payroll share. In the properties of the Payroll share, click the Advanced button under Security. As we expected, the effective permissions of Betty's account show she has no access to Payroll (see Figure 5-7).

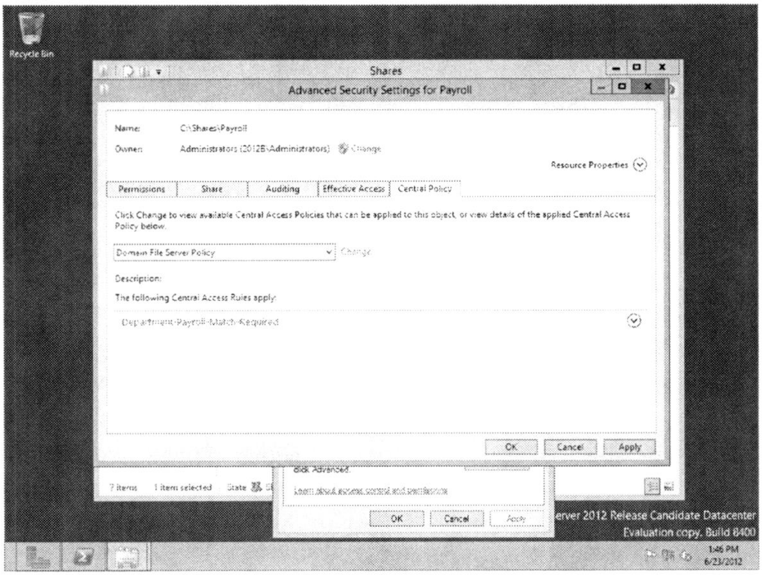

Figure 5-6. Adding a central policy to a folder share

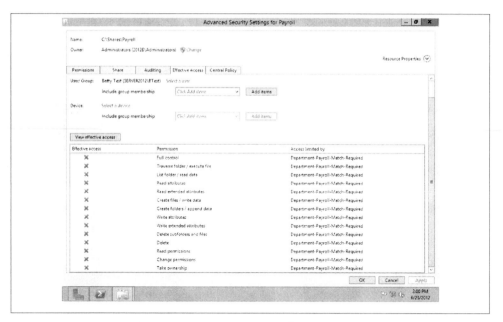

Figure 5-7. DAC gives this user no access to the configured network share

Henry's effective permissions show full access to the Payroll share, so again, DAC is working the way we intended (see Figure 5-8).

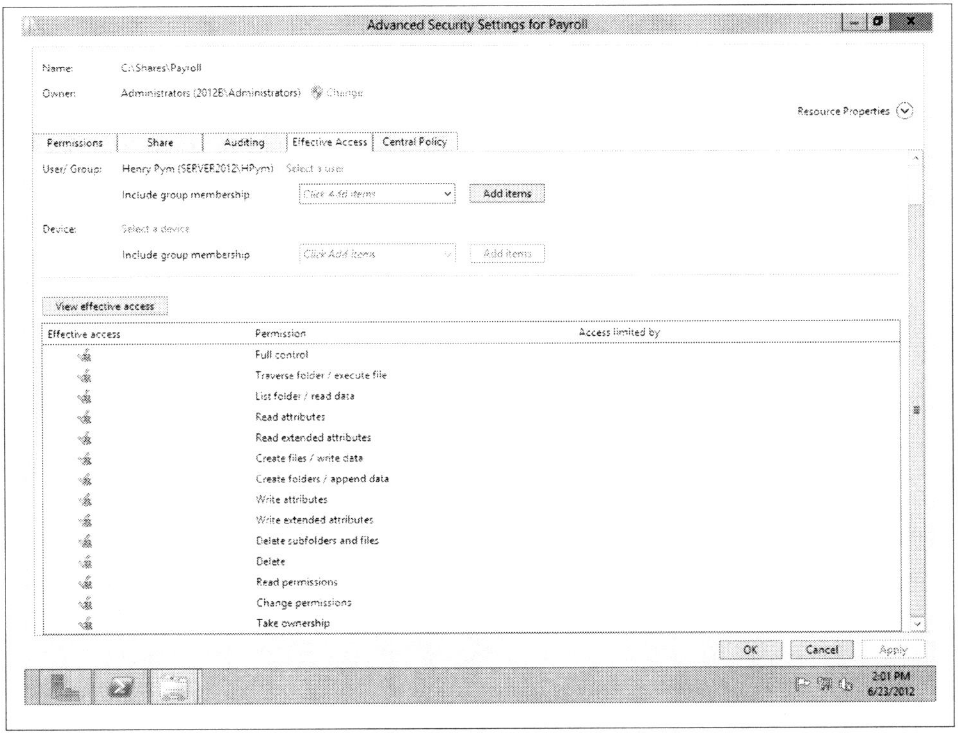

Figure 5-8. This user is granted full permissions to the DAC-configured network share

These are fairly easy DAC deployments, but a good way to get familiar with the basics and first steps of working with DAC.

Access Denied Remediation

Within Dynamic Access Control is the capability to set up the domain such that if a user cannot get into a file or folder because of permissions issues, a customized message displays instructing the user on how to get access. This involves setting up email notification that gets sent to the data owner or IT department (or whoever can approve and give the user access to that data), a functionality known as Access Denied Remediation.

While Microsoft markets this as yet another advancement in DAC (and don't get me wrong, it is), I think a bigger benefit is that Access Denied Remediation allows for quick resolution to problems that may result during DAC deployment. DAC is quite a leap from the way most of us have gotten used to managing permissions in an infrastructure. It's conceivable that there will be growing pains with its deployment. With Access Denied Remediation, permissions issues can be quickly and centrally addressed.

Access Denied Remediation is carried out in three ways. In the first scenario, users can self-assist by requesting access from the owner of that data without involving a server administrator. This is probably the least likely scenario to be carried out in smaller organizations, and more likely in larger ones with massive amounts of data, where having IT grant permissions to every user getting an "access denied" error would be an incredible waste of IT resources. The second remediation option is when, for example, a folder owner receives an email notification that a user requested access. Finally, as we saw in the previous section, administrators can quickly view the effective permissions of any user within a folder or file's properties and configure permissions accordingly.

Deploying Access Denied Remediation

You can configure Access Denied Remediation on individual file servers or throughout an entire domain. The feature is configured in Group Policy for deployment throughout the domain and via File Server Resource Manager on individual file servers.

Group policy deployment

From Group Policy Management, right-click the policy for the domain and click Edit. Navigate to Computer Configuration→Policies→Administrative Templates→System→Access Denied Assistance. You will see two options: "Customize messages" (configure how you want Access Denied Remediation instructions to appear to users) and "Enable access denied assistance for Windows clients" (Access Denied Remediation is supported only on Server 2012, Windows 8, and Windows RT).

File server deployment

To deploy on individual file servers, from the file server, launch File Services Resource Manager. Right-click File Server Resource Manager (Local), select Configuration Options, and then click the Access Denied Remediation tab.

You can enter custom text, or you can use the following built-in macros to create text:

- [Original File Path]
- [Original File Path Folder] (lists the parent folder of the file the user tried to access)
- [Admin e-mail]
- [Data owner email]

See Figure 5-9 for an example of an access denied custom message.

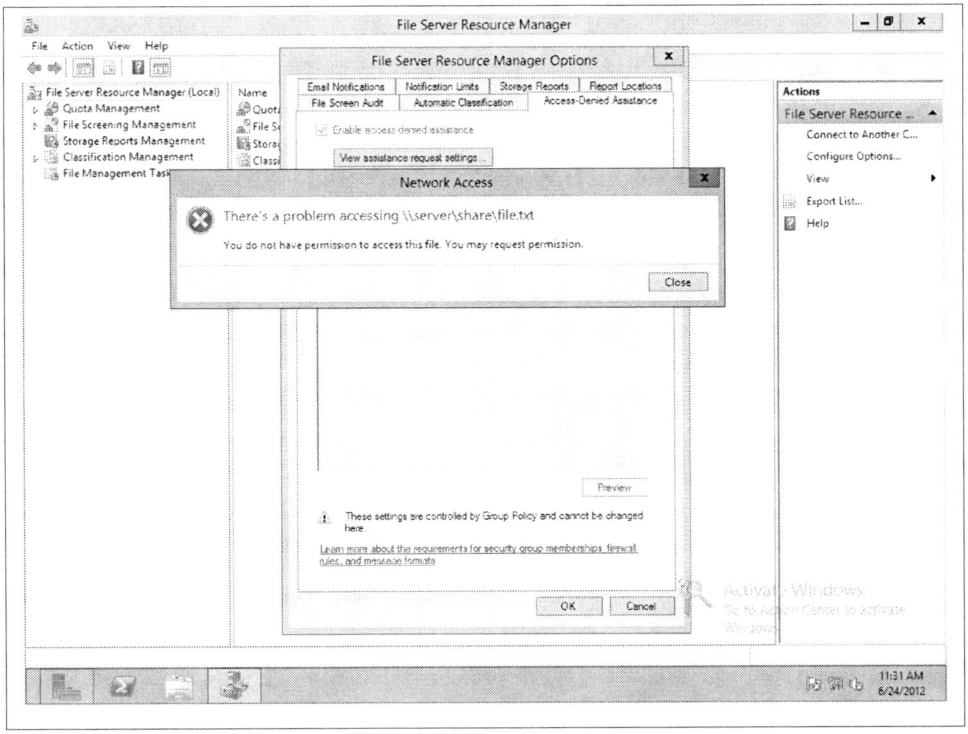

Figure 5-9. Custom access denied assistance message

You have some flexibility with Access Denied Remediation. For example, you can specify a separate access denied message for a specific folder, again using the File Server Resource Manager. You do so by double-clicking File Server Resource Manager (Local) and then expanding Classification Management and right-clicking Classification Properties. Select Set Folder Management Properties.

In the Property box, click Access Denied Assistance Message and then click Add. Browse to the folder you want to apply the message to and create your message or use the macros.

Configure email notification by clicking File Server Resource Manager, right-clicking File Server Resource Manager (Local), selecting Configure Options, and clicking the "E-mail notification" tab.

Auditing

Auditing is yet another component of Dynamic Access Control that, while not new to Windows Server, has undergone a refresh. Windows Server 2008 and 2008 R2 will create audit events anytime a file is accessed, but auditing in Server 2012 is centralized and more sophisticated.

With file access auditing in Server 2012, you can track changes to central access rules and policies, claims definitions, file attributes, and, of course, data access.

If you have been or currently are a Windows server administrator, you already understand the importance of auditing. Auditing is critical for those aforementioned compliance regulations, where federal rules demand that certain organizations know who is accessing what. Auditing is also important for internal security—to protect a company's intellectual property and to prevent data leakage.

While Microsoft has strengthened auditing with Windows Server 2012, the company is going even further, working with partners on solutions for powerful interpretation and analysis of audits. Microsoft's own System Center Operations Manager (SCOM) will work with Server 2012 in providing audit analysis tools.

There are a couple of steps required for configuring auditing in a domain. First, you have to configure a Global Object Access Policy. Launch Group Policy Management and navigate to Computer Configuration→Policies→Windows Settings→Security Settings→Audit Policies→Object Access→Audit File System Properties.

Check the boxes to enable "Configure the following audit events," Success, and Failure. (See Figure 5-10.)

From the navigation pane, under "Audit policies," double-click Global Object Access Auditing. Check the box next to "Define this policy setting," and then click Configure.

The resulting window is the Advanced Security Settings for Global File SACL (security access control lists). Click Add, then "Select a principal." For a global policy, you will typically select Everyone, Full Control, and then Permissions.

Here's where you set the conditions you want to audit. For example, if you want to audit what's happening with Payroll shares and files, you would set:

[Resource][Department][Any of][Value][Payroll]

Now, click OK three times and return to the navigation pane. From there, to finish configuration, click Object Access, double-click Audit Handle Manipulation, and make sure that "Configure the following audit events," Success, and Failure are all checked.

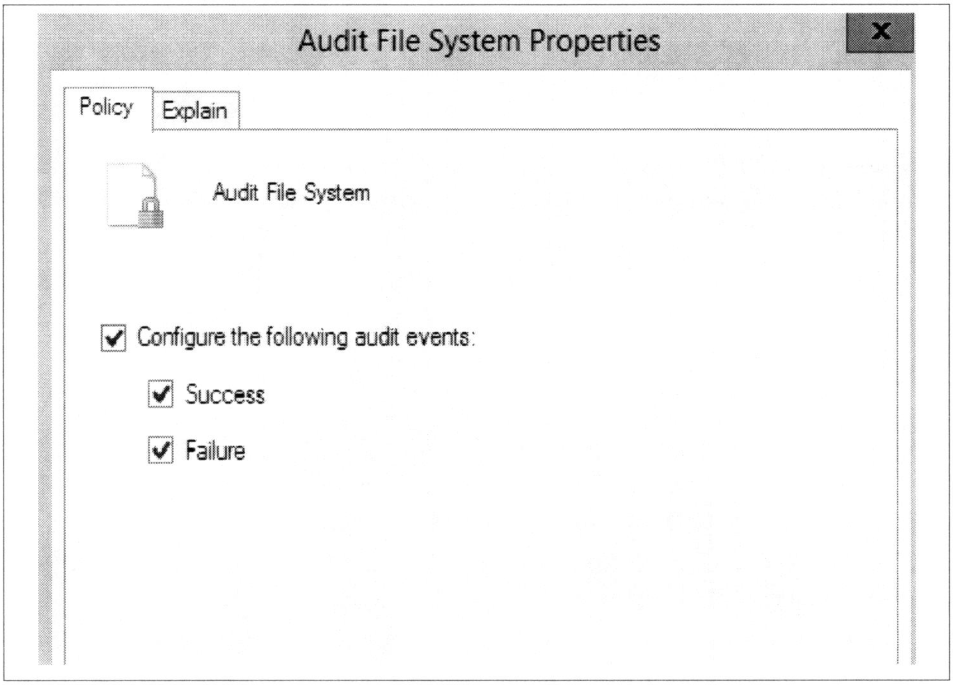

Figure 5-10. Configuring an audit event in Group Policy Management

Once you set up an audit policy for the domain, it's good practice to force a Group Policy update. To verify whether your audit settings are correct—for example, on a shared folder you may have applied against—you modify a file in the share and check the Event Viewer for events 4656 and 4663.

Automatic File Classification

As with auditing, file classification isn't new to Windows Server but has been enhanced in Server 2012. File classification adds to a server administrator's arsenal of management tools with powerful content classification rules.

With a classification rule, you can, for instance, automatically search against a specified set of files to look for the string "Company Confidential." If the string is found in a file, you can set that file's classification to High.

You can also use classification rules to detect sensitive data, such as documents containing Social Security numbers or patient healthcare information.

To deploy automatic file classification, first you need to create resource property definitions. From a domain controller, launch the ADAC. Click Dynamic Access Control, and then Resource Properties. Right-click a property (for instance, Impact), select Enable, and then enable the Personally Identifiable Information resource property.

Next, you create a Content Classification Rule. You do so on the file server with data you want to classify. From the server, as an administrator, run the following command in PowerShell:

```
Update-FSRMClassificationpropertyDefinition
```

This command syncs the property definitions enabled in the DC to file servers. Next, follow these steps:

1. Launch File Server Resource Manager and expand Classification Management, right-click Classification Rules, and click Configure Classification Schedule. Check "Enable fixed schedule" and "Allow continuous classification for new files." Select the day you want to run the rule and click OK.

2. Right-click Classification Rules and select Create Classification Rule. Name your rule Company Confidential.

3. In the Scope tab, click Add and select the folders to be included in the rule. In the Classification tab, configure the following:

   a. "Choose a method to assign a property to files" equals Content Classifier.

   b. "Choose a property to assign to files" equals Impact.

   c. "Specify a value" equals High.

4. Next, click the Configure button under Parameters. In Expression Type, select String. Under Expression, type in **Company Confidential**. You can opt to make the string case-sensitive from the Expression Type drop-down list. Click OK.

5. In the Evaluation Type tab, check "Re-evaluate existing property values" and select "Overwrite the existing values" when a conflict occurs between new and existing values. Click OK.

We now have a new classification rule set against a selected folder that looks for the string "Company Confidential" within documents in that folder. (See Figure 5-11.)

To verify that files are classified correctly, click Classification Management from the File Server Resource Manager. Right-click Classification Rules and then click "Run Classification with All Rules Now."

This runs the Automatic Classification Report to check for classification rules you've established.

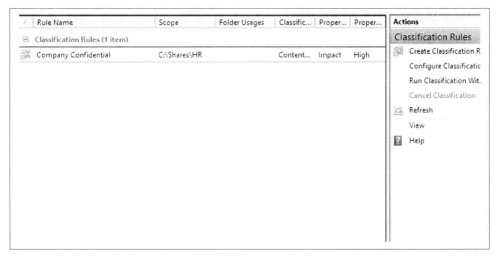

	Rule Name	Scope	Folder Usages	Classific...	Proper...	Proper...
⊟	Classification Rules (1 item)					
	Company Confidential	C:\Shares\HR		Content...	Impact	High

Figure 5-11. "Company Confidential" classification rule

Encrypting Classified Data

Once you have data classified, you can elect to encrypt that data using RMS (rights management server) encryption. Using RMS, you can automatically protect documents based on their classification.

Now, let's create a rule to classify any documents in the *HR* folder to be classified as High if the string "Company Confidential" is found. From the File Server Resource Manager on the file server where the *HR* folder resides, click File Management Tasks and right-click to pull up Create File Management Task.

Give your task the name High Business Impact and the description "Auto RMS protection for confidential docs." From the Scope tab, check Group Files. Select a day from the Schedule tab (the recommendation is to run the task once per week), and under "Continuous operation," choose "Run task continuously on new files." From the Action tab, set Type to RMS Encryption. Next, add the folder you want to run the task against and then run it to verify the configuration.

Summary

Dynamic Access Control can take some getting used to when you first deploy it. There are lots of little steps to wade through and lots of customization options. This is access control that extends way beyond pointing and clicking to set NTFS permissions.

Expect pitfalls, teeth gnashing, and some of Microsoft's infamously cryptic error messages from time to time. Above all, do not attempt to deploy DAC in a live production environment. Test it out first and see if deploying DAC impacts existing permissions.

DAC is a major enhancement from previous versions of Windows Server. Its true power will be most obvious in Windows Server 2012–level domains running Server 2012 domain controllers and file servers and Windows 8 clients. However, you can get started with DAC by deploying a minimum infrastructure with a Windows Server 2012 domain controller and file server.

CHAPTER 6

Storage Management and Clustering

Data accumulation is at an all-time high, as is our dependency on the computer systems we use day to day. This is why storage and high availability of data storage systems are hot topics in technology. Deploying and managing storage and high-availability solutions flexibly and cost-effectively is critical to a well-running IT infrastructure.

Server 2012 delivers key new features and enhancements for storage and for keeping an infrastructure operational in instances of system failure or data corruption. Storage Spaces and ReFS are two major developments in Server 2012 pertaining to storage management.

Storage Spaces is a new feature installed with the File and Storage Services role. Storage Spaces is a low-cost alternative to RAID (but not a substitute, since it's software-based, and many RAID solutions for business depend on actual hardware-based RAID controllers). With Storage Spaces, you can convert any type of disk: SATA, SAS, and even USB, and create storage pools and additional storage space.

Storage is thinly provisioned through the creation of virtual disks. You can configure internal and external drives *storage pools*, virtual hard drives created from physical drives. In turn, these storage pools can be configured with Storage Spaces.

With Storage Spaces, it's possible to dynamically add storage; the feature not only allows for storage scalability, but also can be used for fault tolerance because you can configure the spaces with mirroring and parity redundancy.

Because of the flexibility Storage Spaces offers, organizations can deploy storage solutions such as SANs (storage area networks) with iSCSI targets without the hardware investments typically associated with deploying such solutions.

ReFS (Resilient File System) is a new filesystem introduced with Windows Server 2012. The key to understanding the purpose of ReFS is the word *resilient*. ReFS is all about keeping data integrity—that is, making data less prone to corruption—and thus decreasing the chances of data loss.

ReFS is designed for use with Storage Spaces and specifically, Storage Spaces with mirroring. With mirroring, data corruption is seamlessly repaired across mirrored volumes. Using built-in metadata that gives checksums, ReFS is not only reliable for creating Storage Spaces with virtual disks that provide fault tolerance, but is also scalable. ReFS can also perform automatic repair of data corruption.

The main controversy that I can envision surrounding Storage Spaces is that it really is just software-based RAID, albeit beefed up. While software RAID can work fine as a fault-tolerant solution for many organizations, those needing mission-critical fault tolerance may prefer to still implement third-party hardware RAID solutions. Hardware-based RAID offers some benefits over software RAID because it can be implemented with its own hardware independent of any server and does not cause extra load on server performance. The problem with hardware RAID is that if the RAID controller fails, your entire RAID solution can be destroyed. Of course, with a software solution like Storage Spaces, if your mirrored volumes get corrupted, then all the mirrored data is compromised.

You can deploy Storage Spaces to use as a file server and take advantage of the data protection. This would require deploying a file server attached to a JBOD (Just a Bunch of Disks) configuration using SATA or SAS drives. You also use Storage Spaces as a two-node server cluster for failover.

Storage Spaces can be of great benefit for organizations looking for low-cost storage solutions and can be used for NAS (network-attached storage) and SAN deployments that would otherwise require purchasing additional hardware. The advantages of using Storage Spaces versus a third-party hardware solution ultimately depend on the storage and fault-tolerance needs of your infrastructure.

ReFS Versus NTFS

ReFS is not meant to be used in lieu of NTFS, but rather as a complement to it. You cannot boot an operating system from an ReFS volume, and you can't perform in-place conversions of NTFS volumes to ReFS volumes. You'll want to reserve ReFS for storage to take advantage of the data correction capabilities.

Because ReFS is built from NTFS, the two filesystems share some common attributes, as detailed in Table 6-1.

Table 6-1. NTFS versus ReFS

Attribute	NTFS	ReFS
Maximum single file size	$2^{64}-1$ KB	$2^{64}-1$ KB
Maximum volume size	2^{64} clusters	2^{78} bytes with 16KB cluster size ($2^{64} \times 16 \times 2^{10}$). Windows stack addressing allows 2^{64} bytes.
Maximum number of files in a directory	4,294,967,295	2^{64}

In addition, ReFS supports up to 4 petabytes in a storage pool. There is no fixed limit on the maximum number of storage pools and Storage Spaces you can create.

While there are several deployment scenarios for Storage Spaces, the following section will outline some basic deployment options to get you started.

Creating a Storage Space

You can create a Storage Space from Server Manager using unformatted raw disks. Storage Spaces is installed with the Storage Services feature under the File and Storage Services role. These features and role are installed by default, as part of the "Windows Server with a GUI" install option.

While performing these steps, you can use a simple USB external drive to create the Storage Space. Of course, you could also use USB, SATA, or SAS unformatted, raw drives.

Go into File and Storage Services and create a new volume by clicking "File and Storage Services," then Disks. Right-click the disk and select New Volume. Click Next and then Next again. The New Volume Wizard will bring the raw disk online and initialize it as a GPT (GUID partition table) disk. Specify the size of the volume in the next screen, and then you can choose to assign the drive to a letter or a folder. For most deployments, leave the default and assign the drive as a letter. Click Next. You can format the drive as ReFS from the File System drop-down menu. Click Next and then Create.

Now, let's create a new storage pool for our Storage Space. From File and Storage Services in the Server Manager dashboard, click Storage Pools and then Storage Pools (again).

Under the Storage Spaces view, you will see the disks listed as Primordial. *Primordial* is a standard term that means the disk contains unformatted, unprepared, or unassigned capacity. Click the disk, and from Task select New Storage Pool. This starts the New Storage Pool Wizard. Click Next. Name the storage pool and click Next once more. Check the disks to add to the pool and click Next and then Create. See Figure 6-1 for a confirmation of a created storage pool.

Now you have a new storage pool listed under Storage Spaces. (See Figure 6-2.)

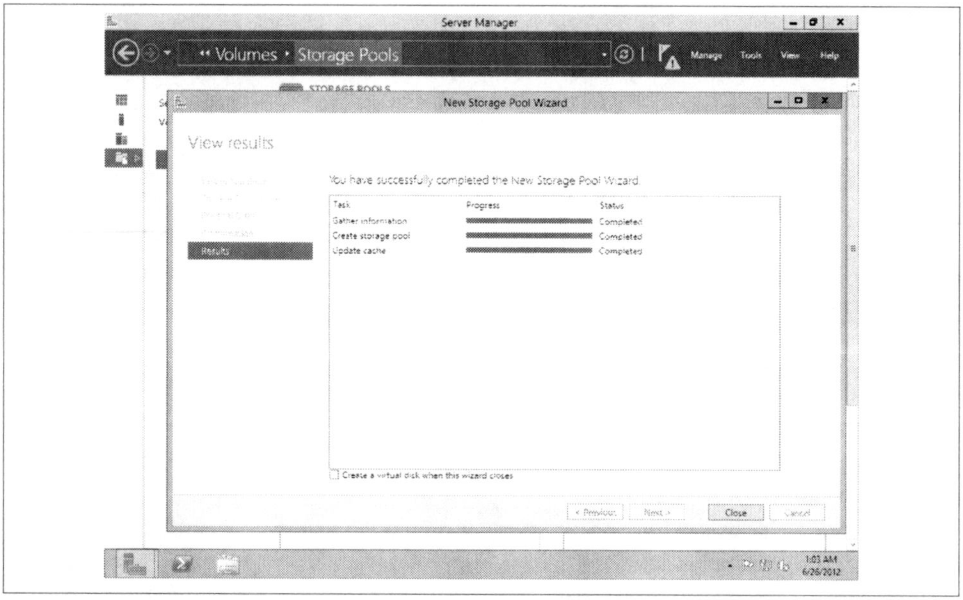

Figure 6-1. New storage pool

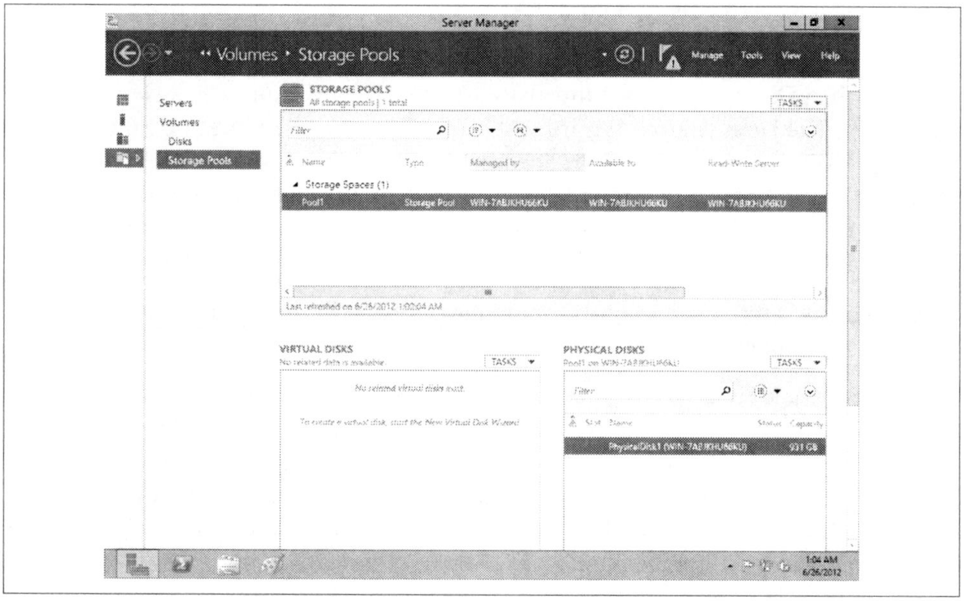

Figure 6-2. New storage space

Next, in your Storage Space, you can create a virtual disk with mirrored parity. From the Virtual Disks window, click Tasks and then New Virtual Disk. Select your storage pool and name your virtual disk. If you want to mirror data kept in your company's department shares, you need to name the virtual disk accordingly, so name it Department Shares, for example, and then click Next.

In Windows Server 2012, you can choose from three storage layouts:

Simple
> This will stripe data across the physical disks that compose your virtual disk. This is equivalent to RAID 0 and is used to boost performance, not for fault tolerance or data redundancy.

Mirror
> This option is usually used in conjunction with Storage Spaces. With mirroring, data is duplicated on two or three disks. This is equivalent to RAID 1 and provides fault tolerance.

Parity
> This is the Storage Spaces version of RAID 5. Parity will offer the most reliable fault tolerance, but it uses more disk capacity to create the configuration than mirroring and requires at least three physical disks in a storage pool.

After selecting the storage layout, you can specify the provisioning type as *thin* or *fixed*. Thin provisioning will dynamically use space as needed up to the size of the volume, while fixed will use only space equal to the volume. If you have an environment where data quickly accumulates, thin provisioning offers benefits as far as scalability.

Now you'll want to specify the virtual disk size and click Next, then Create. This completes the setup of a Storage Space with fault tolerance if configured with parity or mirroring. Storage Spaces are relatively easy and quick to deploy, and serve as an effective storage solution without requiring the purchase of any additional hardware or software.

Clustering

In addition to providing flexible storage solutions that won't make an IT department go over budget, new capabilities in clustering add benefits to help keep a business productive even in the event of a disaster.

Clustering is one of the best ways to provide failover and redundancy in an infrastructure. With clustering, multiple servers (nodes) are grouped together to improve performance through load balancing and allowing for failover, providing high availability (HA). Organizations often cluster mission-critical servers, such as those running databases or line-of-business applications. In a nutshell, clustering is a good solution for any server application where downtime or poor performance could severely impact business productivity and operations.

Because clustering is a feature that comes "in the box" with Windows Server 2012 and requires only installing and configuring services, clustering with Server 2012 is a cost-effective way for organizations to deploy failover of critical systems. Clusters can also be integrated as part of an infrastructure's SAN deployment, supporting iSCSI, Fibre Channel, and SAS storage systems. Of course, clustering is not only about physical machines—virtual machines (VMs) can also be clustered.

Clusters are connected via a LAN or WAN (local or wide area network) and are grouped within the Widows server software. The individual networked nodes function as a single system once they are clustered. Because the servers operate as a single system, if one server running a specific application becomes compromised, a second server within the cluster can seamlessly continue to run that application. Because failover is seamless, you do not have to do any intervening configuration on the recovery node, or any additional user configuration, such as repointing clients to the recovery server.

While clustering is nothing new in Server 2012—the feature first debuted in Windows NT 4.0 Enterprise Server—there are quite a few new capabilities and enhancements designed to make cluster management easier for you.

The name of the game surrounding clustering in Server 2012 is not only high availability, but also high scalability. Server 2008 R2 x64 Enterprise supports up to 16 nodes in a cluster. Hyper-V R2 with Server 2008 R2 SP1 supports up to 1,000 VMs in a cluster (in a five-mode deployment with four active nodes and one failover). Server 2012 supports up to 64 nodes in a cluster, and Hyper-V R3 supports up to a whopping 4,000 VMs in a cluster!

Cluster-Aware Updating (CAU) is a new feature, and one long anticipated by Windows system administrators. CAU allows clustered nodes to receive Windows updates without having to be taken offline.

Cluster Shared Volume (CSV) has also been updated to version 2.0. CSV in Server 2008R2 is a feature that can be enabled with failover clustering and is used with Hyper-V VMs. With CSV, other nodes in a cluster all have access to a CSV-enabled cluster. Nodes that are part of a failover cluster can then all have different VMs that have files on the same volume. With VMs sharing volumes, it's easier to implement SANs. Fewer LUNs (logical unit numbers—used to identify logical units on storage devices in SANs) need to be set up because many VMs can share one volume. This provides even more continuous system availability because each VM can fail over, be migrated to, or be moved independent of other VMs on the same volume. Disk space is used more efficiently because a VHD (virtual hard disk) file does not have to be placed on a separate disk.

CSV 2.0 pushed the technology even further, because now CSV is automatically part of the failover clustering feature. You can enable this feature with a single mouse click, and CSV disks are part of the Failover Cluster Manager Storage view, providing more centralized, and therefore more efficient, management over clusters.

Installing Failover Clustering

Before installing failover clustering, it's important to plan out how many nodes will be in a cluster, and for larger organizations, how many clusters should be created. Failover clusters often require a separate disk or volume to improve cluster availability, referred to as a *quorum disk*. A smaller organization can deploy a two-node cluster with Server 2012, but the install will detect a warning that no appropriate disk could be found for the quorum disk.

Although the purpose of this book is not to teach the intricacies of clustering technology, it's important for you to know the basics of clustering. Quorums can be tricky to understand.

A cluster is considered to be highly available if more than half of the nodes in it are running. These nodes are referred to as the *quorum*. In a nutshell, quorums help to keep nodes communicating with one another in a failover situation.

In Server 2012, you can use the Node and Disk quorum configuration to configure the necessary disk space as a quorum disk if deploying a two-node cluster. Having at least three nodes or an odd number of nodes will set up the appropriate quorum configuration, which Windows will configure with the failover cluster role.

To install failover clustering, from Server Manager click "Add Roles and Features," click Next, and then select the server to be used on the cluster. Click Next again and under "Select features," choose Features from the left-side menu. Select the checkbox next to "Failover clustering" and add the required features (which include the Failover Clustering Tools needed for management). See Figure 6-3.

Click Next again, opt to automatically restart the server, and then click Install.

To launch the Failover Cluster Manager, after install, from Server Manager, click Tools.

Creating a Cluster

To create a failover cluster, select Create Cluster from the Actions menu in the Failover Cluster Manager. See Figure 6-4.

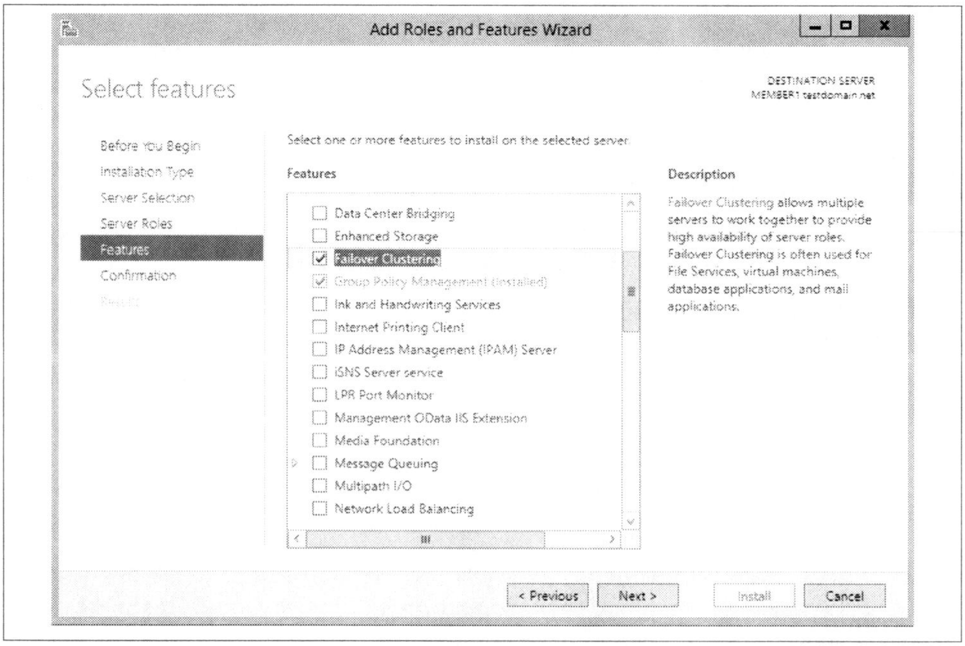

Figure 6-3. Selecting the Failover Clustering feature

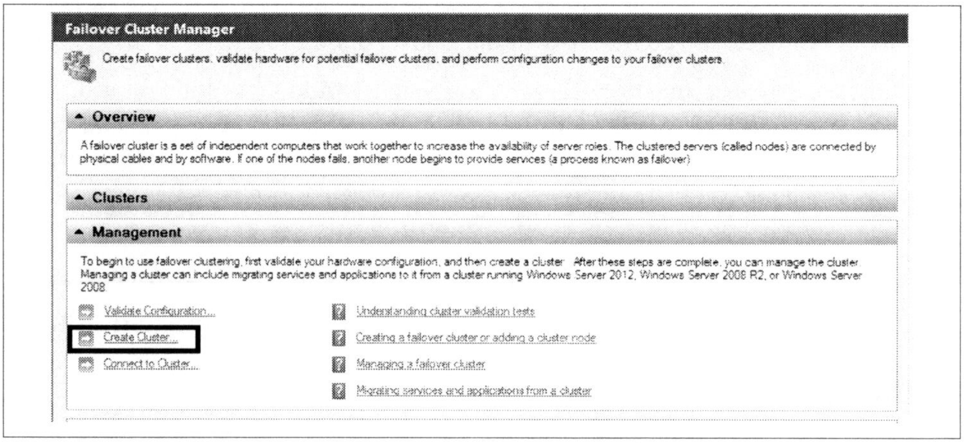

Figure 6-4. The Create Cluster link in the Failover Cluster Manager

To begin creating the cluster, enter the server names for the cluster when prompted by the Create Cluster wizard. See Figure 6-5.

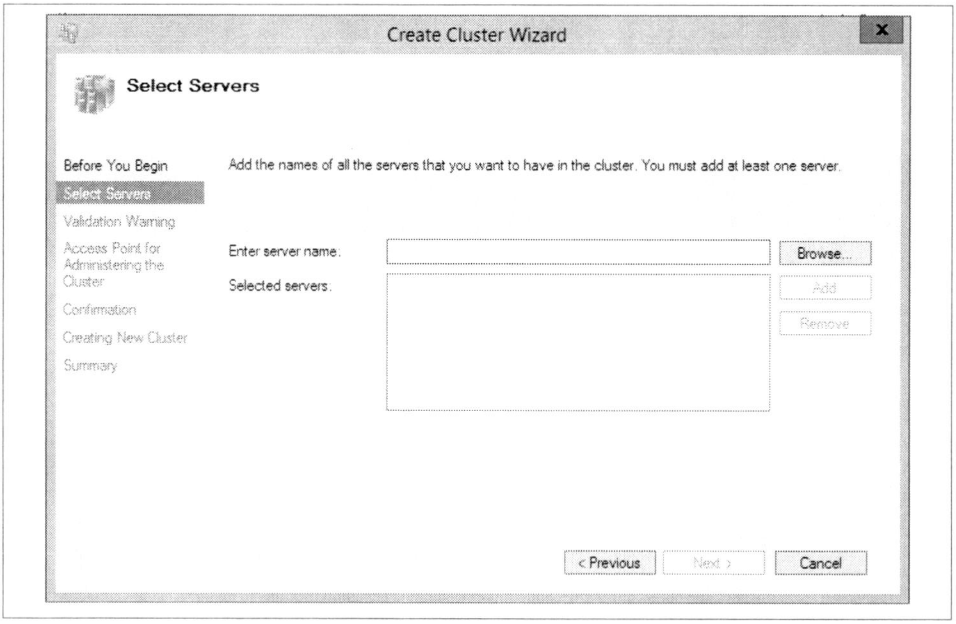

Figure 6-5. Selecting the server to add to the cluster

Then, choose whether or not the cluster should pass validation tests. See Figure 6-6.

> If you are creating a cluster in a business production environment, you will want to opt for the validation tests, because Microsoft supports only clusters that pass validation.

Click Next twice; you'll be presented with the choice to run all validation tests (which is the recommended option) or run only specific tests.

Once the validation tests are run, the system will create a Failover Cluster Validation Report, which details the tests that passed, those that failed, and any warnings (see Figure 6-7).

Finally, name the cluster and then click Finish. After the cluster is created, another report is generated, detailing the cluster creation process and settings.

Any machine that is going to be part of the cluster needs the Failover Cluster Manager installed.

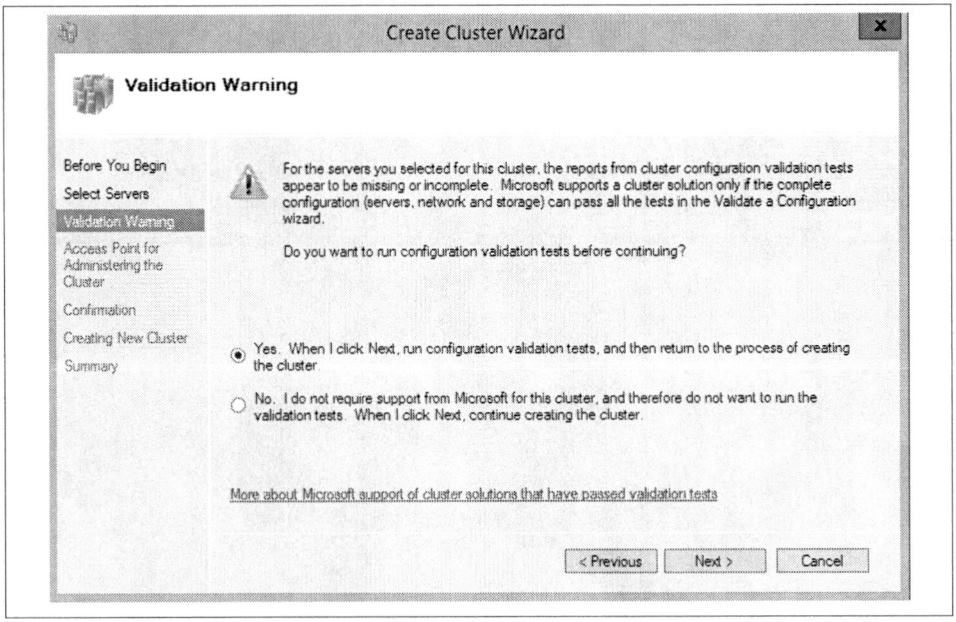

Figure 6-6. Opting to run validation tests

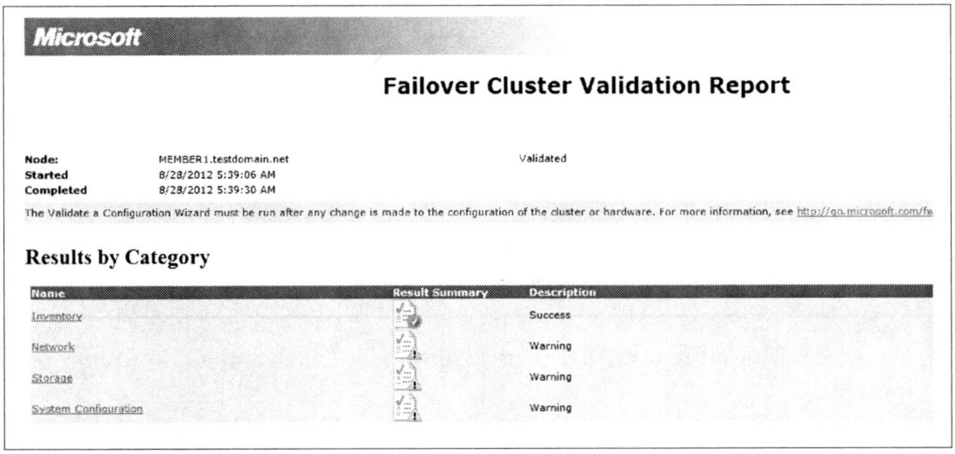

Figure 6-7. Failover Cluster Validation Report

The next step is to add another node to the cluster. From the Failover Cluster Manager, use the Add Node link to add another machine into the cluster. See Figure 6-8.

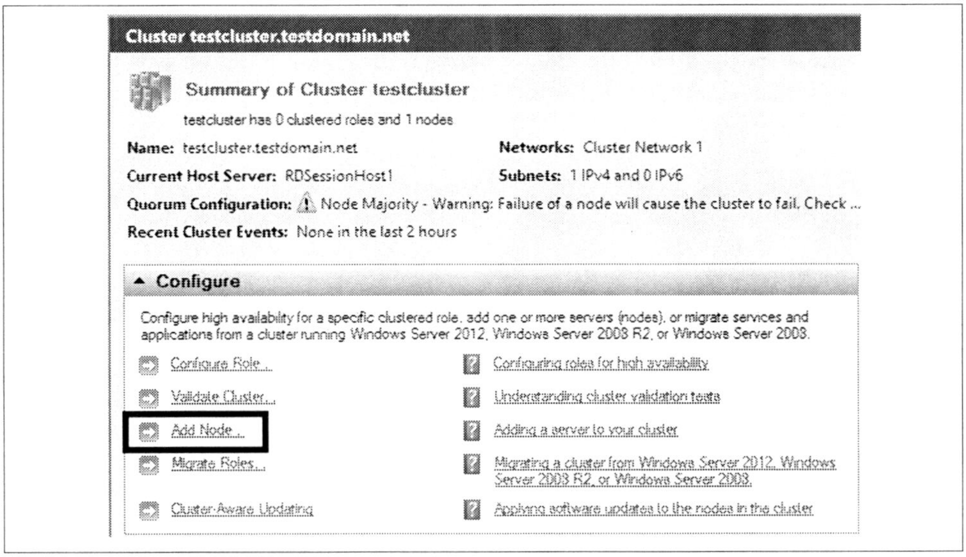

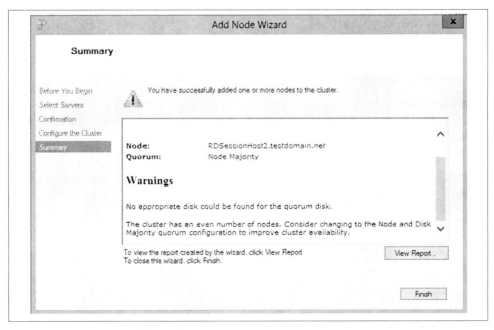

Figure 6-8. Adding nodes to a cluster

If you're creating a two-node failover, after you add the second node, the Add Node Wizard will report the warning message shown in Figure 6-9.

Figure 6-9. A quorum disk configuration warning

To change the cluster to the appropriate quorum configuration, you must edit the properties of the cluster. Right-click the cluster name in the Failover Cluster Manager's left-side menu and then select More Actions. Choose the option Configure Cluster Quorum Settings. See Figure 6-10.

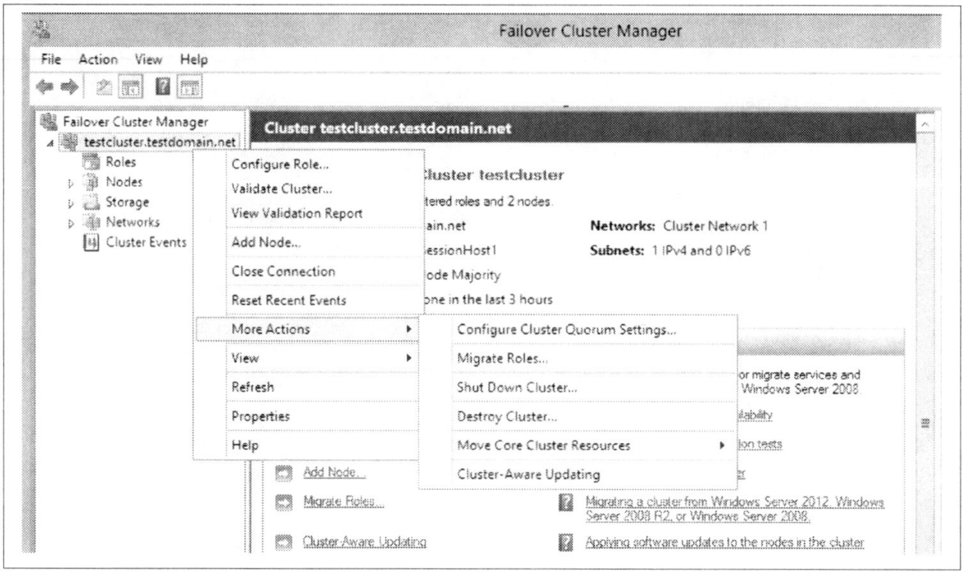

Figure 6-10. Configuring cluster quorum settings

The Configure Cluster Quorum Wizard opens. The wizard gives three quorum configuration options, as shown in Figure 6-11.

Unless there are extenuating circumstances that require a specific quorum configuration, the best course of action is to let the software set up the quorum settings, by selecting the first option, "Use typical settings."

You can set up cluster quorums in Server 2012 in one of four ways, per Microsoft's TechNet whitepaper on failover clustering (*http://technet.microsoft.com/en-us/library/cc770620(v=ws.10).aspx*).

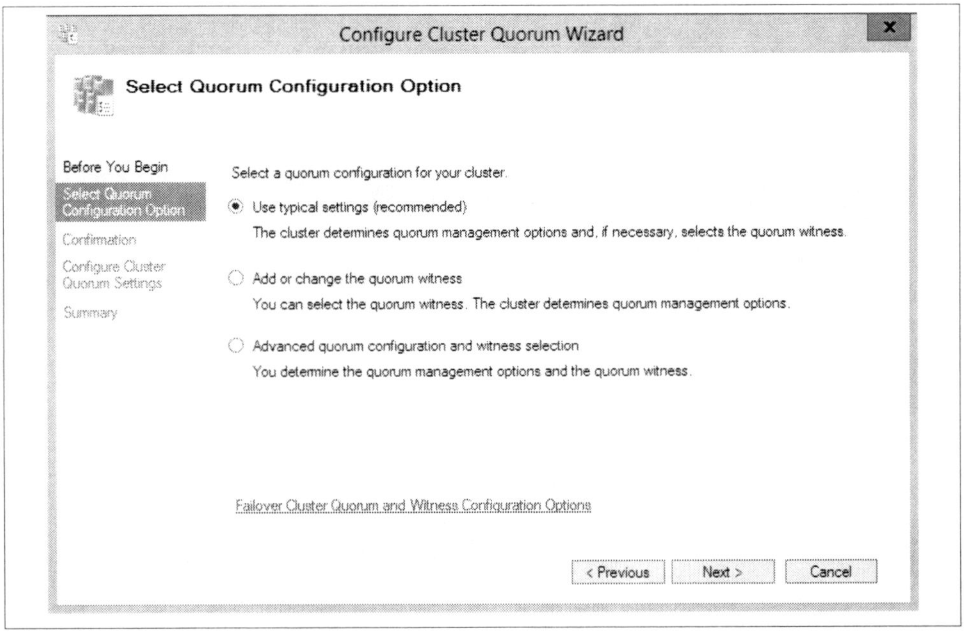

Figure 6-11. Quorum configuration options

Nodes in a cluster can "vote" on whether a cluster achieves quorum:

Node Majority
> Each node that is available and in communication can vote. The cluster functions only with a majority of the votes—that is, more than half.

Node and Disk Majority
> Each node plus a designated disk in the cluster storage (the "disk witness") can vote, whenever they are available and in communication. The cluster functions only with a majority of the votes—that is, more than half.

Node and File Share Majority
> Each node plus a designated file share created by the administrator (the "file share witness") can vote, whenever they are available and in communication. The cluster functions only with a majority of the votes—that is, more than half.

No Majority: Disk Only
> The cluster has quorum if one node is available and in communication with a specific disk in the cluster storage.

Choosing the "Use typical settings" option allows Server 2012 to configure the appropriate cluster quorum.

Cluster-Aware Updating

CAU is set up through the Failover Cluster Manager. From the Configure window, select the Cluster-Aware Updating link (see Figure 6-12).

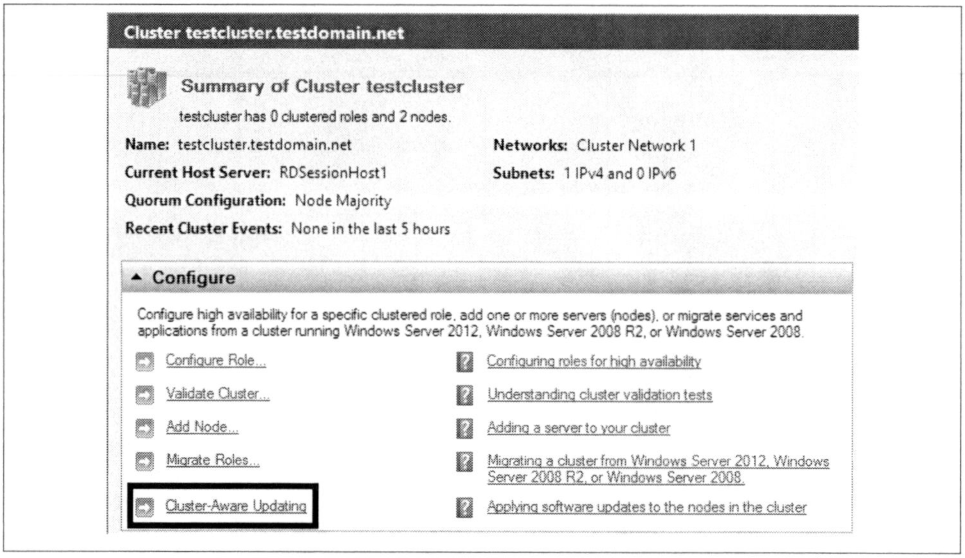

Figure 6-12. Starting the Cluster-Aware Updating configuration

The CAU interface makes applying updates to a cluster very simple. Connect to the cluster and select the configuration options for applying updates, as shown in Figure 6-13. Start the configuration by clicking "Configure cluster self-updating options."

The Configure Self-Updating Options wizard opens. The wizard first walks you through adding the Cluster-Aware Updating clustered role—which is necessary for applying CAU.

In the Add CAU Clustered Role with Self-Updating Enabled window, select the checkbox next to "Add the CAU clustered role, with self-updating mode enabled, to this cluster," as shown in Figure 6-14.

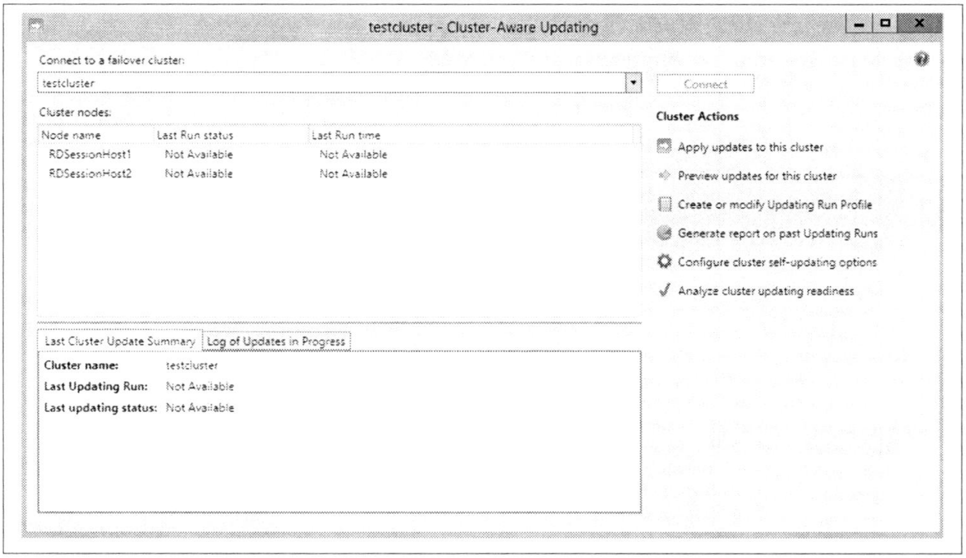

Figure 6-13. Configuring cluster updating options

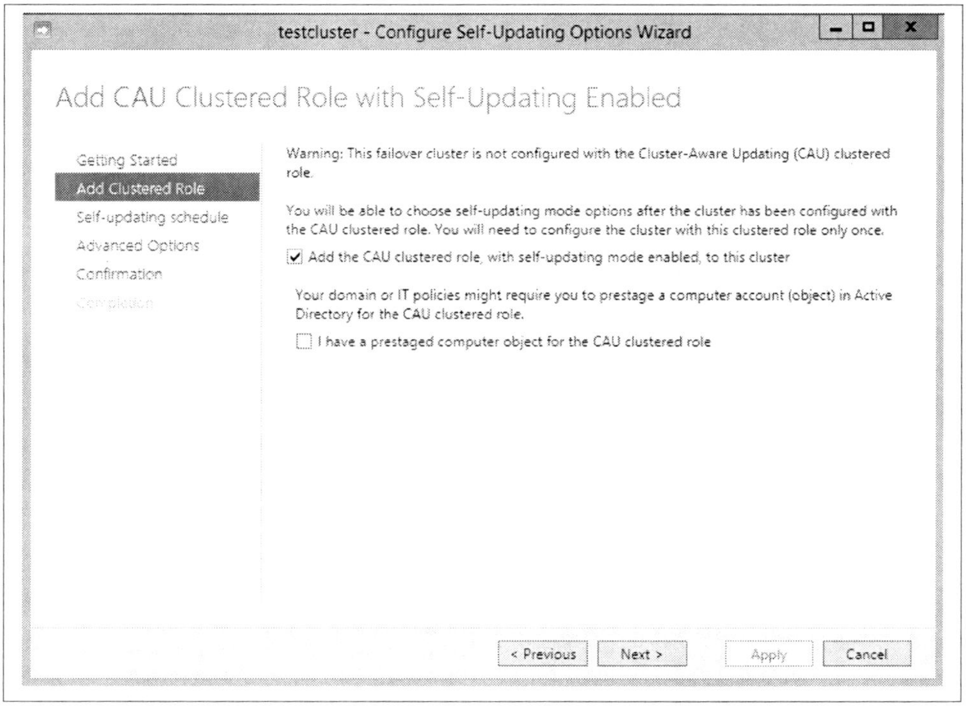

Figure 6-14. Adding the CAU clustered role

Click Next and then set the schedule for updating. By default, the scheduler is configured to update on Microsoft's infamous Patch Tuesday schedule.

Click Next, and then you can enter customizations for CAU, such as running a script before or after updating (see Figure 6-15).

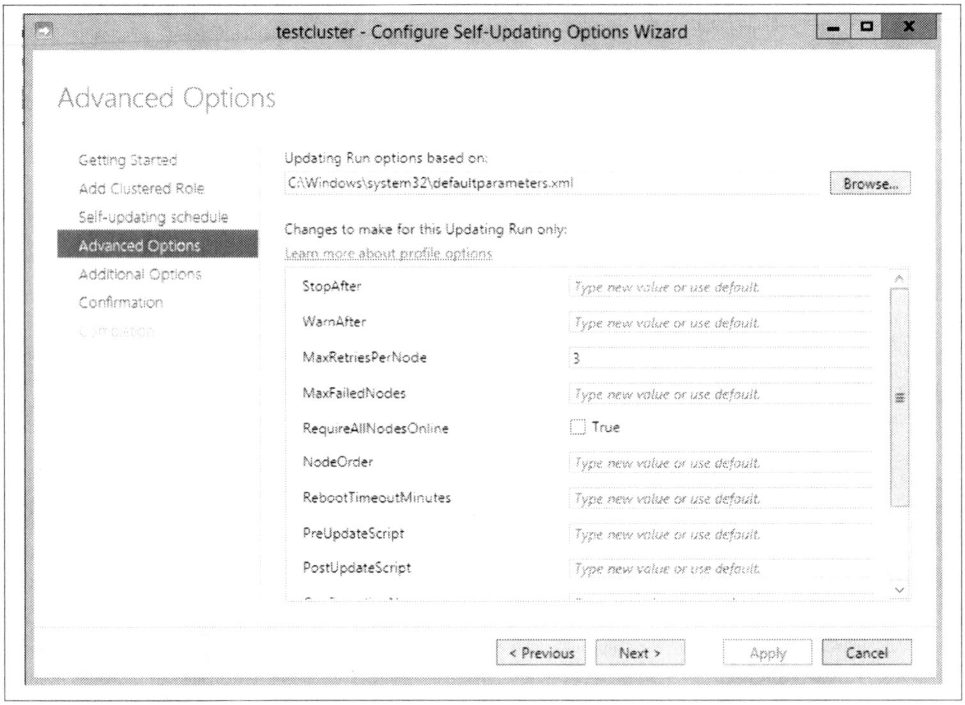

Figure 6-15. CAU advanced options

Click Next again. At this point in the configuration process, you can set CAU to install recommended Windows updates the same way as critical updates. Click Next and then Apply.

Summary

Storage Spaces and ReFS are two new storage features in Windows Server 2012 that provide data integrity and fault tolerance. Although ReFS is more reliable than NTFS, Storage Spaces is essentially robust, software-based RAID and may be subject to the same vulnerabilities as third-party software RAID solutions from a hardware perspective. Your decision to implement Storage Spaces depends on the fault-tolerance needs of your organization.

Also, remember that fault tolerance—regardless of whether you configure mirroring or parity—is not a substitute for backup. Even if you deploy Storage Spaces, you still need a good backup strategy for the ultimate protection of your data.

Clustering is an ideal way to ensure high availability of systems in the event of disk corruption or some other failure. Server 2012 makes configuring a failover cluster very easy, removing a lot of the complexity associated with such a configuration. Cluster Shared Volumes allow for integration with SANs and Hyper-V for even more failover and better use of disk space. Finally, Cluster-Aware Updating allows you to keep a cluster in optimum health since you can install critical and recommended software updates without taking a cluster offline.

CHAPTER 7

Hyper-V

If I had to pick the one sweet spot in Server 2012 that not only is a major impetus for organizations already running Windows to upgrade to Server 2012, but also has the potential to attract new Windows Server 2012 deployments, it would be Hyper-V.

Server 2012 introduces the latest version of Hyper-V: Hyper-V R3. Hyper-V R3 is bundled with Server 2012 and is also available as a free, standalone product.

Microsoft's virtualization solution Hyper-V has gotten many new features and enhancements since Server 2008 R2's release—so much so that Hyper-V has finally evolved into a sophisticated enough virtualization solution to make it a deadly threat for market share against dominant VMware.

Here's a little background on the virtualization space. There are three major players in the virtualization market: Citrix, VMware, and Microsoft. The three have offerings targeted to both SMB (small- to medium-size business) and enterprise. VMware currently has the edge in market share. Microsoft, however, has been persistently making headway, and industry analysts report that Hyper-V is the second most widely used virtualization platform.

Those gains have been made in part from Microsoft's fierce, almost obsessive competition with VMware. VMware has responded in kind, and both companies' marketing machines have been busy churning out tables and charts that painstakingly compare VMware and Microsoft on features, scalability, total cost of ownership, and more. Neither VMware nor Microsoft has been hesitant to disparage the other company's virtualization portfolio.

Amid the bitter battle between the two, the general consensus has been that Hyper-V lacked many of the advanced capabilities of VMware, particularly its enterprise solutions (such as vSphere). For the first time since its release, Hyper-V is a real contender against VMware and is likely to win over market share in the virtualization space, especially in the SMB segment.

Why? Microsoft has introduced several new capabilities in Hyper-V that put it on a level with VMware. Predominant among those features is true live migration. In Server 2008 R2, migrating virtual machines (VMs) from one host machine to another was possible only with clustered VMs or through shared storage. Hyper-V R3 allows live migration of VMs in clusters or between standalone hosts. In addition, R3 allows for the simultaneous migration of several live VMs. These migrations can be performed without any downtime. This flexibility means faster migration without any interruption in productivity, and it even overcomes some of the migration limitations currently in VMware.

Hyper-V also now enables creating and deploying private and public clouds with capabilities that add isolation and multitenancy. Large enterprises that need to create isolated virtual clouds for different segments of a business have the necessary tools at hand. Also, if your business offers management services, new networking capabilities in Hyper-V provide a great way to isolate customers' clouds for better management and for meeting customer service-level agreements (SLAs).

In terms of scalability, Hyper-V has not only caught up with but has outpaced VMware's comparable enterprise vSphere offering. Hyper-V supports up to 64 nodes and up to 4,000 VMs in a cluster versus vSphere's 32 nodes and 3,000 VMs.

You can configure up to 320 logical processors on hardware with Server 2012's Hyper-V, as well as up to 4 TB of physical memory, 64 virtual processors, and up to 1 TB of memory per VM.

Virtualization enthusiasts are also excited about a host of other new features, such as encrypted clusters, live snapshot merging, and resource monitoring—just to name a few.

There's another reason why Hyper-V can potentially overtake VMware in the enterprise: familiarity. Even though VMware currently has more of the virtualization market share, Microsoft's ecosystem is deployed throughout enterprises. System administrators who are already used to working with Microsoft systems have less of a learning curve with Hyper-V than with a new deployment of VMware. There's less cost in training associated with a Hyper-V deployment, and the product is already bundled into Server 2012.

Of course, VMware will still have its loyalists. You may even be reading this and shaking your head, saying, "No way. VMware is the de facto standard for virtualization." I will not argue that VMware makes excellent virtualization products, and one big bonus for going with VMware is that the company eats, sleeps, and breathes virtualization technology—and virtualization only.

So, I absolutely concede: for infrastructures with VMware already deployed, the case to move to Hyper-V is hard to make and probably not very feasible in terms of cost and labor. However, for many organizations that are still just testing the waters of moving systems to virtualized and cloud platforms—and that already have Microsoft products in place—Hyper-V makes an attractive option as these companies move to cloud-based and virtualized systems. Market trends strongly indicate that private and public cloud deployments and the continued transition from physical to virtual infrastructure will significantly grow. Hyper-V is well positioned to be a part of that transition for many organizations.

Although there is a lot that's new and enhanced for Hyper-V, the following sections will acquaint you with its basics and the major new capabilities that are likely to be of interest to most organizations regardless of size or industry. First, let's take a look at the requirements for deploying Hyper-V R3.

Requirements

Hyper-V is included in two of the four editions of Server 2012: Datacenter and Standard. And, as mentioned earlier, Hyper-V is also available as a free, downloadable standalone version.

A Hyper-V host (the system on which you are installing the Hyper-V role or standalone version) requires an x64, virtualization-capable processor (Intel VT or AMD-V). The processor also needs to support DEP (data execution prevention). You may need to enable DEP in the host machine's BIOS.

Microsoft claims that the host machine requires a minimum of 2 GB of memory. Realistically, since VMs also use physical memory, the more VMs you plan to run, the more physical memory the host machine will need for optimal performance. So let's forget about minimum memory requirements and focus on the real world.

Insufficient memory can decimate Hyper-V performance. It is of utmost importance that, before deploying Hyper-V, you have a strong grasp on how much physical memory the host machine needs and how you will allocate memory to VMs.

 There is a rule of thumb for calculating memory allocation in Hyper-V: the total memory of the physical host server should at least equal the sum of memory allocated to each VM. Additionally, Hyper-V optimally needs 300 MB of memory for the hypervisor alone, 32 MB for the first GB of RAM allocated to each VM, 8 MB for every additional GB of RAM allocated to each VM, and another 512 MB for the host operating system.

In Windows Server 2012, VMs now support NUMA (non-uniform memory architecture). A technology originally reserved for high-processing computers, such as machines used in science and academic environments, NUMA helps boost performance. With NUMA, processors access directly attached memory faster than memory attached to another processor in the system. Hyper-V R3 uses existing NUMA topology in a system (typically enterprise-level servers) to maximize performance and scalability without intervention from a user.

There are some other best practices to consider before deploying Hyper-V. To maximize performance, use multiple network adapters on a Hyper-V host. With multiple NICs (network interface cards), one physical adapter is dedicated to Hyper-V management, and another can be used by VMs. System administrators will also often use dedicated NICs for iSCSI storage and clustering.

It's also a good idea to keep VM files off the system partition. Either create another partition for storage, or better yet, put them on a separate disk.

Installing the Hyper-V Role

Deploying Hyper-V in Server 2012 requires adding the Hyper-V role. As with other roles and features, this is done in Server Manager. And as with most of the instruction throughout this book, the focus is on performing tasks through the GUI. Keep in mind, however, that you can also perform all of these tasks through PowerShell.

From the Server Manager dashboard:

1. Click "Add roles and features," then click Next and select "Role-based or feature-based installation." Click Next until you get to "Select server roles."

2. Scroll and select the Hyper-V server role. By default, the Hyper-V Module for Windows PowerShell and Hyper-V GUI Management tools are also installed. Opt to include management tools by leaving the checkbox selected and then click Add Features.

3. Click OK to select the destination computer. The Next button will enable. Click Next until you see the window Create Virtual Switches. This is where you select the network adapter installed on the physical host that will be used to create a virtual switch. The virtual switch provides network connectivity to virtual machines. By default, all the network adapters installed on the Server 2012 box are listed. Select the network adapter you want to use (see Figure 7-1).

   Finish this step by clicking Next.

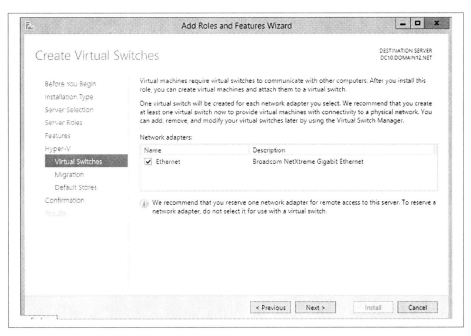

Figure 7-1. Selecting the network adapter

4. Now you'll see the window for Virtual Machine Migration (see Figure 7-2). In this screen, you can enable the server for live migration. If you plan to use live migration on the server in the network for which you are installing Hyper-V, check "Allow this server to send and receive live migrations of virtual machines." Do not select this option if, for example, you plan to set up clustering or a *heartbeat network*—a private network between clustered machines within a cluster. You can select a specific network after installing Hyper-V from network settings instead.

5. If you are performing a relatively simple deployment of Hyper-V without clustering, you can opt to allow the server to do live migrations. You also have to select the protocol to use to authenticate live migrations—either CredSSP (credential security support provider) or Kerberos.

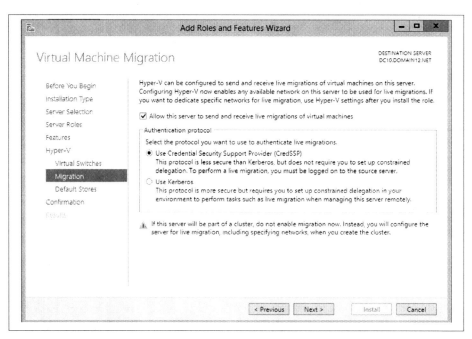

Figure 7-2. Configuring the authentication protocol for live migration

CredSSP and Kerberos are both SSPIs (security support provider interfaces) used for authentication in Windows environments. Most Windows, Active Directory–based infrastructures use Kerberos. CredSSP is used in environments where Kerberos can't be used. For example, CredSSP is used when system admins have to remotely execute PowerShell commands related to clustering—a scenario that would cause various issues in environments where Kerberos is deployed.

6. The Hyper-V Role Wizard then lets you select the default location for the virtual hard disk files and virtual machine configuration files. You can also modify these filepaths after install. Click Next, and then you can choose to automatically restart the server if required (as is the case with the Hyper-V role). Click Install.

   When the server comes back from reboot, some final installation tasks are automatically performed.

Creating and Configuring Virtual Machines

While anyone who has experience creating virtual disks in Server 2008 R2's Hyper-V should have little to no trouble figuring out how to create VMs and virtual disks in Hyper-V R3, there are some new features available in the procedures. One of the most significant is a new file format for virtual disks.

Configuring Virtual Disks

Hyper-V R3 uses a new file format for virtual hard disks: *.VHDX*. In Server 2008 R2, the file format is *.VHD*. VHDX supports virtual hard disk storage capacity up to 64 TB (VHD supports up to 2 TB). Virtual disks are storage resources for VMs, and the great thing about them is that they dynamically expand—seamlessly—as you add content to the VMs.

> Traditionally, hard drives have used 512 KB disk sectors. To accommodate the demand for huge storage capacity and the latest in storage technology, vendors developed drives that use 4 KB disk sectors, which is now the standard.

Of course, you can also use physical disks for VM storage: disks that are installed on the host machine or use a LUN (logical unit number) in a SAN (storage attached network) solution. In this example, we're creating a virtual disk that dynamically expands. From Server Manager, click Tools and then Hyper-V Manager. From the right-side Actions menu, click New and Hard Disk. This launches the New Virtual Hard Disk wizard. The first option is to choose the disk format, either VHD or VHDX. Although VHDX supports larger capacities and gives better data protection, the format also supports only Windows Server 2012. If your virtual environment requires the use of legacy Windows Servers, you will have to use VHD. See Figure 7-3 for the New Virtual Hard Disk wizard's Choose Disk Format window.

The next configuration option is selecting the disk type. There are three types of virtual disks that you can create:

Fixed
Fixed disks provide the best performance. If you'll be using the virtual disk with heavy I/O applications, such as a database with a high level of transactions, this is the best choice. Planning the size of a fixed disk is critical, because whatever capacity a fixed disk is created in is the capacity it remains, no matter how much data gets added.

Dynamically expanding

A dynamic virtual disk will automatically expand as capacity needs increase. As long as it's used for applications that are not I/O heavy and don't consume lots of disk resources, for many infrastructures it's probably the most common option.

Differencing

Differencing virtual disks is associated with another disk, which acts as a parent disk. Changes can be made to the child/differencing disk without affecting the parent disk. Differencing disks are typically used in testing and development environments, where changes will be written to a disk in testing and then the testers want to deploy an identical image without the changes to retest. Differencing disks are likely the least common disk type deployed in production environments.

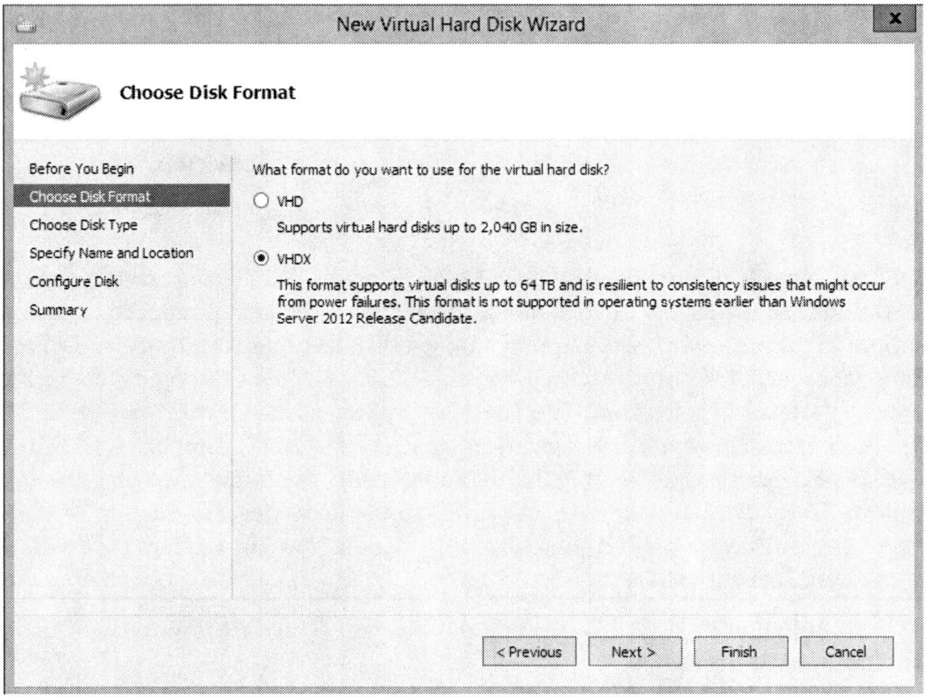

Figure 7-3. Choosing the virtual disk format

Now select "Dynamically expanding" and click Next. In the "Specify Name and Location" window, name the virtual disk and select a location for the files.

In the Configure Disk window, you can create a blank virtual disk and specify its size, or you can copy the contents of a physical disk attached to the host, or from another virtual disk—great time savers if you have images on another disk that you want to add to a new virtual disk. Click Next, and the disk setup is complete.

Creating Virtual Machines

The following steps detail creating a new VM:

1. Click New and then Virtual Machine. The first option is to name the VM; and, if you want to store the VM in a location other than the default location defined in the Hyper-V setup, you do so in this screen (see Figure 7-4).

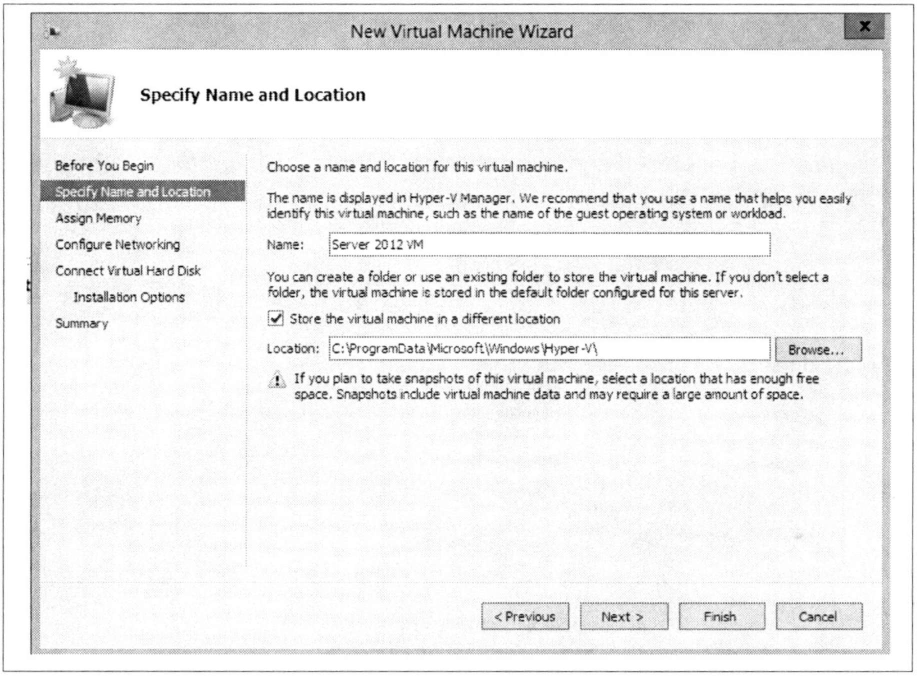

Figure 7-4. Defining the name and location for the VM

The next step is to assign memory. You can also choose to use dynamic memory for the VM.

Memory configuration has a big impact on Hyper-V performance. With dynamic memory, VMs that require more memory are allocated memory resources from VMs that require less, such as those in an idle state. Smart paging is a feature of dynamic memory and works in very much the same manner as a page file on a physical disk: when memory runs low, memory resources are given to active applications. You can select dynamic memory when creating a VM; however, you may not get true performance gains unless you are running a lot of VMs at once.

2. The New Virtual Machine wizard then displays the Configure Networking screen. This is where you select the network adapter the VM will use. After you do so, the wizard walks you through connecting a virtual disk. The options are to create a new virtual disk, connect an existing one, or attach a virtual disk later.

3. Under Installation Options, you can choose to install an operating system from a boot image or disk, perform a network installation, or opt to install the OS later. In Figure 7-5, I am installing a virtual guest Windows Server 2012 as the operating system for the VM from an *.iso* image.

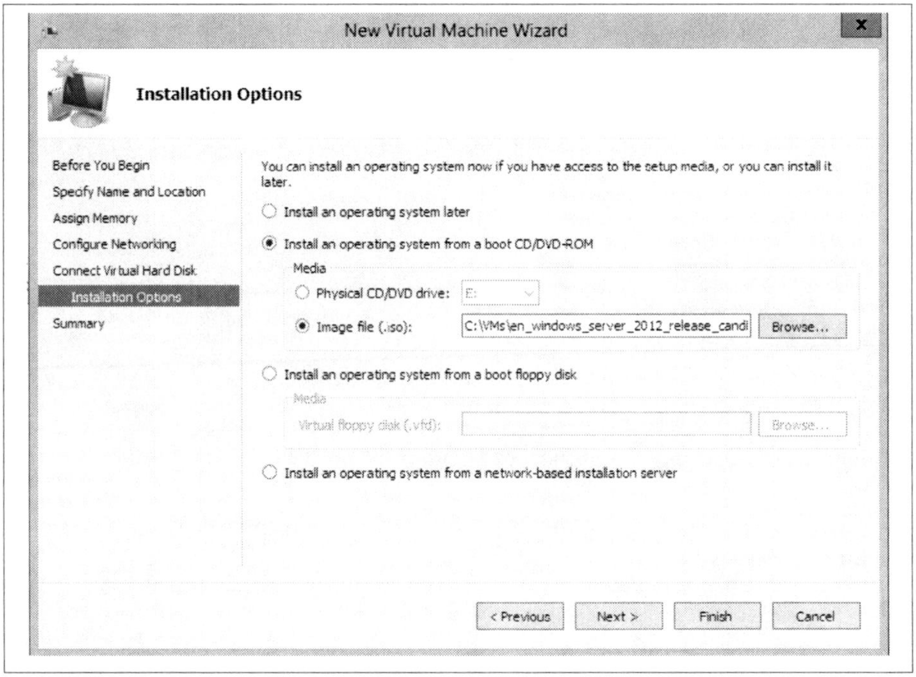

![New Virtual Machine Wizard dialog showing Installation Options with "Install an operating system from a boot CD/DVD-ROM" selected and an Image file (.iso) path of C:\VMs\en_windows_server_2012_release_candi]

Figure 7-5. Installing an OS on a VM

4. Click Next and then Finish to complete the VM setup. The new VM is displayed in Hyper-V Manager in an off state. Right-click the VM and click Start and then Connect to complete the guest OS install.

Managing Virtual Machines and Virtual Disks

The following sections give step-by-step walk-throughs on some of the most important features in Hyper-V R3.

Live-Migrating Virtual Machines

Hyper-V R3 marks a big improvement with live migration—that is, moving VMs from one physical host to another without downtime. That improvement is the ability to migrate VMs without shared storage or having both hosts in a cluster, either of which is required for live migration in Windows Server 2008 R2.

Simpler live migration is a must-have feature in virtualized environments. Being able to quickly transfer over a VM from one physical host to another is critical to quickly getting up and running in the event of a disaster. If one host goes down, you can move a VM to another host.

To run live migration, you must have two or more servers running Hyper-V. The servers must have the same make of virtualization-supported processor (either all AMD or all Intel—if the processors are different, the VM will have to be shut down before migration); the servers must belong to the same domain or to domains that have a trust relationship with each other; and the VMs must be configured to use virtual storage or virtual Fibre Channel disks.

To live-migrate VMs, you must be logged in as a domain administrator or with an account that has proper permissions. You can perform live migrations locally, through Remote Desktop, though a remote PowerShell session, or by using remote management tools from a Windows 8 client.

In the following steps, Server 2012 VM is migrated from one physical Server 2012 box to another. Both hosts are on the same subnet on the same physical network, and the migration is performed locally.

1. To migrate a VM, right-click the VM from Hyper-V Manager and click Move and then Next. Select "Move the virtual machine" in the Choose Move Type window. Click Next.

2. Next, you must specify the name of the destination computer. You can browse to locate it in Active Directory (see Figure 7-6).

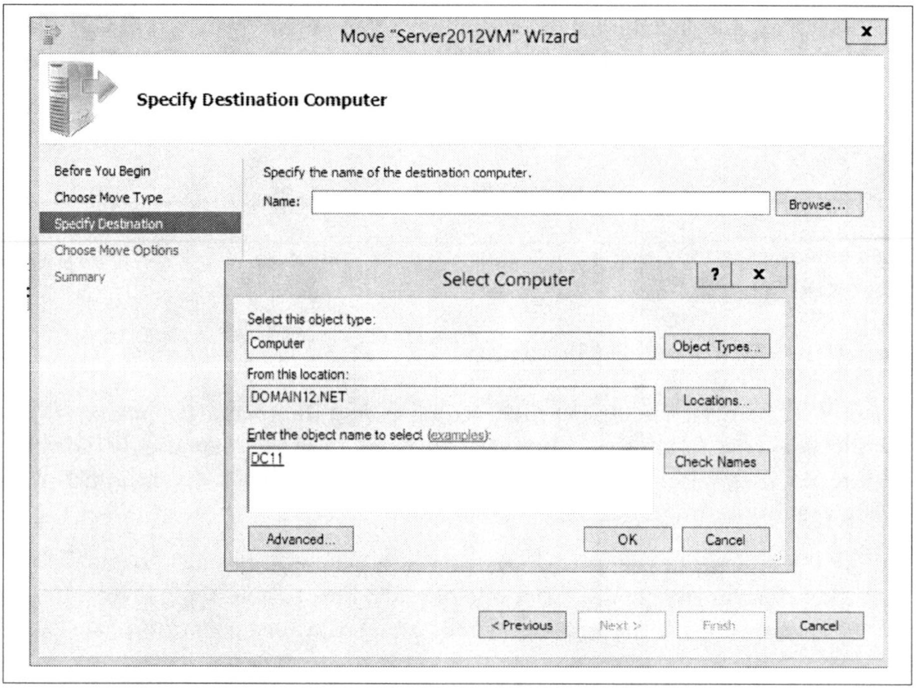

Figure 7-6. Specifying the destination server for live migration

3. Click Next, and the Move wizard displays the Choose Move Options window. The choices are moving the entire VM and its associated data (such as the virtual hard disk, snapshots, and its paging file), move only the VM, or move the VM and its associated storage resources consumed to different locations. In Figure 7-7, I've selected "Move the virtual machine's data to a single location" to move the data and the VM to the destination.

4. You then choose where to store the VM on the destination folder. (See Figure 7-8.) Click Next and then Finish.

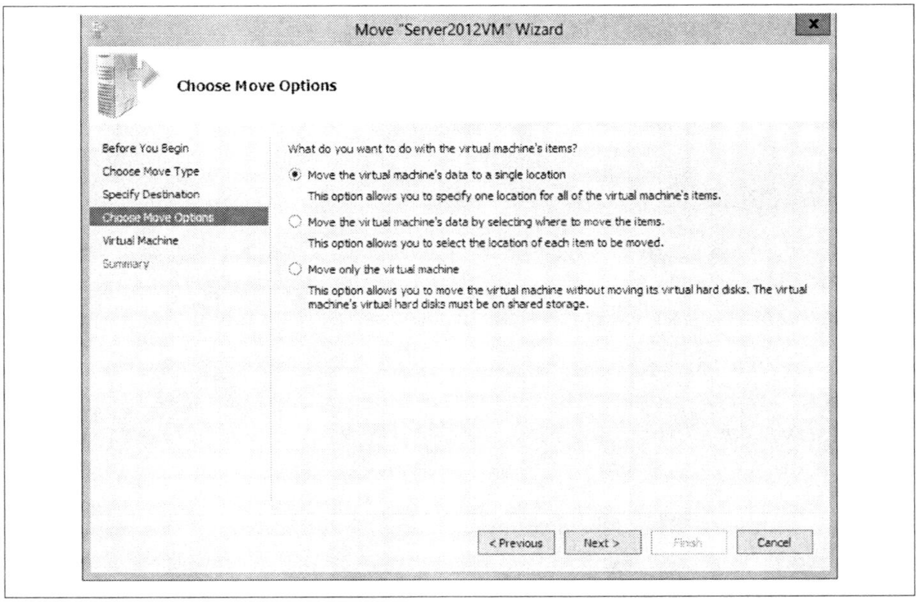

Figure 7-7. Selecting move options

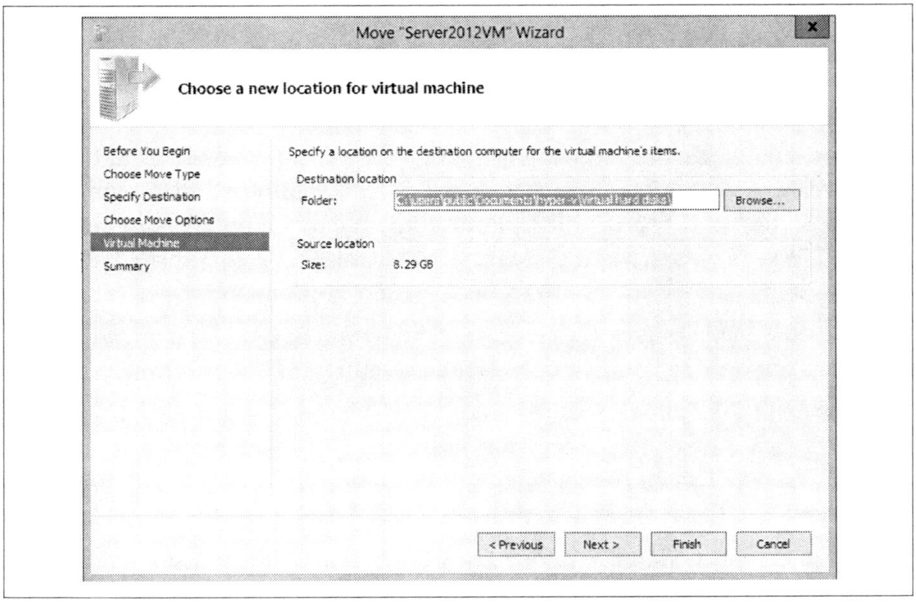

Figure 7-8. Selecting a location for the migrated VM

You can also move virtual storage devices (VHD and VHDX files) for one or more VMs from one host to another without shutting anything down. This capability gives you more flexibility with virtual storage. System admins can use live storage migration to upgrade storage, troubleshoot storage issues, or reconfigure storage loads.

Hyper-V Replica

Hyper-V Replica is a new feature in Server 2012 that allows for the *asynchronous replication* of VMs (a fancy way of stating that you are replicating a VM from one host machine to another), which is great for times when you are having issues with a host.

Keep in mind that this isn't migrating, because you aren't moving a VM from one Hyper-V server to another. Instead, you are making an exact copy of a VM and placing it on another server. As with live migration, the Hyper-V machines do not have to have shared storage or be in a cluster. They just have to be able to communicate on a network.

1. First, to create a VM replica, you have to enable replication. From Hyper-V Server Manager, right-click the VM that's to be replicated and select Enable Replication. This opens up yet another wizard.

2. The next order of business is to specify the replica server. In Figure 7-9, I have selected the server that will receive the replicated VM; however, I get an error that the specified replica server is not configured to receive replication.

   Hyper-V gives us the option to configure the replica server, which we can do remotely, from the host machine that has the VM to be replicated. Once the error message appears, a Configure Server button is displayed.

3. In the Enable Replication window that opens, select the checkbox next to "Enable this computer as a Replica server." Next, select the authentication method for replication traffic. Kerberos will replicate without encryption, but you can opt to use HTTPS so that the data sent from one host to another is encrypted. Finally, choose the servers that are allowed to replicate within the domain.

   Save time and configure the servers you know will be used for replication after you set up Hyper-V by going into the Hyper-V settings of that server.

4. Now that the destination server is configured for replication, click Next to display the Specify Connection Parameters window. Here, you confirm whether to use HTTP or HTTPS for the replication traffic, and you can opt to compress the data transmitted (this is enabled by default). Click Next.

   The next screen (Figure 7-10) gives you the option to deselect any virtual disks you do not want replicated.

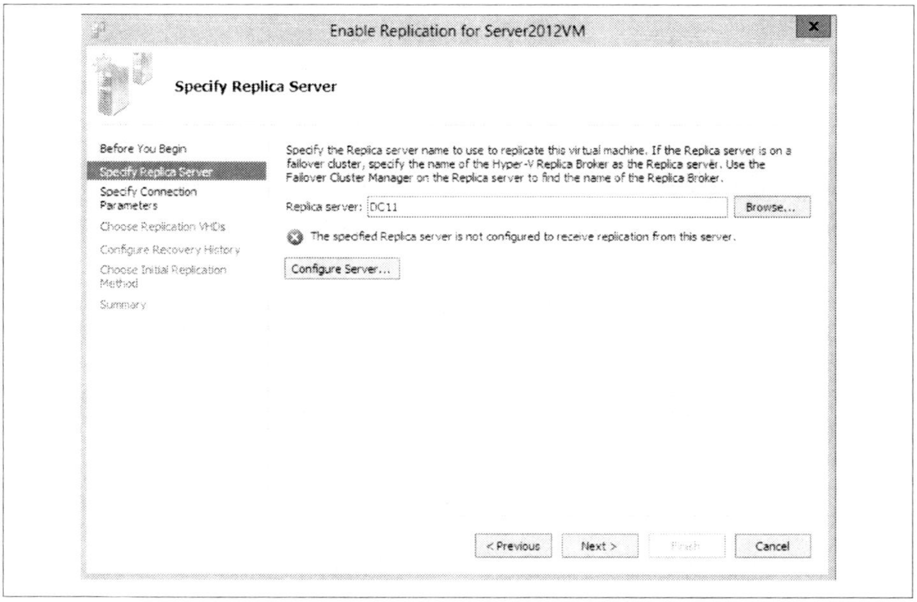

Figure 7-9. Hyper-V replica error

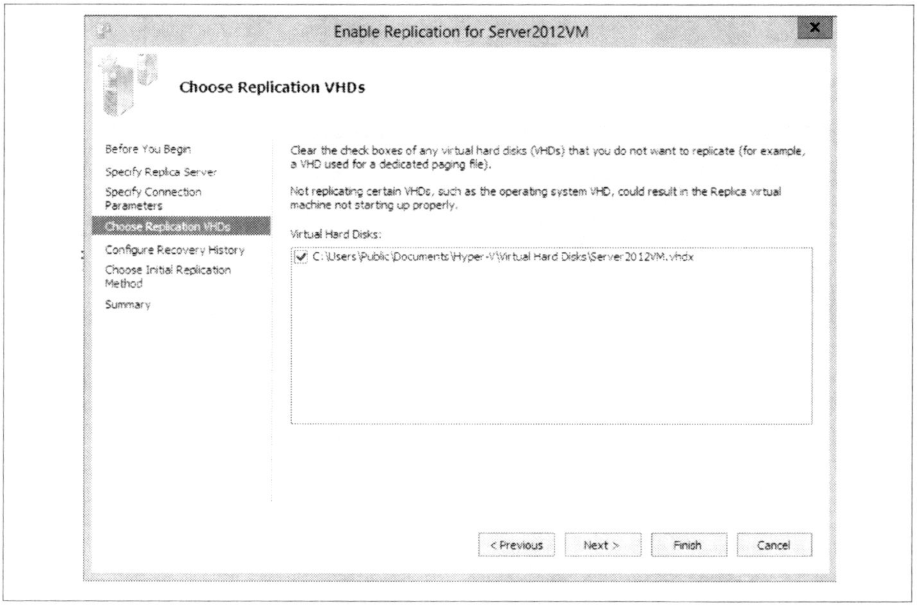

Figure 7-10. Select the virtual hard disks to be included for replication

The wizard then lets you configure recovery history. Configuring recovery means choosing which recovery point of the VM being replicated you wish to store. The default option is to store only the latest recovery point (which saves on disk space), but you can also store additional recovery snapshots.

5. The final configuration option before the actual replication is to set how the VM should be replicated. By default, the replicated VM is sent from host A to host B over the network. However, in cases where bandwidth is limited, a replicated VM can be exported to external media and then sent over the network at a later time. A third option exists if you have already restored the same VM on the replica server. That restored machine can be used for initial replication. This option conserves replication time and bandwidth, because only the changes made to the replicated VM since the VM was restored to the destination replica server are sent over the network.

Set replication to start immediately or schedule the process, and click Finish.

 Make sure the firewall on the replica server is configured to accept inbound replication traffic. If it isn't, you'll get an "Unable to replicate" error. For Windows Firewall and Kerberos and certificate-based (HTTPS) authenticated replication traffic, enable the "Hyper-V Replica HTTP Listener (TCP-In)" rule in Inbound Rules in the Windows Firewall settings.

6. Upon successfully configuring replication, you will see the status "Sending Initial Replication" within Hyper-V Manager (see Figure 7-11); click Merge. Once you've done that, the VM will be in the Hyper-V Manager of the replica server.

Cloning Virtual Domain Controllers

While cloning virtualized domain controllers is nothing new in Windows Server, Server 2012 does deliver improvements that make cloning DCs easier.

There are a number of benefits to DC cloning. First, it's an ideal way to scale up a growing Windows infrastructure, because you can quickly deploy DCs without investing in additional hardware. It also saves IT time, because there's no need to reconfigure a DC. Also, the ability to clone a DC is a good strategic part of a disaster recovery plan.

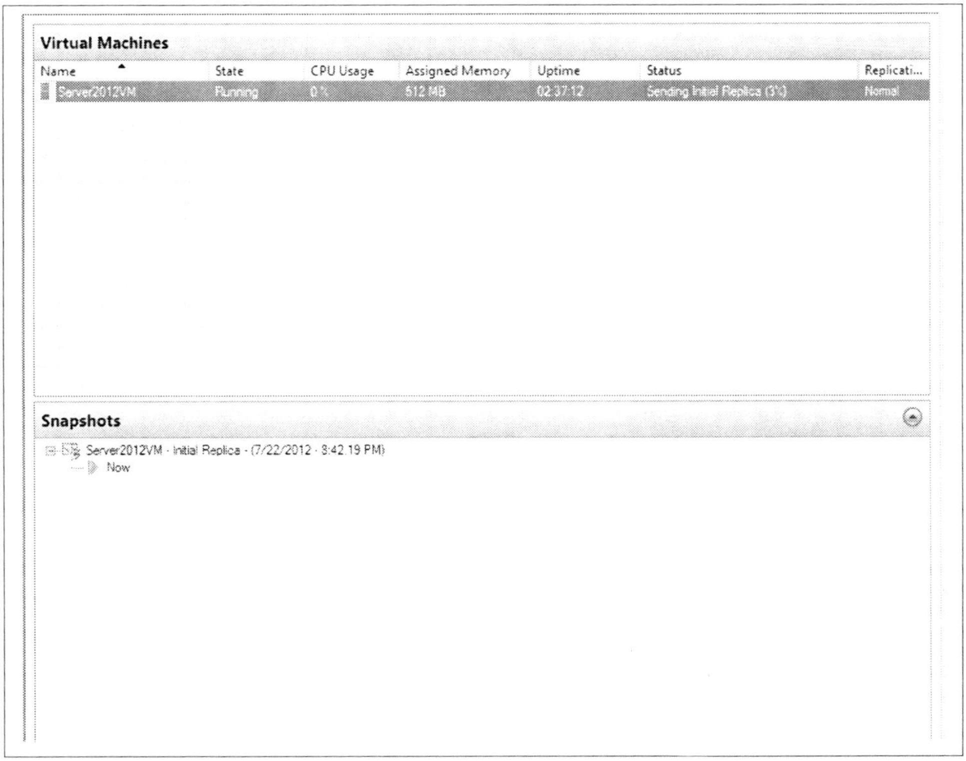

Figure 7-11. Replication in progress with source VM running

There are some checks and preparations to make before you can clone a virtual DC. For instance, you have to authorize a DC for cloning. You do so by adding the DC to the Cloneable Domain Controllers group in Active Directory. This is a group under the Users container in AD.

System administrators also have to make sure that the DC serving the FSMO (flexible single master operation) role as PDC (primary domain controller) emulator is running Windows Server 2012. In addition, you must check to make sure that any applications running on the DC can be cloned.

Checking application "clone compatibility" is easy—simply run this PowerShell command:

```
Get-ADDCloningExcludedApplicationList
```

This cmdlet runs on the DC to be cloned. The command checks against a list of common apps that can be cloned in a virtual setting. The output of the file displays apps that have not been verified as safe to clone for either licensing or functionality reasons. If you run the file and an app you have installed on a DC appears on the output list, you can contact the app's vendor and ask if it is safe to clone, or you can remove the app from the DC and reinstall after cloning.

You then need to run another cmdlet. Run `New-ADDCloneConfigFile` on the virtual DC to be cloned. This cmdlet creates a configuration file for the clone process. The command has to be typed with specific parameters, including the DC's computer name, IP address, DNS address, gateway, subnet mask, WINS Server IP address, and domain name.

For example, the virtual domain controller we want to clone is named VMDC1. The VM is configured with static IPv4 addressing, and the domain name is Domain12.net. The syntax for the configuration file is therefore:

```
New-ADDCloneConfigFile –Static –IPv4Address "192.168.1.12" IPv4DNSResolver
"192.168.1.10" –Ipv4SubnetMask "255.255.255.0" –CloneComputerName "VMDC1"
–IPv4DefaultGateway "192.168.1.1" –PreferredWINSServer "192.168.1.10"
–SiteName "DOMAIN12.NET"
```

The VM getting cloned is then shut down. Right-click the VM in Hyper-V Manager and select Export and you'll be prompted to save the exported VM. Click Export, and Hyper-V Manager will display the status of the export. A subfolder gets created in the directory to which the exported VM is saved. The subfolder is created with the same name as the exported VM. In the subfolder are three more folders: *Snapshots*, *Virtual Hard Disks*, and *Virtual Machines*. These are all the associated data elements that get exported with the VM.

The final step is to import the virtual DC. From Hyper-V Manager's Actions menu, click Import Virtual Machine. Browse to the location where you have the exported VM file saved. Select the VM to import. Click Next and then select the type of import to perform. There are three options (see Figure 7-12):

Register the virtual machine in-place
This is a new option in Hyper-V R3 for the import process. This option uses the existing unique ID. If the VM you are importing already has its associated data files where you want them and all you want to do is fire up the VM in Hyper-V, then go with this option.

Restore the virtual machine
If the VM's files are saved on a network folder or external disk, Hyper-V will move the VM's files to the appropriate location and then register the VM.

Copy the virtual machine
If you want to import the VM more than once, this is the option to choose because the VM is given a unique ID.

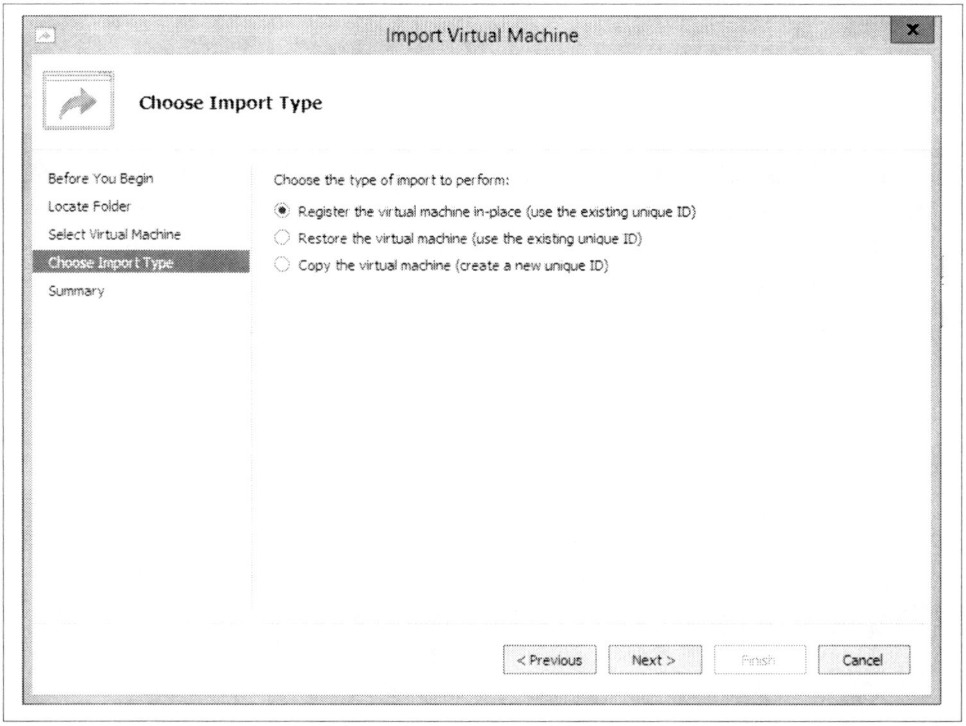

Figure 7-12. Select the appropriate import type

Merging Snapshots

Snapshots are data files used to restore a VM to a past state. These files are mostly used in testing environments, but they come in handy if you've made a change to a VM that caused a problem with it, such as applying an update, and now you want to revert the VM to its state before the update.

Snapshots, of course, are not a new feature in Server 2012. What *is* new is that a snapshot can now be merged into a VM without shutting down that VM. This is a major change in technology from Hyper-V on Server 2008 R2, which required the VM be powered off to merge snapshots.

To revert a running VM to a previous state, from the Actions menu in the Hyper-V Manager, right-click the VM and select Revert. The Revert Virtual Machine dialog box appears, confirming the revert selection. In Figure 7-13 you can see the reversion process happening while the VM runs.

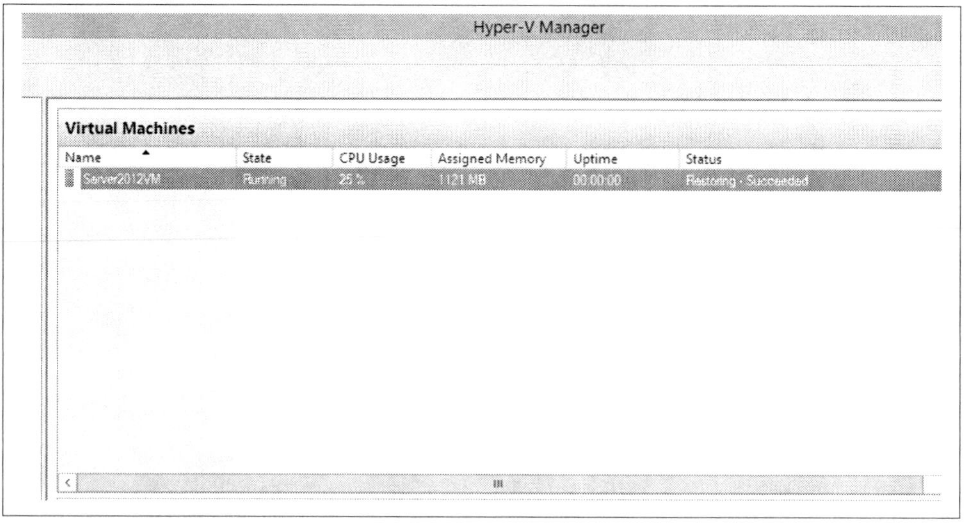

Figure 7-13. Live snapshot merging

Performance and Virtual Network Management

Besides creating and managing VMs, system administrators are also responsible for monitoring the performance and health of VMs, just as with physical machines.

Hyper-V delivers not only improvements in monitoring virtual environments, but also new features that are worth getting familiar with.

Resource Metering

Resource metering is a new feature that gives you information on the CPU, memory, storage, and network resources that a VM is consuming. Consider it a Performance Monitor for virtualization.

Besides giving insight into how well or poorly a virtual infrastructure is running, resource metering provides another important purpose: customer billing. As companies increasingly provide services to customers via cloud deployments, they need a way to bill those customers for service usage. With resource metering, a business can create an in-house strategy for billing customers for usage based on metrics provided. Previously, most companies had to rely solely on third-party solutions to bill for cloud services.

Resource metering provides:

- Average CPU usage, measured in megahertz over a period of time
- Average physical memory usage, measured in megabytes
- Minimum memory usage (lowest amount of physical memory)

- Maximum memory usage (highest amount of physical memory)
- Maximum amount of disk space allocated to a virtual machine
- Total incoming network traffic, measured in megabytes, for a virtual network adapter
- Total outgoing network traffic, measured in megabytes, for a virtual network adapter

To execute resource metering, run the following cmdlet in PowerShell (see Figure 7-14):

```
Get-VM -ComputerName <name of Hyper-V host machine>|Enable -VMResourceMetering
```

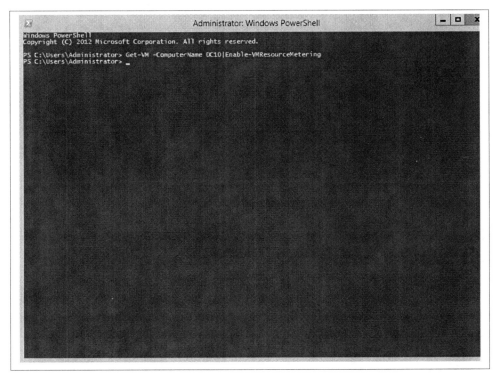

Figure 7-14. Resource metering cmdlet

The default time to collect data for performance metrics is an hour. You can change this interval. The following cmdlet sets the data collection time to under a minute:

```
Set-vmhost –computername <Hyper-V host name>
-ResourceMeteringSaveInterval 00:01:00
```

To display all the data collected for VMs, run this command (see Figure 7-15):

```
Get-VM –ComputerName <name of Hyper-V host>|Meaure-VM
```

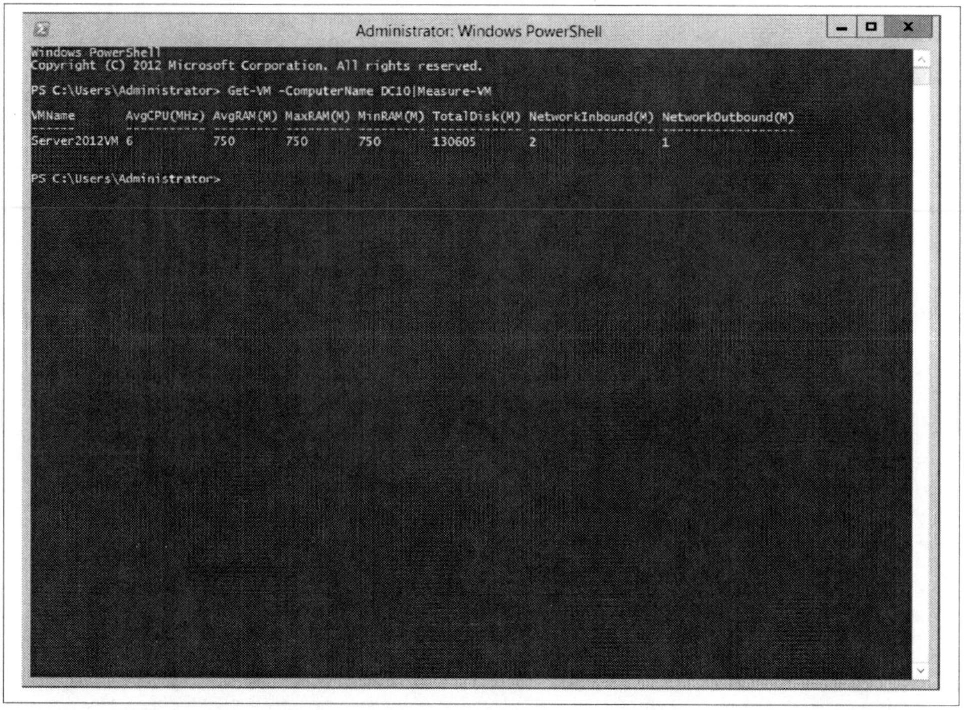

Figure 7-15. Displaying the Resource metering data

You can also just get metrics on a specific VM. In the following example, we specify a VM named Server2012VM on a Hyper-V host, DC10:

```
Get-VM –ComputerName DC10 –Name "Server2012VM"|Measure-VM
```

Since cloud computing is at the forefront of Server 2012 and Hyper-V R3 marketing, there's a good chance that organizations will take a close look at the two solutions if they do have billable cloud services. Resource metering is a good way to see usage within a virtualized environment, but Microsoft's options for exporting the data you get from running these PowerShell commands is rather weak. I would prefer a GUI component that provides rich reporting and data visualization capabilities. Currently, the best way I can determine to extract data when you run resource metering cmdlets is to use the output command to create a CSV (comma-separated value) file.

Summary

Hyper-V R3's new capabilities center on easier, yet more robust, management of virtual environments. Live migration, live merge of snapshots, and Hyper-V replication are all ways to deploy VMs quickly for scalability, troubleshooting, or disaster recovery. Features such as resource metering make Server 2012 and Hyper-V attractive for hosted service providers.

Many of the steps in this chapter also apply to clustered VMs. You can perform everything covered here—including live migration and Hyper-V replication—with PowerShell.

As a system administrator, you must become familiar with virtualization. This chapter detailed the major new features in Hyper-V, but these are certainly not all of the new capabilities. In the next chapter, we'll look at new networking capabilities in Server 2012 not only for physical networks, but for Hyper-V as well.

CHAPTER 8

Networking

Windows Server 2012 introduces new features in network management that are designed to meet the shift many organizations are undergoing—from traditional LANs/WANs (local and wide area networks) to cloud infrastructures.

Before delving deeper into these new features, it's important to make the distinction between traditional networking and "the cloud." A LAN is, essentially, computers behind a firewall that share a physical or wireless link for communicating with one another. In a LAN, servers and applications are deployed onsite and managed by IT. Upgrading a LAN for scalability, more storage, additional systems, or other resources requires action by IT.

With cloud computing, components of an IT infrastructure—such as servers, storage, memory, and network and computing resources—are virtualized within an organization's private intranet or in a hosted service provider's network. Cloud computing allows for quicker deployment of infrastructure components as well as unprecedented scalability, and because there is little to no extra hardware investment, it is more cost-effective than managing and upgrading a traditional LAN. In cloud computing, resources are always "on demand."

There's a lot of eyebrow raising and snickering about *cloud computing* being an overhyped marketing catchphrase. While the technology industry has no shortage of hype and annoying marketing terms, cloud computing is not one of them. Cloud computing isn't composed of new technology. Think about the technology that makes cloud computing capable: high-speed Internet access, high-capacity storage, and hardware and network virtualization. These technologies have been around for some time. What makes cloud computing new and exciting is that it takes existing technology capabilities and provides a new way to quickly deliver highly scalable infrastructure, applications, and services. Cloud computing is rapidly overtaking the 20th-century style of computer networking because it's so flexible and cost-effective.

There are three types of cloud service delivery models:

IaaS

Infrastructure as a Service is the delivery of traditional hardware that makes up an infrastructure via the cloud. With IaaS, customers have hosted servers, storage, networking resources, and some control over the configuration of those resources. Amazon Web Services and Google Compute Engine are examples of IaaS.

PaaS

Platform as a Service is the delivery not only of traditional hardware components, but also operating systems, database, web, and other (typically server) software. PaaS also usually provides a development environment. Microsoft's Azure and Amazon Electric Beanstalk are PaaS solutions.

SaaS

Software as a Service is the delivery of applications through the cloud. Microsoft's Office 365 and Salesforce.com (*http://salesforce.com*) are two SaaS offerings.

There are three ways of implementing cloud computing: as private, public, or hybrid clouds. Private clouds, like a traditional LAN, exist behind an organization's firewall and have no public access. Public clouds are hosted services from a provider that are shared by multiple customers. Companies are increasingly purchasing subscriptions to hosted networking services from IaaS providers such as Amazon. Finally, most organizations aren't placing their entire infrastructure in the cloud, instead opting for the hybrid cloud —using the public cloud for some services yet retaining some systems within a private cloud, perhaps for privacy, compliance, or compatibility concerns. For example, an organization may opt to use Azure for its development platform but may keep applications built in Azure within its private intranet.

While cloud computing offers many benefits, it also presents some management challenges. Security is vital. It's also necessary to efficiently allocate and monitor bandwidth requirements as outlined in a customer's service-level agreement.

With Hyper-V R3 and new networking capabilities in Server 2012, organizations have the tools not only to create their own internal, private clouds, but also to provide hosted services to customers. Server 2012 also allows system administrators to meet some of the challenges of managing a cloud computing environment by allowing control over virtual networks.

It's important to remember that the underlying technology of cloud computing is virtualization. Many of the new networking features are not just for the physical networks, but virtual ones. First, let's look at two of the most significant new network features in Server 2012.

IPAM

IPAM (Internet protocol address management) is a new tool for managing IP addresses on a network. With IPAM, system administrators can automatically discover IP addresses within the infrastructure, create reports on IP address data, and audit IP address changes.

IPAM is an important new feature because as networks become more virtualized and as cloud deployments increase, IP addresses are assigned to remote and virtual machines (VMs), not just local physical nodes on a network. With physical, virtual, and cloud networks all possible within one infrastructure, managing IP addressing can get a bit messy. IPAM provides a way to centrally keep tabs on both the physical and virtual machines in a network's IP addressing space. IPAM also integrates with DHCP (Domain Host Configuration Protocol), DNS (Domain Name System), and Active Directory, so it's an all-encompassing network management utility.

IPAM retains three years of IP address information, including IP address leases, MAC addresses, and user login and logoff information, in a Windows internal database. Unfortunately, as of now, it's not possible to set that database to be purged automatically or on a schedule—system administrators must manually purge it.

Although IPAM supports IPv4 and IPv6, there are some limitations in IPAM with IPv6. IPAM will track utilization trends only for IPv4 addresses. Also, IP *address reclaiming* —where DHCP will try to reclaim an abandoned IP address when a client makes a request—through IPAM is supported only with IPv4 addresses.

An IPAM server can be deployed at every site, or an organization can set up a central server. The deployment option depends on the organization's size and number of network nodes. A large enterprise with branch offices and thousands of clients will likely deploy one IPAM server per site, while a smaller organization with hundreds or fewer clients can get away with a central IPAM server. One IPAM server supports up to 150 DHCP servers, 500 DNS servers, 6,000 DHCP scopes, and 150 DNS zones.

Installing IPAM

There are a few requirements for deploying IPAM, as well as some limitations:

- IPAM installation requires 512 MB of RAM.
- Server 2012 must be installed on the machine running IPAM.
- IPAM supports only domain controllers, DHCP, DNS, and NPS at Windows Server 2008 level and higher.
- Only Windows internal database is supported.
- IPAM supports only the Windows internal database.

IPAM works best if it's installed on a dedicated, domain-joined Windows Server 2012 machine with no other roles. It's not recommended to install IPAM on a domain controller or a server running DHCP.

To install IPAM, follow these steps:

1. From Server Manager, click "Add roles and features." Select "Role-based or feature-based installation." Click Next. Select the server for the IPAM install. Click Next.

2. From the left menu in the "Select server roles" window, click Features. Scroll down in the Features menu and click the checkbox for "IP Address Management (IPAM) Server."

3. Installing IPAM requires additional features, which Server Manager will automatically install. Click "Add features." Click Next and choose to restart the server automatically if desired. Click Install, and the IPAM install process initializes.

   When install completes, IPAM is listed in the Server Manager dashboard.

Configuring IPAM

When you open IPAM in Server Manager for the first time, you'll need to complete a few tasks to set up the server. These tasks are conducted through a series of wizards (see Figure 8-1).

Once you've connected to the IPAM server from Server Manager, the next step is provisioning the IPAM server. This involves setting up a manual or Group Policy–based provisioning method to configure the required access needed to manage DCHP, DNS, NPS servers, and DCs. Most Windows infrastructures can use Group Policy provisioning for its seamless integration with Active Directory.

To set up IPAM for Group Policy provisioning, select the "Provision the IPAM server" link in the IPAM Server Tasks window. Click Next, and then select Manual or Group Policy Based as the provisioning method.

If creating Group Policy provisioning, you must create a GPO (Group Policy object) prefix name. This prefix is used in the Group Policy objects added to the servers that IPAM will manage. The prefix is added to the GPO entries in DHCP, DNS, NPS servers, and DCs. There must be one unique GPO for each IPAM instance running in an AD forest.

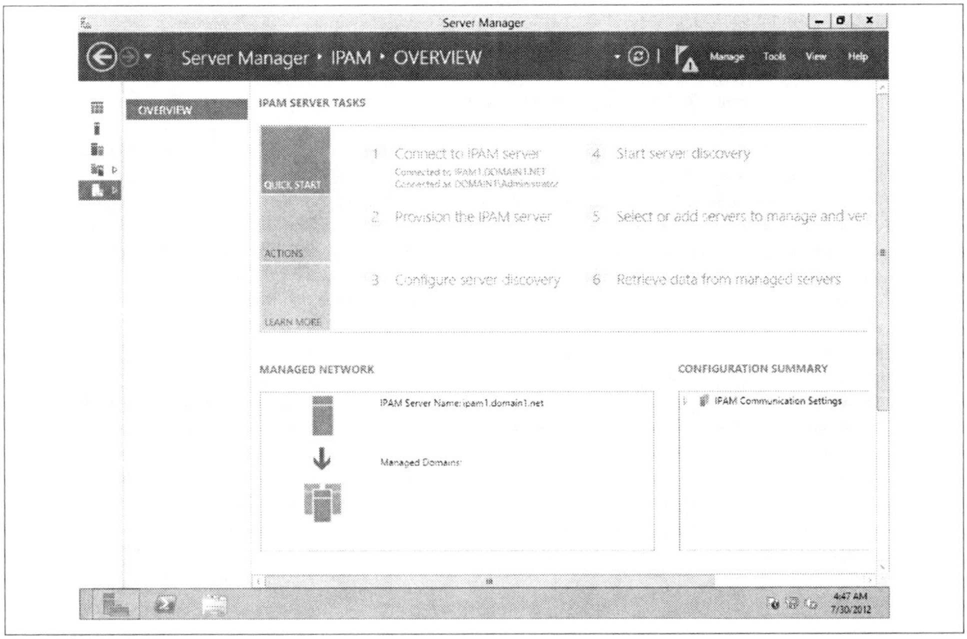

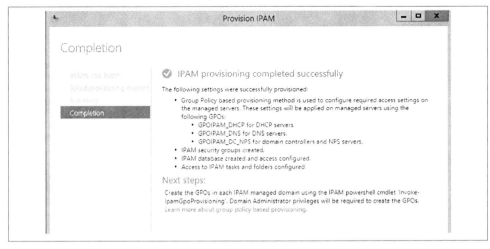

Figure 8-1. IPAM configuration wizard

In Figure 8-2, the GPO prefix name is GPOIPAM, meaning there will be a GPO created for DHCP with the naming convention GPOIPAM_DHCP. Click Next and then Apply after confirming the settings to complete the provisioning. When IPAM is successfully provisioned, a confirmation window displays.

Figure 8-2. IPAM provisioning completed

For multidomain environments, you can execute the PowerShell command `Invoke-IpamGPOProvisioning` at the command prompt. You must execute this cmdlet with an account that has domain administrator privileges so that the necessary GPOs are created in each domain.

Once IPAM is provisioned, the next step is configuring server discovery. From the IPAM Overview screen in Server Manager, select the link for "Configure server discovery" (see Figure 8-3).

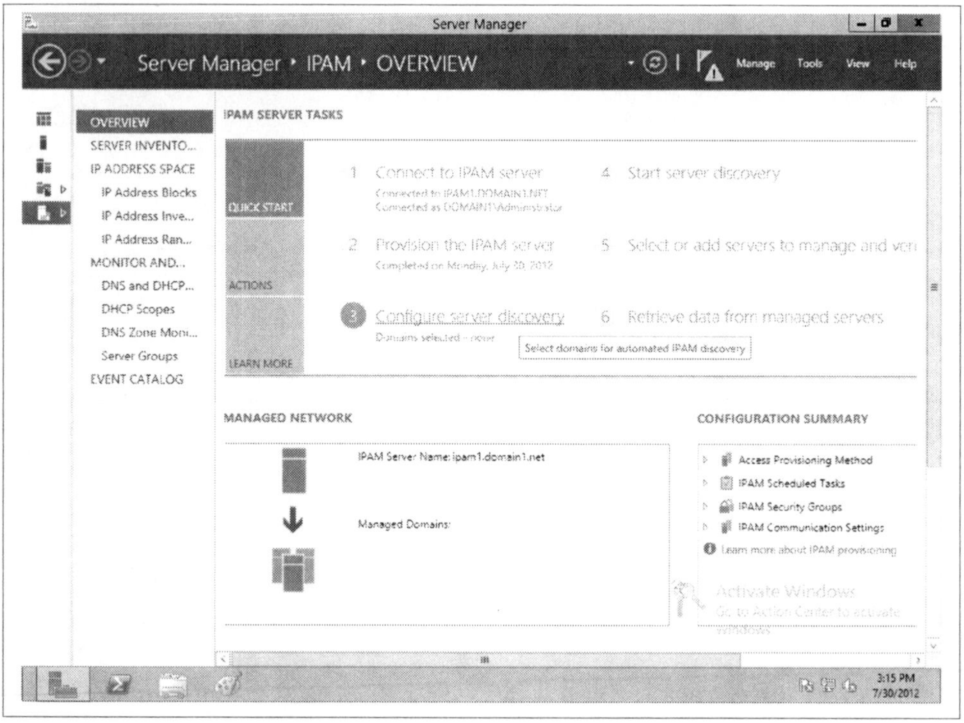

Figure 8-3. Launching IPAM's Configure Server Discovery wizard

From the Configure Server Discovery window, select the domain(s) to discover. Click Add and OK (see Figure 8-4).

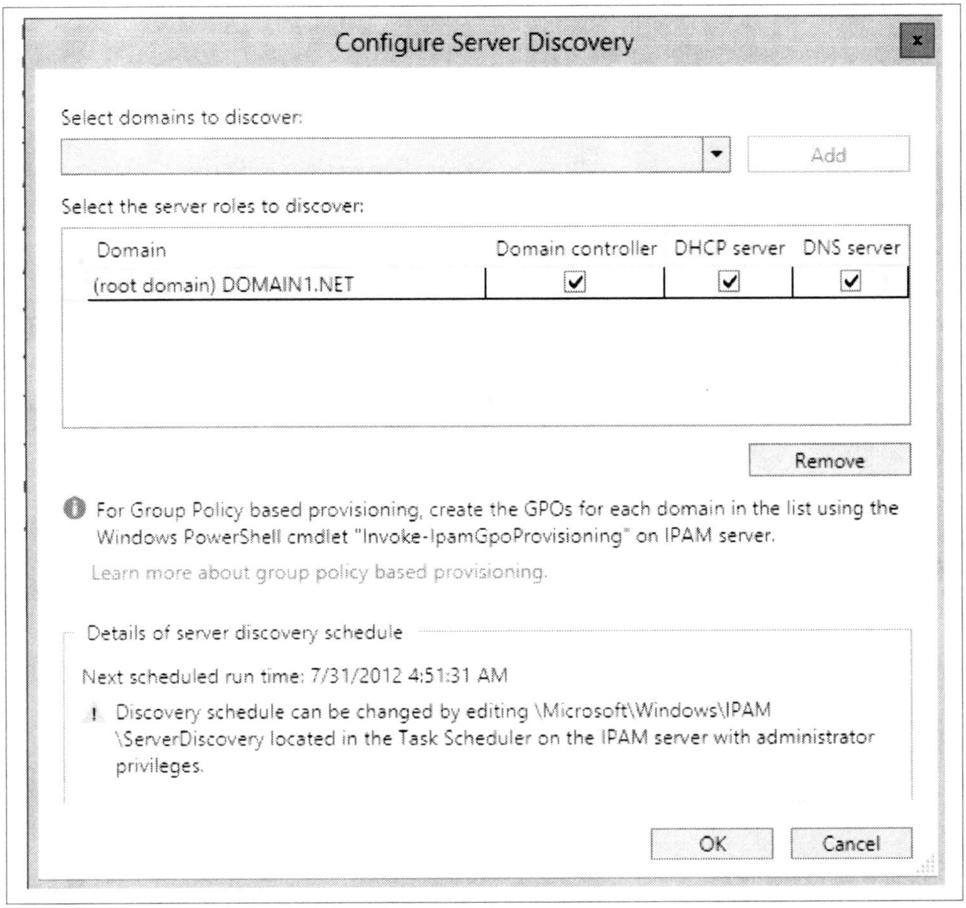

Figure 8-4. Selecting domains for discovery

Click Start Server Discovery from the IPAM Overview windows in Server Manager. Server Manager will display a notification stating, "There are one or more IPAM tasks still running in the Task Scheduler. Please wait for their completion." When discovery is complete, the notification message will show the time that servers were discovered.

After discovery, click the link "Select or add servers to manage and verify IPAM access" from the IPAM Overview window. This opens a server inventory of IP addresses. The DHCP and DCs should be listed. The servers listed will likely have a manageability status set to Unspecified and an IPAM access status of Blocked. Here is where you need to check a few configuration options, from Group Policy Management on the IPAM server, drill down to Domains→Group Policy Objects. Check to ensure there are three objects created:

- GPO Prefix Name_DC_NPS
- GPO Prefix Name_DHCP
- GPO Prefix Name_DNS

If those objects are not created, run (as a domain administrator) `Invoke-IpamGpo Provisioning` in PowerShell again.

If the objects are in Group Policy Management, go back to Server Manager and Server Inventory in the IPAM Overview. Right-click the first server listed and select Edit Server (see Figure 8-5).

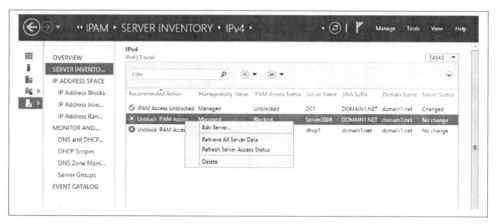

Figure 8-5. Editing a server's manageability status

From the drop-down list for the "Manageability status" field, select Managed and then click OK. Do this for all the servers IPAM is to manage.

At this point in configuration, a red *x* will indicate the servers that still have IPAM access blocked. To unblock access, run `gpupdate/force` from PowerShell on each server. After Group Policy updates, IPAM access is unblocked (see Figure 8-6).

 If IPAM access continues to be blocked, make sure you have firewall settings configured correctly and rerun `gpupdate`.

The last step in configuring IPAM is to click "Retrieve data from managed servers" from the IPAM Overview window to pull IP address information from the managed servers.

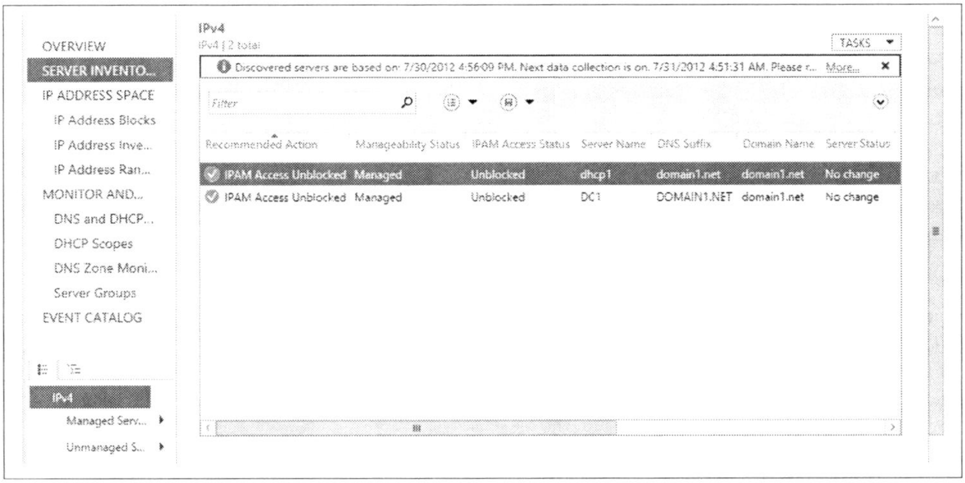

Figure 8-6. Editing a server's manageability status

Using IPAM

Once IPAM is configured, at-a-glance information about an infrastructure's IP address space is displayed. IPAM can automatically discover IPv4 and IPv6 range information for all active DHCP scopes on managed DHCP servers. IP addresses on nonmanaged or non-Microsoft devices can be added manually or imported from a CSV (comma-separated value) file.

Clicking IP Address Blocks provides information such as the start and end IP addresses on a network, the IP address type (public or private), static IPs, and the number of IP addresses used within an address block. Some particularly handy data is IP utilization level; insight into how IP addresses are being used across an organization helps in planning IP addressing schemes as nodes are added to a network.

IPAM also provides a centralized console for monitoring and managing DHCP and DNS scopes and zones, so you don't have to flip between Server Manager views. You can't perform the management options for DNS and DHCP through IPAM, but right-clicking either server in IPAM gives you the option to open up the management console for either DHCP or DNS.

IPAM features

The main features in IPAM include server inventory, IP address space management, utilization statistics, DNS and DHCP management and monitoring, and auditing and event tracking.

Server inventory displays all Windows 2008 and later servers managed by IPAM. Server information is collected through Active Directory. By default, server inventory will discover and include all DCs registered in domains, as well as Microsoft DNS and DHCP servers. NPS servers will not be autodiscovered but can be added manually.

Servers are arranged in a hierarchical view. At Level 1 are servers displayed by IPv4 and IPv6 addresses. Level 2 shows servers by manageability status (managed or unmanaged). Level 3 displays by subnet in multisubnet environments (see Figure 8-7).

Figure 8-7. Editing a server's manageability status

As mentioned previously, you can add servers manually into IPAM. Right-click the IP address version of the server to configure its manageability. In Figure 8-8, an NPS running on a Windows Server 2008 R2 server with a static IPv4 address is being added. The option Add Server appears.

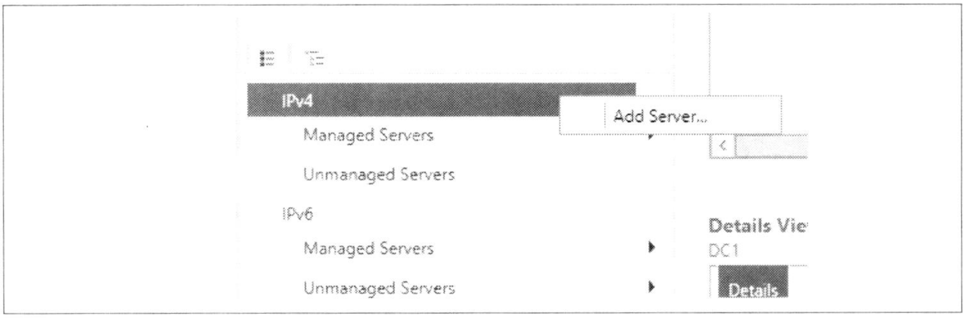

Figure 8-8. Adding a server

Enter the IP address or FQDN (fully qualified domain name) of the server, enter the server type, and select the Manageability status (choose Managed if the server's IP information is to be managed by IPAM). Click Verify (see Figure 8-9).

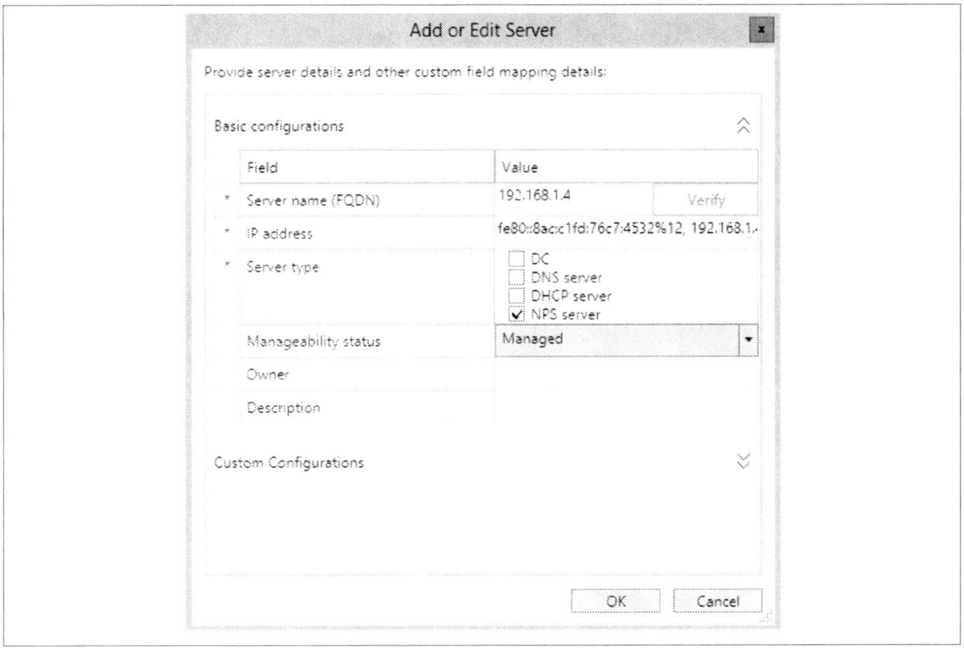

Figure 8-9. Entering properties of a manually added server

The NPS server is now included in the server inventory list. To manage fully with IPAM, you need to unblock the IPAM access, as outlined earlier in the chapter (see Figure 8-10).

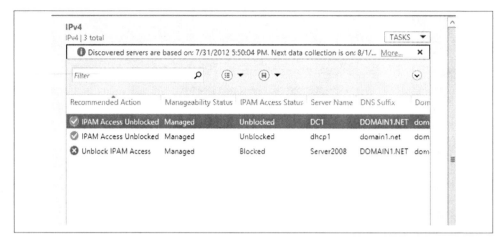

Figure 8-10. Allowing a manually added server IPAM access

Right-clicking a server within the Server Inventory view displays a menu with options to retrieve server data (collect IP address information), delete the server, edit its properties (such as the IPAM manageability status), or refresh the server status (see Figure 8-11).

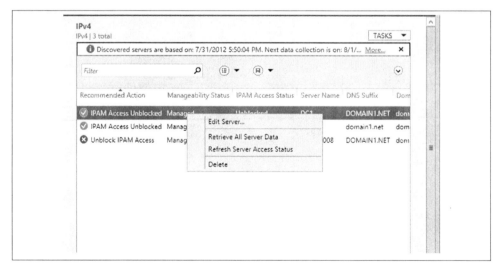

Figure 8-11. Context menu in IPAM

IP address space management lets you track, audit, manage, and report on the IP addresses in an infrastructure. IP address space management is a useful tool to organize the IP addresses in a network. With IPAM, IP address spaces are organized into IP address blocks. Blocks can be broken into IP address ranges, which can in turn be used to allocate IP addresses to devices on the network. Larger organizations even have the ability to organize IP address ranges into range groups and place IP addresses into custom, user-defined groups.

Creating an IP address block is a fairly straightforward process in IPAM, and a good starting point for organizing IP addresses. To create a new IP address block:

1. Click the Tasks drop-down menu and select Add IP Address Block, as shown in Figure 8-12.

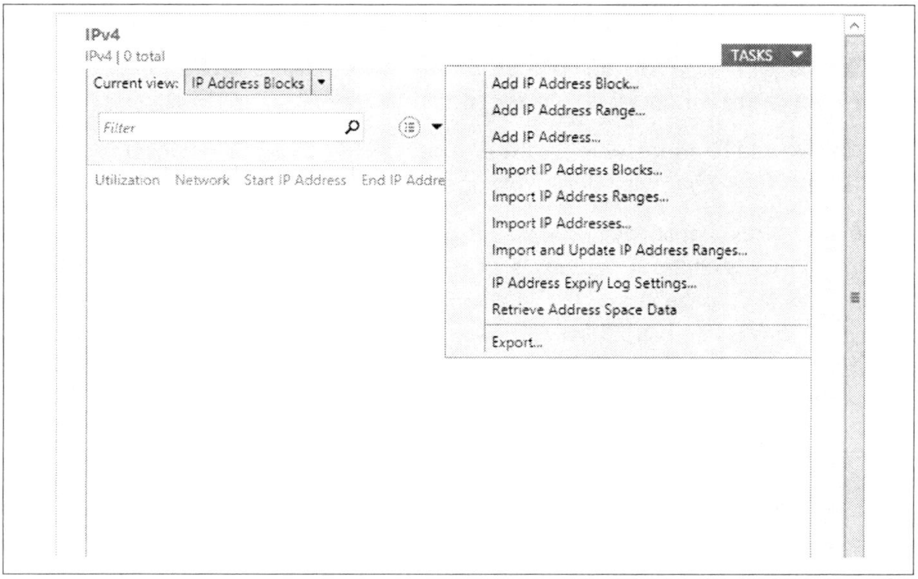

Figure 8-12. Selecting Add IP Address Block from Tasks

2. In the window that displays, under Network ID, type in the starting range of the IP addresses to be blocked. For Prefix Length, select /24, which will include IP addresses up to 192.x.x.254. Click OK. You will now see a defined IP address block as well as the percentage of IP addresses within the block that are currently in use. The utilization level of IP addresses in the block is also displayed (see Figure 8-13).

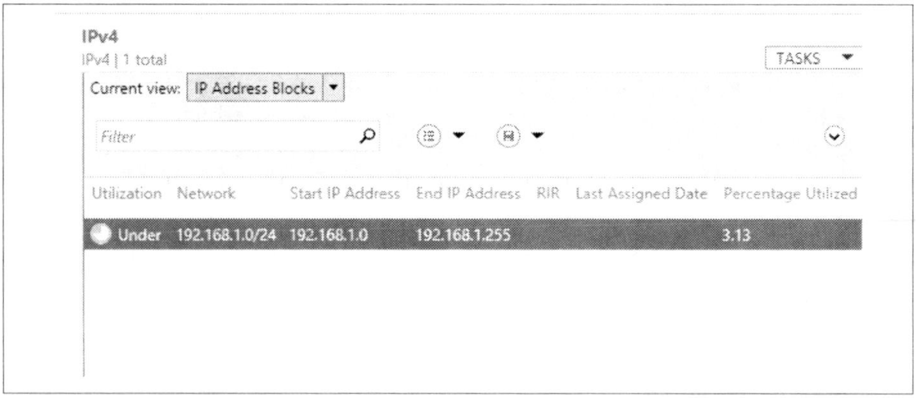

Figure 8-13. Adding an IP address block

The Details View in IPAM displays additional information, such as how many IP addresses within the server block are assigned throughout the network.

You can also add IP address blocks for IPv6 and public IP addresses. You can even place IP addresses into other user-defined groups.

IP address spaces enable you to see ranges and blocks of IP addresses allocated by DHCP. They won't pick up static IP addresses, third-party devices like routers, or mobile devices that may connect to the network. IPAM apparently lacks the ability to do comprehensive network discovery across all devices using SNMP (Simple Network Management Protocol), but you'll find this capability in some third-party network utility solutions from companies such as SolarWinds and Cisco.

You can manually add IP addresses either through IPAM or by importing a CSV file. For example, let's say you have a Windows Server 2008 R2 member server in the domain assigned a static IP address. It's not a DC, so IPAM can't autodiscover it. Still, you can add that server in IPAM by following these steps:

1. From IPAM in Server Manager, click to highlight IP Address Inventory. Click Tasks and select Add IP Address (see Figure 8-14).

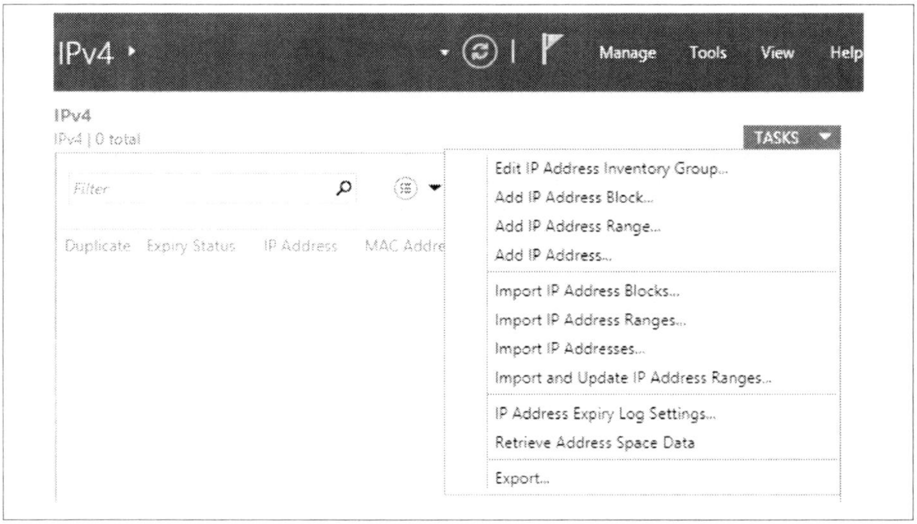

Figure 8-14. First step in adding an IP address

2. In the Add IPv4 Address window, enter the IP address and the device's MAC (media access control) address. You can also add other properties, such as the type of IP address assignment (dynamic or static), as shown in Figure 8-15.

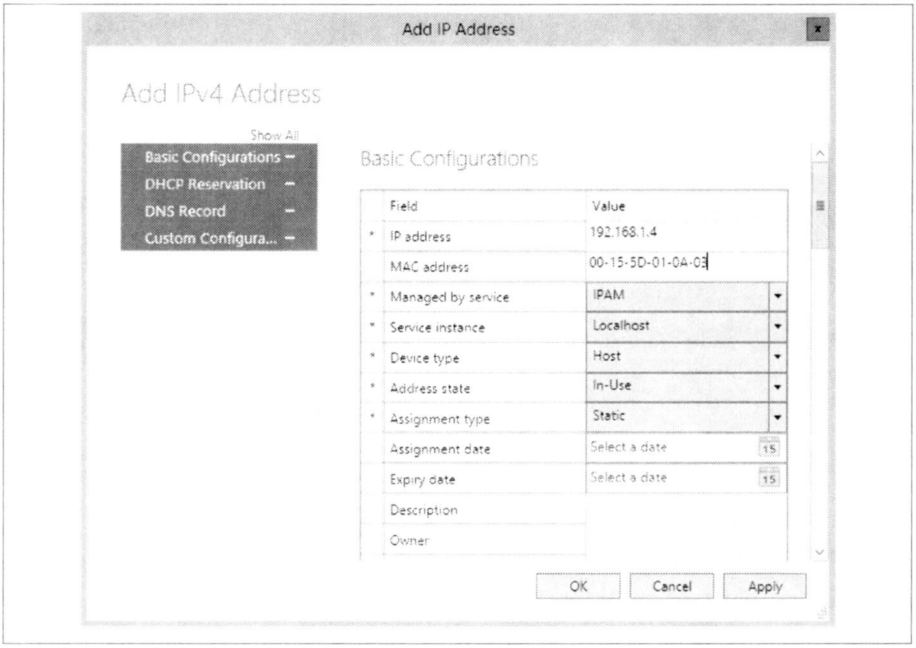

Figure 8-15. The Add IPv4 Address window

You can now see the manually added address in the IPv4 Private Address Space view in IPAM (see Figure 8-16).

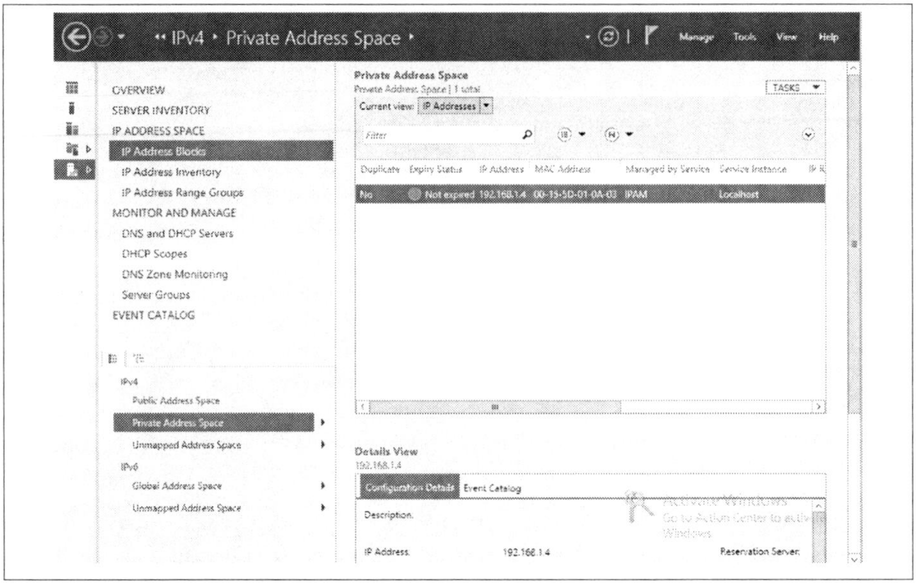

Figure 8-16. A manually added IP address

Instead of manually adding IP addresses in IPAM, you can import them into IPAM as a CSV file. The file has to be properly formatted as follows:

1. From the DHCP server, go into DHCP Manager. In the left menu, expand the Address Leases folder under IPv4 or IPv6, depending on which address types are to be imported into IPAM.

2. Right-click Address Leases and select Export List. Save the exported DHCP information as a CSV file.

3. From IPAM, add at least one IP address into IPAM's IPv4 address space, as outlined previously. Once you've created that IP address, click Tasks and then Export. This will export the IP address into a CSV file that is properly formatted.

Now you're ready for the import into IPAM.

1. Copy and paste the contents of the CSV file exported from DHCP into the exported IPAM file. In Figure 8-17, the exported information from IPAM is above the space, and the copied exported information from DHCP is below.

```
"Duplicate","Expiry Status","IP Address","MAC Address","Managed by Service","Service Instance","IP Range",
"Device Name","Device Type","IP Address State","Assignment Type","Expiry Date","DHCP Reservation Sync",
"DNS Host Record Sync","DNS PTR Record Sync","Assignment Date","Owner","Serial Number","Asset Tag","Description",
"Reservation Name","Reservation Description","Reservation Type","Reservation Server","Reservation Scope Name",
"Reservation Scope Details","Forward Lookup Primary Server","Forward Lookup Zone","Reverse Lookup Primary Server",
"Reverse Lookup Zone","AD Site","Country or Region","Microsoft Server Role","Region","RIR","Type of Network",
"VMM DNS Suffix","VMM IP Pool Name","VMM Logical Network"
"No","Not expired","192.168.1.4","00-15-5D-01-0A-03","IPAM","Localhost","","","Host","In-Use","Static","","Not Att


Client IP Address,Name,Lease Expiration,Type,Unique ID,Description,Network Access Protection,Probation Expiration,
192.168.1.2,,8/13/2012 1:25:16 AM,DHCP,b407f9ae54a1,,Full Access,N/A,None,
192.168.1.27,Client8.DOMAIN1.NET,8/12/2012 9:00:28 AM,DHCP,00155d010a00,,Full Access,N/A,None,
192.168.1.28,Client7.DOMAIN1.NET,8/12/2012 5:41:44 PM,DHCP,00155d010a01,,Full Access,N/A,None,
192.168.1.29,android_cdf93ef3465b4113.DOMAIN1.NET,8/12/2012 6:35:28 PM,DHCP,c8aa21410bdf,,Full Access,N/A,None,
192.168.1.40,SLynn.DOMAIN1.NET,8/12/2012 3:12:56 AM,DHCP,002710af4f5c,,Full Access,N/A,None,
192.168.1.42,HP-HP.DOMAIN1.NET,8/12/2012 3:13:34 AM,DHCP,0015005d12b0,,Full Access,N/A,None,
```

Figure 8-17. Data exported from IPAM is above the space; data exported from DHCP is below

2. Next, you want to import the six IP addresses shown in the information from DHCP, so you copy the 192.168.1.4 line from IPAM five times and then copy and paste the DHCP IP addresses and MAC address information into the copied lines (see Figure 8-20). Save the file in *.csv* format.

3. Next, let's import the six IP addresses shown in the information from DHCP (in this example, I have only six addresses assigned by DHCP in my small testbed; you will import whatever number of DHCP-assigned addresses are in your network). Copy the 192.168.1.4 line from IPAM five times and then copy and paste the DHCP IP addresses and MAC address information into the copied lines. (See Figure 8-18.)

```
"Duplicate","Expiry Status","IP Address","MAC Address","Managed by Service","Service Instance","IP Range",
"Device Name","Device Type","IP Address State","Assignment Type","Expiry Date","DHCP Reservation Sync",
"DNS Host Record Sync","DNS PTR Record Sync","Assignment Date","Owner","Serial Number","Asset Tag","Description",
"Reservation Name","Reservation Description","Reservation Type","Reservation Server","Reservation Scope Name",
"Reservation Scope Details","Forward Lookup Primary Server","Forward Lookup Zone","Reverse Lookup Primary Server",
"Reverse Lookup Zone","AD Site","Country or Region","Microsoft Server Role","Region","RIR","Type of Network",
"VMM DNS Suffix","VMM IP Pool Name","VMM Logical Network"
"No","Not expired","192.168.1.4","00-15-5D-01-0A-03","IPAM","Localhost","","","Host","In-Use","Static","","Not Att
"No","Not expired","192.168.1.2","b4-07-f9-ae-54-a1","IPAM","Localhost","","","Host","In-Use","Static","","Not Att
"No","Not expired","192.168.1.4","00-15-5D-01-0A-03","IPAM","Localhost","","","Host","In-Use","Static","","Not Att
"No","Not expired","192.168.1.4","00-15-5D-01-0A-03","IPAM","Localhost","","","Host","In-Use","Static","","Not Att
"No","Not expired","192.168.1.4","00-15-5D-01-0A-03","IPAM","Localhost","","","Host","In-Use","Static","","Not Att
"No","Not expired","192.168.1.4","00-15-5D-01-0A-03","IPAM","Localhost","","","Host","In-Use","Static","","Not Att


Client IP Address,Name,Lease Expiration,Type,Unique ID,Description,Network Access Protection,Probation Expiration,
192.168.1.2,,8/13/2012 1:25:16 AM,DHCP,b407f9ae54a1,,Full Access,N/A,None,
192.168.1.27,Client8.DOMAIN1.NET,8/12/2012 9:00:28 AM,DHCP,00155d010a00,,Full Access,N/A,None,
192.168.1.28,Client7.DOMAIN1.NET,8/12/2012 5:41:44 PM,DHCP,00155d010a01,,Full Access,N/A,None,
192.168.1.29,android_cdf93ef3465b4113.DOMAIN1.NET,8/12/2012 6:35:28 PM,DHCP,c8aa21410bdf,,Full Access,N/A,None,
192.168.1.40,SLynn.DOMAIN1.NET,8/12/2012 3:12:56 AM,DHCP,002710af4f5c,,Full Access,N/A,None,
192.168.1.42,HP-HP.DOMAIN1.NET,8/12/2012 3:13:34 AM,DHCP,0015005d12b0,,Full Access,N/A,None,
```

Figure 8-18. Formatting the file for import into IPAM

You should save the file in *.csv* format. This properly formats the file for import into IPAM, as shown in Figure 8-19.

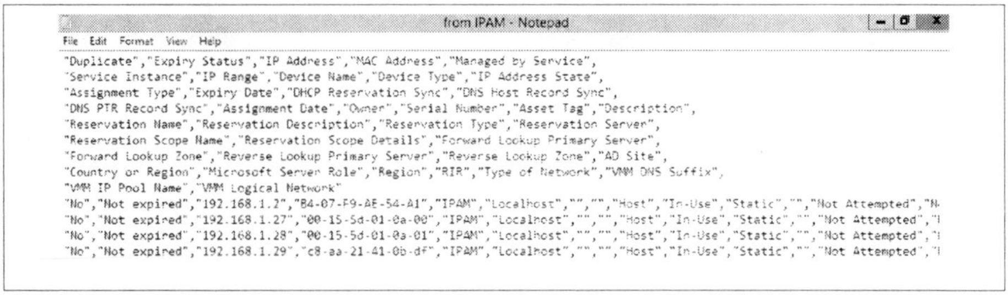

Figure 8-19. File prepared for import

4. Next, import the prepared CSV file into IPAM. From IPAM in Server Manager, click to highlight IP Address Inventory and then click IPv4 or IPv6 at the bottom menu, depending on which type of addresses are being imported. Click Tasks, then Import IP Addresses, and browse to the CSV file.

IPAM will confirm when the addresses are imported. If there are any issues with the import, the confirmation will note that as well.

Now, instead of only the IP address we manually added into IPAM before, the addresses from the CSV file are listed under the IPv4 Private Address Space view. (See Figure 8-20.)

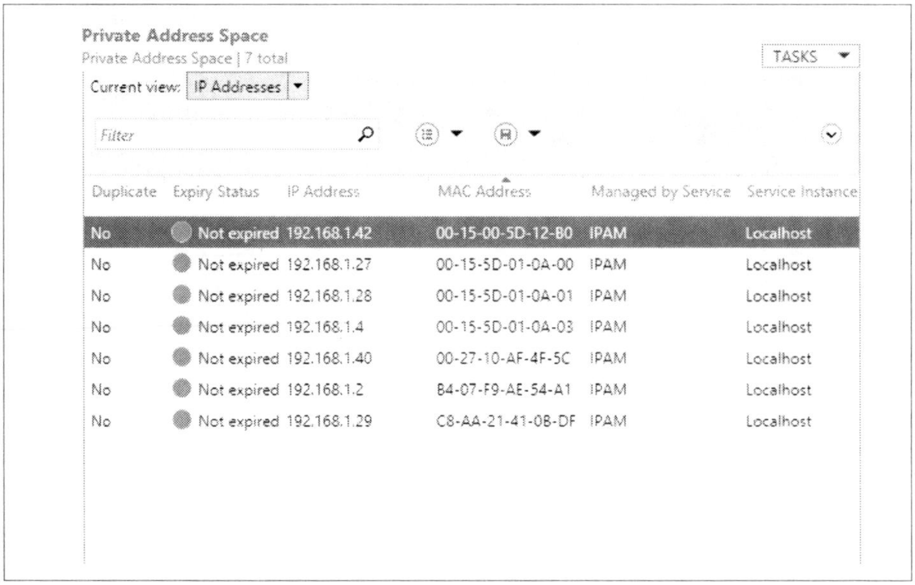

Figure 8-20. IP addresses added from the CSV file

Of course, importing IP addresses in a network with hundreds of clients is inefficient. While Microsoft provides decent overall management of IP addresses, enterprises may want to use (or continue to use) third-party IP management or network discovery tools in conjunction with IPAM for granular management over all IP addresses in the network. Smaller organizations with fewer than 100 network nodes should find IPAM and its capability to import IP addresses sufficient for IP address space management.

IPAM utilization

One of the key features of IPAM is visualization of IP address usage. IPAM provides usage information on IP address ranges, IP address blocks, and IP range groups.

Clicking into the IP address range groups in IPAM will show whether IP addresses in that range are over- or underused, or at optimal utilization level. You can also display a line graph in the Details View. The graph shows utilization trends over a specified period of time. (See Figure 8-21.)

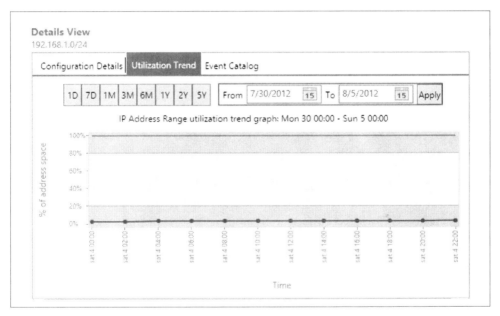

Figure 8-21. IP address utilization trend

The "Find and Allocate Available IP Address" feature will be appreciated by any system administrator who has spent time figuring out which IP address is free to allocate to a new device. Right-clicking an IP address range group gives you the option to find and allocate an available IP address. When you select that option, the Find and Allocate Available IP Address window displays (Figure 8-22). IPAM pings a request to IP addresses not in use and attempts to resolve them through DNS.

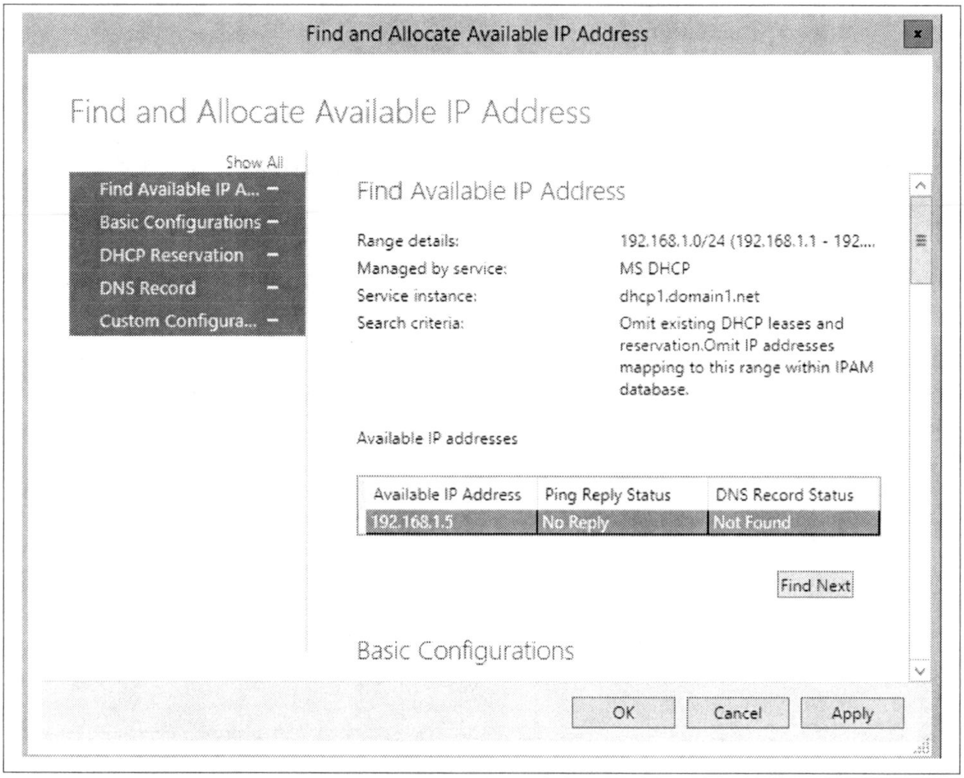

Figure 8-22. Finding and allocating unused IP addresses

Just as handy as finding unused IP addresses is that once an available address is found, you can make it a DHCP reservation, add it to a DCHP scope, or perform other tasks, such as creating a DNS record for the IP address entry—all from within IPAM and without needing to access the DNS or DHCP servers.

IPAM also allows for reclaiming leased IP addresses that are no longer being used. You access this option by right-clicking the appropriate IP address group and selecting Reclaim IP Address.

DHCP and DNS management and monitoring through IPAM

As mentioned earlier, IPAM provides DHCP and DNS management from the IPAM console, saving you administrative time. Within the IPAM console, you can create or delete DHCP reservations for IP addresses as well as DNS-pointed records.

Other tasks that you can perform from IPAM include editing DHCP server options and creating DHCP scopes.

Auditing and events

IP address auditing is provided with two additional, major capabilities in IPAM: IP address tracking and event catalog. With tracking, you can build and schedule queries that include searches against IP addresses, MAC addresses, hostnames, or usernames. Tracking allows you to search for specific IP address–related events in a specific time period.

IPAM will also log events such as configuration changes made to DHCP and IPAM servers.

As with other Windows Server management roles, you can manage IPAM remotely using the IPAM client that is part of the Server Manager RSAT, which can be downloaded from the Microsoft download center and installed on any Windows 8 client machine. Remote administrators must be members of the WinRMRemoteWMIUsers group on the IPAM server and members of the appropriate IPAM security group (or local administrators group).

NIC Teaming

Network interface card (NIC) teaming is now a native feature in Windows Server 2012. With NIC teaming, multiple NICs can be consolidated to provide bandwidth load balancing and network connection failover without requiring third-party hardware or software.

Load balancing via NIC teaming provides bandwidth aggregation. For example, a Server 2012 system with two network adapters that each connect at 1 Gbps will give 2 Gbps throughput when teamed.

Windows Server 2012 network adapter teaming is designed to work with any vendor's network cards. For aggregation or failover, both adapters have to support the same network speed.

Teaming is pretty straightforward to enable. In the following steps, we will create a networking team by connecting a system with a built-in interface to an additional interface, with both interfaces connecting at 1 Gbps. To configure both for aggregation:

1. From Local Server view in Server Manager's dashboard, click Disabled next to NIC Teaming (see Figure 8-23).

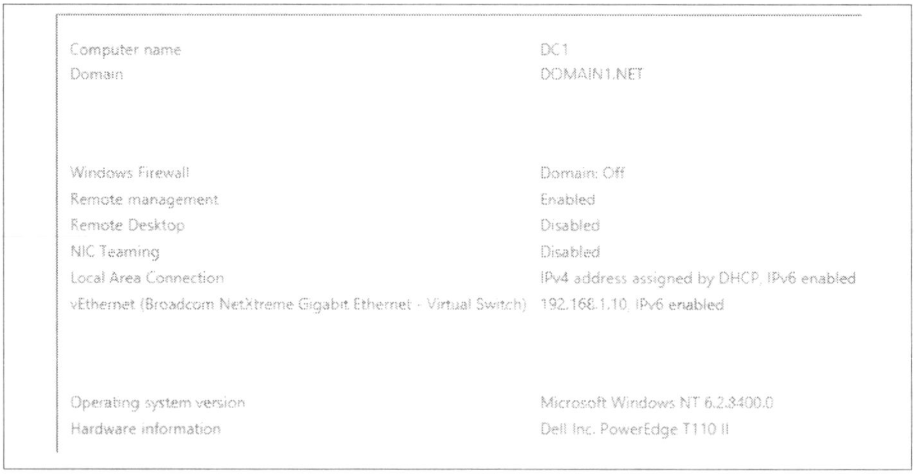
Computer name
DC1
Domain
DOMAIN1.NET
Windows Firewall
Domain: Off
Remote management
Enabled
Remote Desktop
Disabled
NIC Teaming
Disabled
Local Area Connection
IPv4 address assigned by DHCP, IPv6 enabled
vEthernet (Broadcom NetXtreme Gigabit Ethernet - Virtual Switch)
192.168.1.10, IPv6 enabled
Operating system version
Microsoft Windows NT 6.2.8400.0
Hardware information
Dell Inc. PowerEdge T110 II

Figure 8-23. Enabling NIC teaming in Server Manager

2. The NIC Teaming window opens. Under Teams, click the drop-down menu for Tasks and select New Team (see Figure 8-24).

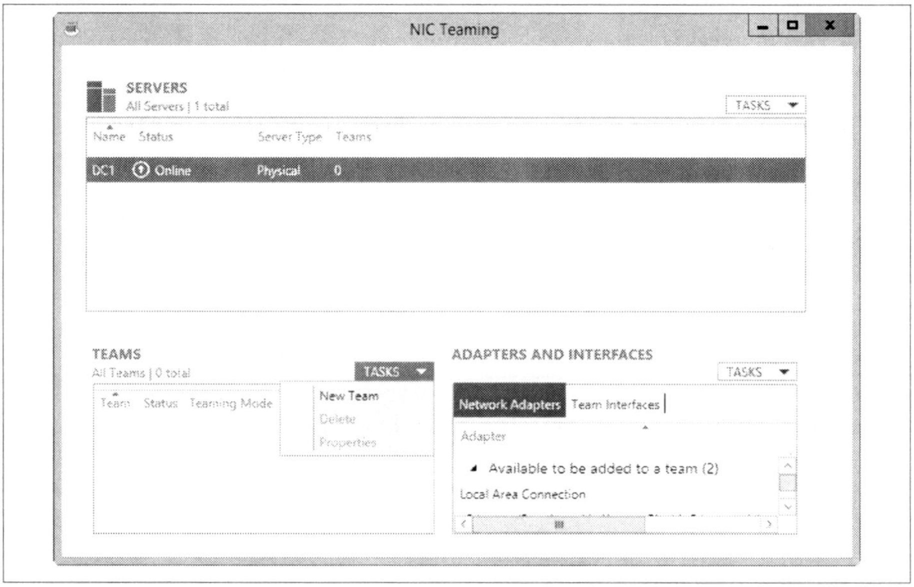
NIC Teaming
SERVERS
All Servers | 1 total
TASKS
Name
Status
Server Type
Teams
DC1
Online
Physical
0
TEAMS
All Teams | 0 total
TASKS
Team
Status
Teaming Mode
New Team
Delete
Properties
ADAPTERS AND INTERFACES
TASKS
Network Adapters
Team Interfaces
Adapter
Available to be added to a team (2)
Local Area Connection

Figure 8-24. Creating a new team

3. Name the team and select the adapters to include (see Figure 8-25).

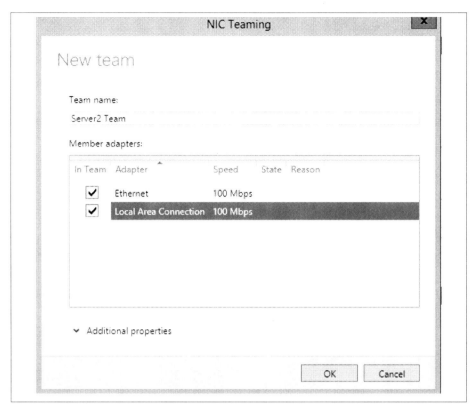

Figure 8-25. Configuring a NIC team

Additional properties are available to configure the teams. Properties you can select are Switch Independent, which means no additional switch configuration is needed and adapters can be connected to different switches to team; Address Hash, which enables load balancing and bandwidth aggregation; and Standby Adapter, which uses a specified NIC for failover in case one fails.

Before teaming, the two network interfaces in this example were connected to a 10/100 Ethernet switch and had individual bandwidth speeds of 100 Mbps.

After the NICs are teamed as Switch Independent and with Address Hash, the server displays the NICs as a team with an aggregated bandwidth of 200 Mbps (see Figure 8-26).

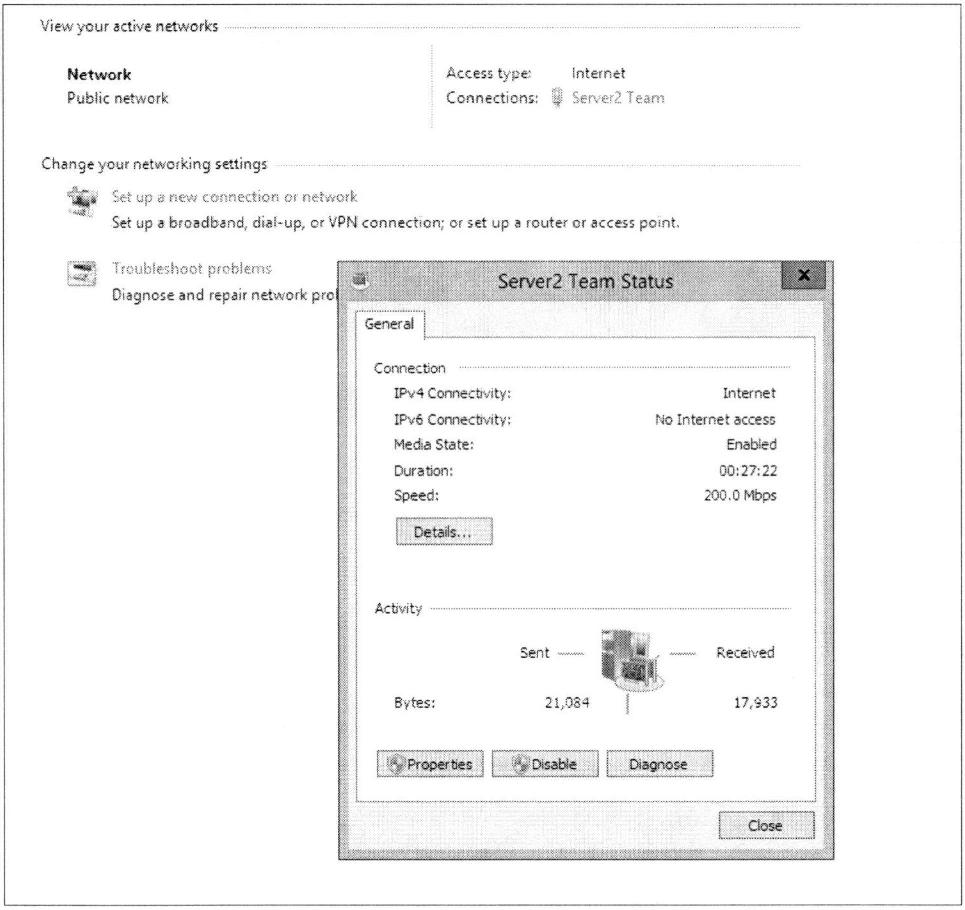

Figure 8-26. NICs teamed for bandwidth aggregation

You can perform NIC teaming with VMs as well. For example, you can connect more than one virtual adapter to a Hyper-V switch for failover purposes in case one of those adapters gets disconnected.

Quality of Service

Quality of Service (QoS) is a feature typically associated with networking hardware such as routers. QoS works the same with routers as in Windows Server 2012. It's used to prioritize traffic; for example, networks that have a VoIP (Voice over IP) solution deployed can set QoS to give bandwidth priority to VoIP traffic, improving the call quality of VoIP communication. Network administrators can use QoS to throttle traffic and measure bandwidth performance.

QoS is not a new feature in Server 2012. With Server 2008 R2, you enable QoS by creating policies. What is new, however, is a set of QoS management capabilities now in Hyper-V. There are two use cases for QoS in Hyper-V. For the corporate network, QoS can help solve performance issues. For businesses that provide hosted cloud services, QoS can help them meet performance requirements as outlined in customer service-level agreements (SLAs).

Hyper-V QoS provides a way to specify minimum bandwidth QoS policies and other controls over network traffic. In Server 2008 R2, QoS control was limited in that you were able to set only maximum bandwidth, which meant you'd face performance problems if different types of network traffic exceeded that level. With minimum bandwidth, the set level cannot be reduced to a lower level. A specific amount of bandwidth is defined.

To begin QoS deployment in Hyper-V, when setting up a VM, click "Enable bandwidth management" and set minimum and maximum bandwidth in Mbps. (See Figure 8-27.)

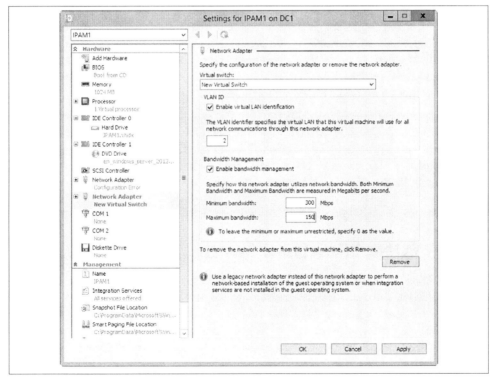

Figure 8-27. Enabling bandwidth management for QoS

You can also enable minimum bandwidth QoS through hardware; you use a network adapter that supports *data center bridging* (DCB) to configure service levels on specific types of traffic.

QoS Policies

You can create QoS policies in Windows Server 2012 through the GUI Policy wizard or through PowerShell. To create a new QoS policy using the wizard:

1. Launch Group Policy Management. Right-click to edit the Default Domain Policy. Expand either Computer Configuration or User Configuration, depending on which objects (computers or users) the QoS policy is to be configured against (generally, QoS computer configurations are applied to servers), and then navigate to Policies→Windows Settings→Policy-based QoS.

2. Right-click "Policy-based QoS" and select "Create a QoS Policy." Specify a DSCP (differentiated services code point) value. This value assigns different levels of service to network traffic; values from 0 through 63 are allowed. Routers use the DSCP value to classify network packets and queue them appropriately; the higher the value, the higher the priority for the packet. For example, if an organization's traffic consists of video, and that traffic has high priority, you can create a policy for that video app and set DSCP to 34 (the recommended value for video), and create another policy for all other traffic set to the default value of 0.

3. Next, specify outbound throttle rate. If traffic is high priority, clear this box so that throttling is disabled; otherwise, leave the defaults. Click Next and then select the application(s) to which the policy will be applied. Then specify the source and destination IP addresses to apply the policy to, click Define to define the protocol and ports for the policy, and then click Finish.

Remember, you can configure QoS through PowerShell as well.

Hyper-V Extensible Network Switch

Hyper-V R3's Extensible Switch is another killer feature in Windows Server 2012 networking. With it, third parties can create plug-ins to enhance Hyper-V management. Even before Windows Server 2012 was released in its final version, vendors started creating and marketing extensions for Hyper-V that can do tasks ranging from aiding system admins in easily mounting virtual drives to securing virtualized environments.

Configuring Private VLANs

The Hyper-V network switch also provides network management features just like any physical hardware switch. For instance, VMs can be isolated from other VMs, giving organizations the power to deploy a multitenant cloud. You can isolate VMs by placing them in private virtual LANs (PVLANs). PVLANs aren't only for isolating tenants using an organization's hosted services; they are also used to secure access and communications within a network, between VMs on a physical host.

Figure 8-28 shows a Hyper-V host with four VMs all connected to the same Hyper-V virtual switch.

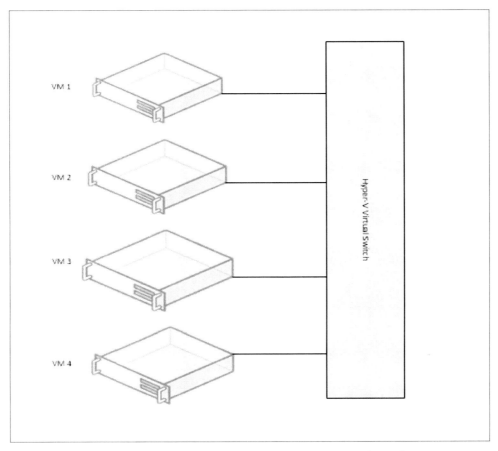

Figure 8-28. Four virtual servers connected to the Hyper-V virtual switch

VMs 1 and 2 have applications and data that the Sales and Marketing departments use. Data transfer and communication has to happen between the two VMs. VM 3 runs a database with which all the other VMs in the VLAN need to communicate. VM 4 runs the finance and accounting application, with which no other VMs should communicate. To configure these four VMs as PVLANs, follow these steps:

1. First, assign a VLAN ID for all the VMs. To accommodate the preceding scenario, we'll configure all the VMs on the same VLAN with VLAN ID set to 2. There are two ways to set a VM with a VLAN ID. The first is by going into the network adapter settings of the VM and enabling virtual LAN identification. The ID number by default is 2, but it can be changed. (See Figure 8-29.)

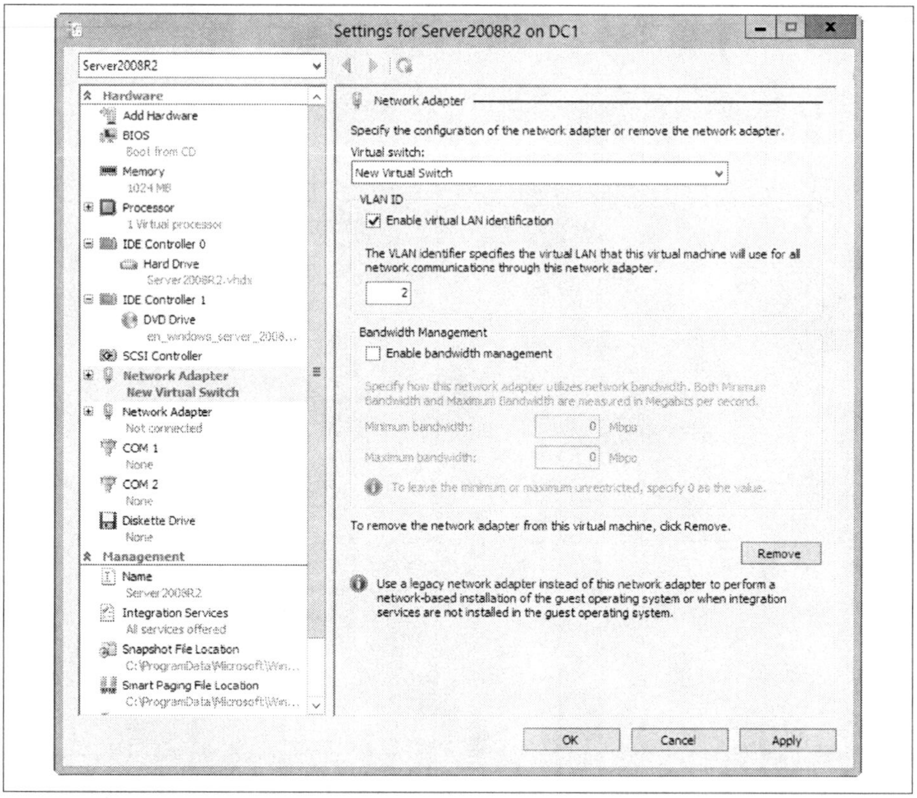

Figure 8-29. Configuring a VLAN ID

You can set a VLAN ID using this PowerShell cmdlet:

```
Set-VMNetworkAdapterVlan –VMName <VM name> -Access –Vlan
<VLAN ID number>
```

2. Next, you need to assign each VM a secondary VLAN ID that correlates with a PVLAN mode. There are three modes in which PVLANs can be set:

Promiscuous

VMs can communicate with any other VM, including an isolated one.

Community

>VMs can communicate with other community ports and their promiscuous ports.

Isolated

>VMs are isolated; traffic is forwarded only to promiscuous ports.

Let's say you want VM1 and VM2 to interact with each other because Sales and Marketing access and transfer data among the apps running on them. We set those VMs to Community mode, and give them a secondary VLAN ID of 5. We do so using the following PowerShell line (in the example, the name of the VM is "VM1") against both VM1 and VM2:

```
Set- VMNetworkAdapterVlan -VMName VM1 -Community -PrimaryVlanID 2
-SecondaryVlanId5
```

Since no other VMs should communicate with VM4, we'll configure it in Isolated mode and place it in its own PVLAN set to ID 4:

```
Set- VMNetworkAdapterVlan -VMName VM4 -Isolated -PrimaryVlanID 2
-SecondaryVlanId4
```

VM3 needs to communicate with all VMs, including VM4, which is isolated, so we'll configure it in Promiscuous mode and give it both PVLAN IDS of 4 and 5:

```
Set- VMNetworkAdapterVlan -VMName VM3 -Promiscuous -PrimaryVlanID 2
-SecondaryVlanIdList 4-5
```

Be aware that the virtual network switch delivers other features, such as private access control lists (PACLs) and security defenses that include protection against ARP (address resolution protocol) spoofing, rerouting of traffic from rogue DHCP servers, port mirroring, and a trunk mode that can consolidate traffic from multiple VLANs.

Summary

With new networking features, Windows Server 2012 gives organizations the tools they need for cloud computing deployments. The foundation of cloud computing is virtualization. Many of these new features lend themselves to virtual networking.

One of the most significant new features is IPAM, which helps IT corral IP address management into a centralized console. NIC teaming is a long-awaited feature that lets system administrators pair multiple NICs to provide connectivity failover and bandwidth aggregation.

New Quality of Service (QoS) capabilities allow for traffic shaping and giving bandwidth priority to the most critical applications an organization runs.

Finally, the Hyper-V extensible network switch allows third parties to write extensions to bring even more network management to the Hyper-V infrastructure. Native properties in this virtual switch allow for the same type of configurations in any physical switch. VMs can be placed into PVLANs to isolate VMs and control communications to them. Inherent security mechanisms in the virtual switch also guard against various threats.

CHAPTER 9

Remote Access

One of the most common deployments in Windows Server infrastructures is remote access. Employees need a way to access the corporate network when they are away from the office. Remote access is implemented in Windows environments with two features: Routing and Remote Access (RRAS) and DirectAccess.

RRAS has been around since Windows 2000, built from RAS (Remote Access Service), which allowed remote access over modem lines in Windows NT 4.0. RRAS not only provides VPN (virtual private networking) and dial-up connectivity in Windows servers, but it also functions as a software-based router offering LAN, WAN, or over-the-Internet routing services.

DirectAccess was introduced in Windows Server 2008 R2 and provides a relatively easy way to connect Windows 7 domain-joined clients to a corporate network remotely and lets IT manage those client computers without the hassle of setting up a traditional VPN solution. Microsoft Forefront Unified Access Gateway (UAG)—Microsoft's proprietary VPN and reverse proxy gateway solution, launched in 2010—provides even more manageability and easier deployment of remote access. With DirectAccess, clients are seamlessly connected to the company network once connected to the Internet, even before authenticating. DirectAccess gives VPN to Windows 7 and Windows 8 clients. RRAS provides VPN to legacy clients.

Unified Remote Access

Server 2012 takes remote access a step further with Unified Remote Access. In Server 2012, RRAS and DirectAccess are combined into one Remote Access server role. There are myriad improvements in both DirectAccess and RRAS in Server 2012. Some of the most significant are:

- Coexistence of both DirectAccess and RRAS on the same server.

  Because of security conflicts between RRAS and DirectAccess, having both on the same box caused problems with DirectAccess connections. This mostly had to do with security conflicts between the two. DirectAccess uses IPv6 to establish client connections. This didn't mean that the feature could not be deployed in IPv4 networks, since DirectAccess uses IPV4-to-IPv6 transition technology. However, RRAS blocks this type of transitioned network traffic, causing problems with DirectAccess functionality. DirectAccess also has built-in security mechanisms to protect the internal network against DoS (denial of service) attacks, also causing problems with functionality when RRAS is deployed. Unified Remote Access alleviates the issues that occur when DirectAccess and RRAS are on the same box.

- Easier deployment with a new Setup wizard and fewer prerequisites for deployment.

  One requirement that has been eliminated is having to deploy PKI (public key infrastructure) for certificate authentication. Instead, DirectAccess now uses HTTPS-based Kerberos. You don't really need to know the ins and outs of the HTTPS-based Kerberos proxies, because the new Getting Started wizard configures this authentication method automatically.

- There's no longer any need to deploy UAG to allow access to IPv4-only resources on the corporate network. Built-in IPv6-to-IPv4 protocol translation allows that access.

- Better remote management.

  DirectAccess clients are connected to the corporate network as soon as they have an Internet connection. Therefore, system administrators can remotely manage machines. This remote management includes applying patches and upgrades and enforcing corporate compliance on these remote clients.

- Load balancing.

  Windows Server 2012 introduces built-in support for Windows Network Load Balancing (NLB), delivering high availability and scalability for DirectAccess and RRAS. Load balancing is set up via the new Setup wizard.

- Integration with NAP (Network Access Protection).

  NAP is a deployable platform in which a client meets a company-defined set of requirements before it is allowed access to the corporate network. For example, your company's corporate compliance technology policy may require that a client must have a certain version of antivirus software before it is given full access to the network. With NAP integrated with Windows Server 2012 DirectAccess, NAP can be enforced on remote clients. NAP enforcement is enabled through the Remote Access Setup wizard.

- Unified Remote Access can be installed in Server Core mode and managed with PowerShell v3.
- A new Remote Access Server Management Console provides you with insight into the performance, user activity, and resource consumption of the remote clients.
- New diagnostics capabilities include event logging and packet tracking.
- Windows Server 2012 Unified Remote Access provides in-the-box reporting and accounting on information such as user statistics when used with a RADIUS server or Windows Internal Database (WID).

There are a couple of scenarios where remote connections will still not be able to access IPv4 resources:

- If the resources (folder shares, for example) reside on legacy systems that are not fully IPv6-capable, such as Windows Server 2003 file servers.
- In networks where IPv6 has been disabled.
- IPv4 resources in applications that do not support IPv6.

Other new and improved features include the ability to deploy DirectAccess behind a NAT device and support for multiple domains and sites.

Requirements

Deploying Unified Remote Access with Windows Server 2012 requires a domain-joined Windows Server 2012 server, deploying the Remote Access role, and clients running Windows 7 or Windows 8. At least, this is what Microsoft states as the requirements. However, as of this writing, DirectAccess is fully functional only on Windows 8 Enterprise clients or on a Windows Server 2012 Server acting as a client.

DirectAccess

DirectAccess has its own requirements. A DirectAccess server needs TCP port 443 open on the firewall.

DirectAccess can use a server authentication certificate for TLS (transport layer security) issued by a certificate authority (CA) that is trusted by the DirectAccess clients. CAs issue digital certificates. These certificates are used for security and, in a nutshell, verify that the public key associated with the digital certificate is held by the organization it's been issued to. It's public identity validation.

Commercial CAs charge to issue certificates, but there are public CAs that will issue certificates at no cost. DirectAccess will support certificates issued by a public CA.

If an organization has no certificate, DirectAccess can handle that. Windows Server 2012's DirectAccess server setup process will configure the necessary IP-HTTPS and KDC (key distribution center) proxy certificate automatically as a self-signed certificate.

Deploying DirectAccess

The first step in deploying DirectAccess is to *plan*. Determine which clients and servers will use DirectAccess. By default, when DirectAccess is installed, DirectAccess Group Policy objects are created and applied to mobile devices, which are part of the domain computer's Active Directory group. Typically, DirectAccess clients are mobile devices, but if they will be desktops, you'll need to create a DirectAccess Active Directory group and add them.

As a best practice, install the Remote Access role on a domain-joined member server not running other roles.

To install:

1. From the Server Manager dashboard, click "Add roles and features." Select the Remote Access role to install. Click "Add features" and then Next.

2. The install wizard will prompt for the install of the DirectAccess and VPN (RAS) and the Routing Service role. The DirectAccess install option is selected by default. Click Next three times and then Install.

 Install the Routing Service role to make the Windows Server a router. For example, smaller and test networks will often use a multihomed server with two NICs connecting two subnets for testing.

The Remote Access role installs the following features in addition to DirectAccess and VPN:

- Group Policy Management
- RAS Connection Manager Administration Kit (CMAK)
- Remote Server Administration Tools (RSAT)
- IIS
- Windows Internal Database

After a successful install, the Server Manager dashboard will display Remote Access and IIS in the menu list (see Figure 9-1).

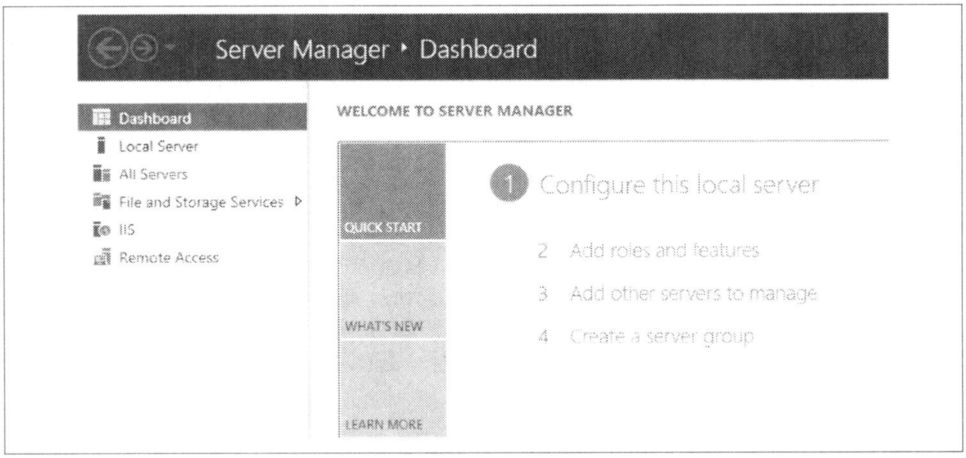

Figure 9-1. Successful install of Remote Access and IIS

Configuring DirectAccess

You can configure DirectAccess using the new Getting Started wizard. The link to open this wizard is displayed after you install DirectAccess in Server Manager as a post-deployment task alert. (See Figure 9-2.)

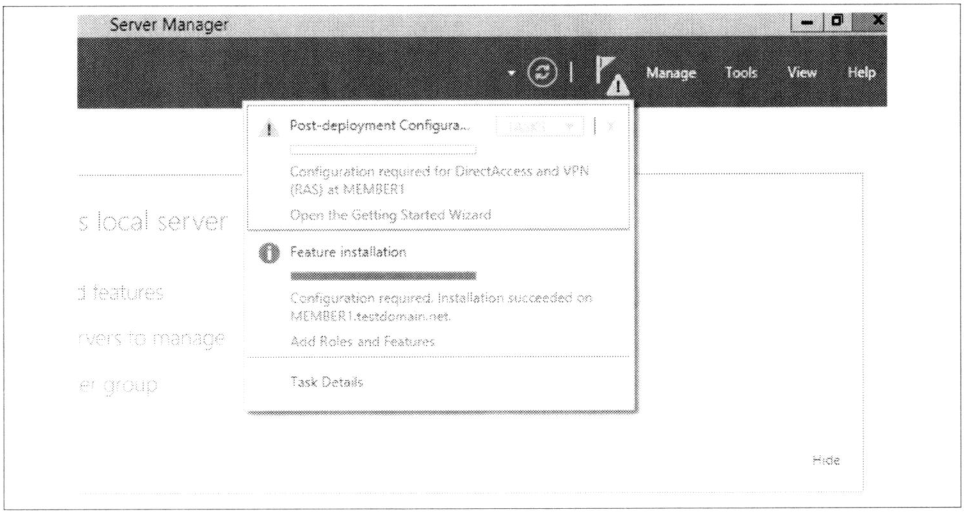

Figure 9-2. The Getting Started wizard

You can also launch the wizard by clicking Tools from Server Manager and opening Remote Access Management.

In the Remote Access Setup wizard are two links. The first is for running the Getting Started wizard. This will install DirectAccess with the default recommended settings. The second is "Run the Remote Access Setup Wizard," which will allow a custom setup. Since Windows Server 2012 is likely to be a new experience for you, you may want to initially configure DirectAccess with the Getting Started wizard and then tweak settings later.

Clicking the link for the Getting Started wizard gives you the option of installing Direct-Access and VPN, DirectAccess only, or VPN only. If an infrastructure has a mix of machines that need to use VPN as well as DirectAccess—for instance, legacy Windows clients that aren't supported by DirectAccess have to use VPN—then deploy Direct-Access and VPN. For all legacy Windows environments, go with VPN only, and for those rare infrastructures that are all Windows 8 and Windows Server 2012, only deploying DirectAccess will do. Here we'll deploy both DirectAccess and VPN, the Microsoft-recommended option.

The next step prompts you to choose how the Remote Access server is deployed. There are three options. If the Remote Access server is a server with two NICs—one connected to the Internet and the other connected to the internal network that sits on the edge of the internal network—select the Edge configuration. For a server with two NICs that sits behind an edge device (such as a firewall), select the "Behind an edge device." Finally, for a Remote Access server connected only to the internal network with a single NIC, select "Behind an edge device (with a single network adapter)." Enter the public-facing hostname or IP address that clients will use to connect to the Remote Access server.

At this point of the installation, you can configure additional properties, including GPO settings, AD groups, adapter settings, and DNS properties. For example, you may want to deploy DirectAccess not for all domain users, which is the default setting, but only for the Sales team with employees always on the road. You'd configure this type of specification in additional properties.

If you don't need to configure any of these settings, click Finish.

A successful install and configuration is indicated by all green checkmarks next to the components in the Operations Status screen in the Remote Access Management Console (which is launched from Server Manager). See Figure 9-3.

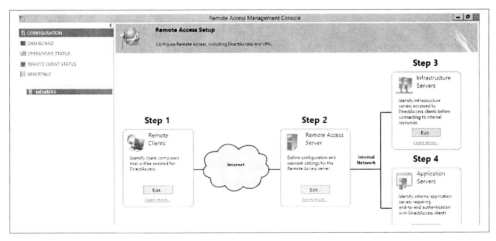

Figure 9-3. DirectAccess post-install view in the Remote Access Management Console

If a question mark or error is displayed next to any of the listed components, you can review and edit the DirectAccess configuration by clicking Configuration in the Remote Access Management Console.

The console opens up to a handy graphic outlining the steps needed to get remote access set up. (See Figure 9-4.)

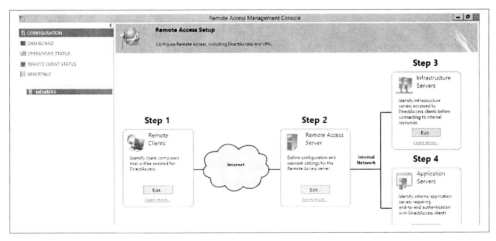

Figure 9-4. Configure Remote Access steps

Next you'll connect mobile clients who will be using DirectAccess to the corporate network, and join any desktops using DirectAccess to a DirectAccess group that you, as the administrator, have created in AD.

To test clients for DirectAccess preparedness, you can execute a few client-side cmdlets:

- `Get-DNSClientNrptPolicy` displays the Name Resolution Policy Table (NRPT) for DirectAccess. This is a good way to confirm that the Getting Started wizard created the proper DNS entries for DirectAccess and for creating the Network Location Server.

- `Get-NCSIPolicyConfiguration` displays the connectivity settings for DirectAccess clients, including the domain location determination URL (displayed as Domain-LocationDeterminationURL) that clients use to connect when they are outside the corporate network. When you're configuring DirectAccess, the URL will follow the convention *https://DirectAccess-NLS.domainname*.

- To test client connections, run the cmdlet `Get-DAConnectionStatus` from clients. This cmdlet will show if the clients are connected locally or remotely. With Direct-Access, clients should be able to reach the corporate network's resources, no matter how they are connected.

You can configure DirectAccess manually instead of using the Getting Started wizard. You may find the wizard easier to get DirectAccess deployed, but you can use the manual steps to backtrack through the wizard's settings to perform any troubleshooting with the wizard's install.

Manual configuration

Manual configuration is done through the Configuration option in the Remote Access Management console and involves four primary steps:

1. Select a deployment scenario.

    The Remote Access Manager gives two options for deploying DirectAccess. The first option is to perform a full client and remote management deployment. This is the scenario most organizations are likely to go with, because not only does it deploy DirectAccess to clients and let those clients connect to the corporate network, but it also allows you to remotely manage clients connected to the Internet. The second option allows you only to remotely manage clients connected to the Internet. To demonstrate the full capabilities of DirectAccess, let's install DirectAccess for client access and remote management, the first option I've just mentioned. (See Figure 9-5.)

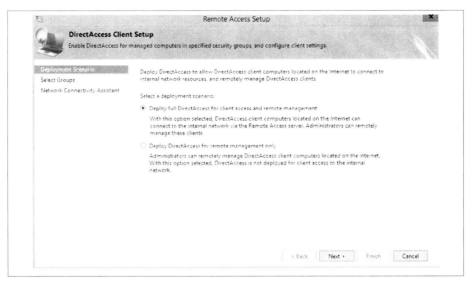

Figure 9-5. Selecting the DirectAccess deployment scenario

Then, select the computer groups to which DirectAccess will be applied. This is where you can select the DirectAccess group for desktop computers in addition to the default Domain Computers group. If desktops are going to use DirectAccess, be sure to clear the checkbox next to "Enable DirectAccess for mobile computers only."

You can also select the option to use force tunneling in this screen (see Figure 9-6). Use this option to force clients to connect from the Internet to the corporate network through a web proxy server.

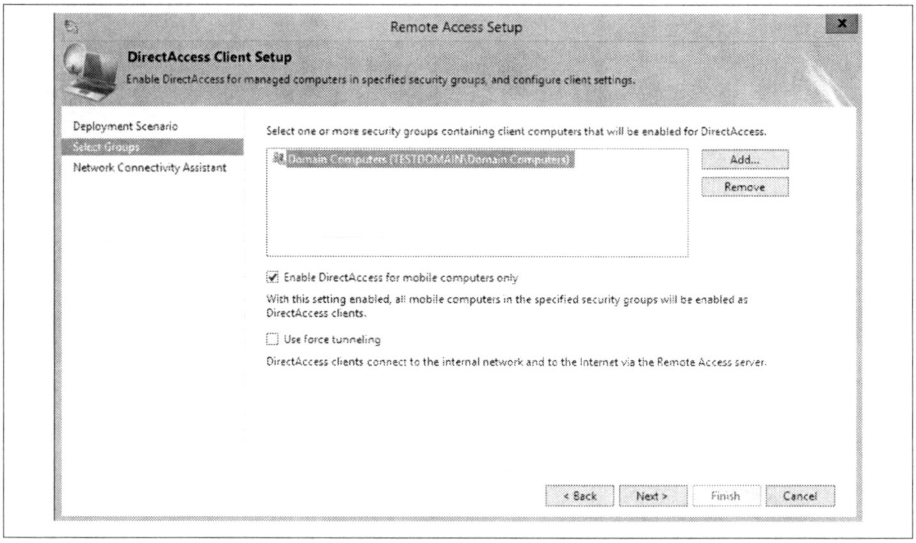

Figure 9-6. Configuring DirectAccess group settings

The next screen displays the resource URL used by clients to connect to the internal network. These clients will run the Network Connectivity Assistant (NCA), which provides you with information about client connectivity, diagnostics, and support. Additional configuration options on this screen include defining an email address for clients to send helpdesk requests, setting the DirectAccess connection name, and allowing clients to use local name resolution for connecting.

2. Configure the Remote Access server.

We completed this step earlier when deploying DirectAccess. Be aware, though, that you can deploy remote access without configuring DirectAccess and return to this step at a later time to configure DirectAccess.

3. Identify any servers DirectAccess clients should access before connecting to resources on the corporate network.

For example, administrators can opt to have DirectAccess clients connect to a network location server. This server is used by clients to confirm if they are connected to the corporate network, and can help make managing connection issues easier, especially for a larger number of clients. Here is where you can also define the DNS servers that connected DirectAccess clients should use, as well as any server IT may use to update or manage remote clients.

4. Configure application servers.

This is where you can set end-to-end authentication for DirectAccess clients to connect to specific application servers. This is useful in granting access to servers containing sensitive data that require an added layer of security.

Be aware that although Server 2012 makes the entire process of getting DirectAccess deployed easier than ever (since installation and configuration is essentially automated), proper deployment still requires proper configuration of DNS and IP addressing. So, make sure all servers and DNS are in order before deploying Direct-Access.

BranchCache

Unified Remote Access also provides site-to-site connectivity. Many organizations and businesses have branch offices in different locations. You can configure Windows Server 2012 RRAS and DirectAccess to provide site-to-site VPN. The performance of the connection between sites is largely dependent on the type of WAN connection that exists between branch offices (T1 lines provide a fixed 1.5 Mbps bandwidth, but combining T1s or Ethernet-over-Copper connections give faster speeds).

Yet, even with adequate bandwidth between sites, issues with latency, file syncing, and pokey performance can persist. BranchCache, which debuted with Server 2008 R2, is a feature that attempts to address issues with performance between sites. With Branch-Cache, data at a main site is cached at the remote site, so that users at the remote site are accessing data locally rather than across the WAN.

Windows Server 2012 BranchCache improvements include the ability to deploy multiple hosted cache servers in a site as well as managing BranchCache with PowerShell and Windows Management Instrumentation (WMI).

In addition, deployment is now easier because you no longer need to create a separate Group Policy object for each site; all that's required is a single Group Policy object. Clients that connect to BranchCache servers are automatically configured as cache clients, so client-side configuration is seamless. There are also security improvements with data encryption that does not require added PKI certificates or other encryption technologies.

In addition to Windows Server 2012 and Windows 8 clients, Server 2008 R2 also supports the new features of BranchCache, so you could deploy a Server 2012 BranchCache-hosted server at a main site and partner it with a Server 2008 R2 machine. Windows 7 clients can also connect to Windows Server 2012 BranchCache, as long as they are installed with certificates that support TLS. Server 2008 R2 and Windows 7 clients can't take advantage of the data-hashing and -chunking features in Server 2012's Branch-Cache, which are used to optimize performance of data replication between sites.

Requirements

BranchCache can be used to deliver data to remote clients from web servers, from file servers, or to application servers.

- For BranchCache on web servers, IIS is required and needs to be configured with HTTP or HTTPS.
- File servers with BranchCache require both the File Service role and the Branch-Cache for Network File Services role to be installed.
- Application servers used with BranchCache require BITS (Background Intelligent Transfer Service) to be installed as well as BranchCache. An example of an application server that can be used in a BranchCache scenario is a Windows Update Services Server from which remote sites can get Windows updates.

Integrating Group Policy with BranchCache and using hosted cache automatic discovery requires an Active Directory domain, but a domain is not required for individual machines to use BranchCache. For automatic discovery of hosted cache servers, the client and server must belong to the same AD site.

Deploying BranchCache

Before installing BranchCache, you must figure out how it is best deployed. There are two deployment modes for BranchCache, and if you are familiar with BranchCache in Server 2008 R2 you will be familiar with the deployment options, because the modes are the same: distributed cache mode and hosted cache.

Smaller organizations with a few branch offices can benefit from the distributed cache mode because it requires less hardware. This is because in distributed cache mode, a BranchCache server resides in the main office. Clients in branch offices receive cached data from a content file server in the main office.

The second deployment mode is hosted cache. This is where, in addition to a Branch-Cache server in the main office, another hosted cache server is deployed in the remote office. Client computers receive data from the local hosted cache server. This mode offers more performance benefits for larger organizations and those with lots of data moving across the WAN, but it does require more hardware and software in branch offices.

To deploy BranchCache:

1. From a domain controller, launch Group Policy Management. Drill down to the target domain or OU (organizational unit), right-click, and select "Create a GPO in this domain, and Link it here."

2. Next, name the new Group Policy object (GPO) and click OK. The GPO is now listed under the domain or OU. Right-click the newly created GPO and select Edit. (See Figure 9-7.)

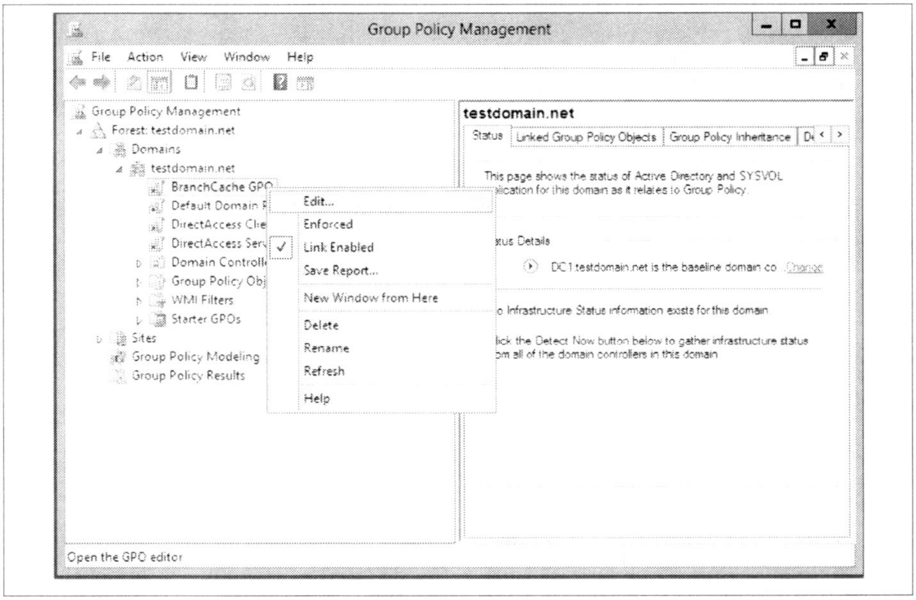

Figure 9-7. Editing the BranchCache GPO

3. Now drill down to Computer Configuration→Policies→Administrative Templates:Policy definitions (ADMX files) retrieved from the local computer→Network→BranchCache (see Figure 9-8).

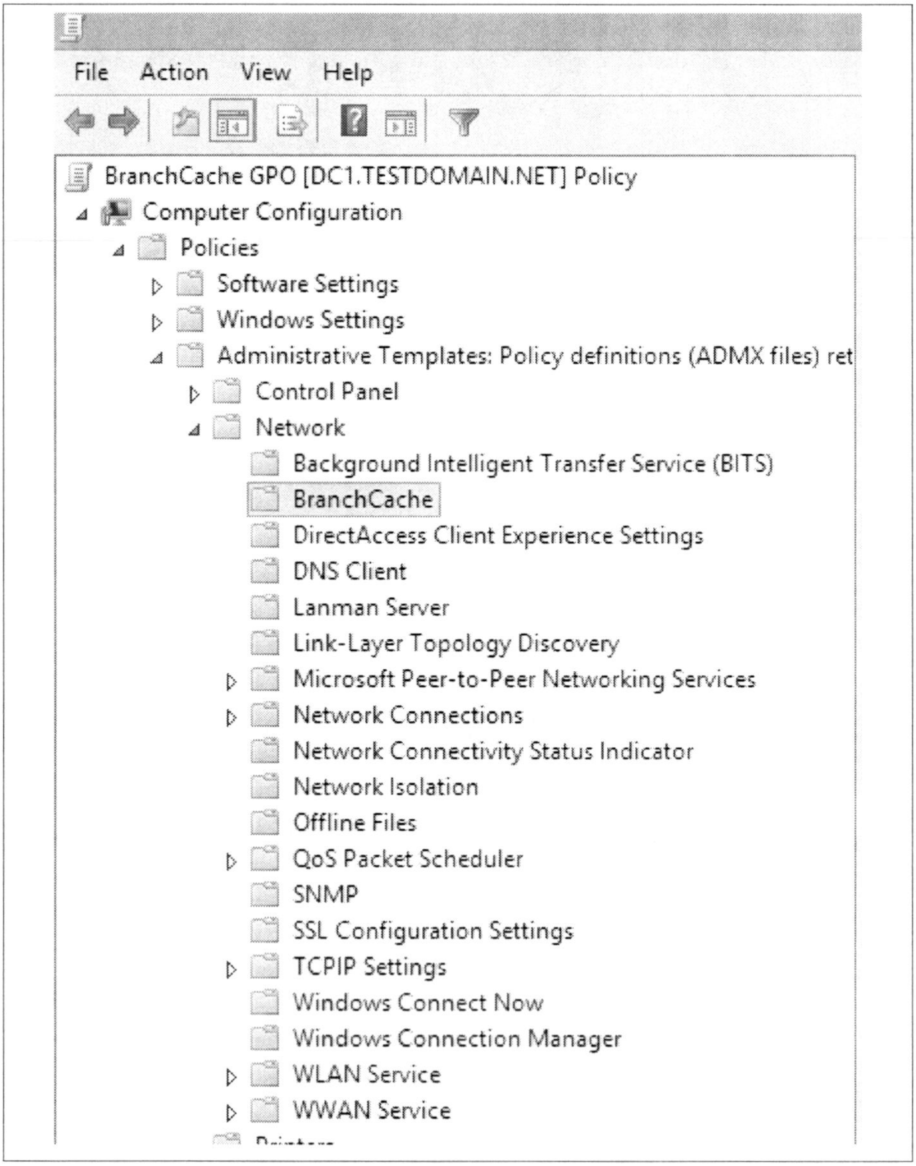

Figure 9-8. Navigating to the BranchCache policy settings

4. Under this GPO path are nine BranchCache policy settings. For initial deployment, enable "Turn on BranchCache" by right-clicking, choosing Enabled, clicking Apply, and then clicking OK. Do the same for "Set BranchCache Distributed Cache mode," and "Enable Automatic Hosted Cache Discovery Service Connection Point."

For BranchCache on file servers, enable "Configure BranchCache for network files" in the GPO settings. For hosted cache deployment modes, select the option "Set BranchCache Hosted Cache mode" instead of "Set BranchCache Distributed Cache Mode."

Configuring the Windows Firewall

Windows Firewall also has to be configured to allow BranchCache traffic. From Control Panel and then System and Security, open Windows Firewall. Click Advanced Settings and double-click to open Inbound Rules.

There are preconfigured rules created for BranchCache that are listed when Inbound Rules are displayed. Look for the predefined "BranchCache Content Retrieval (HTTP-In) Rule." Right-click, and select Properties. Check the box to enable this rule and select "Allow the connection." (See Figure 9-9.)

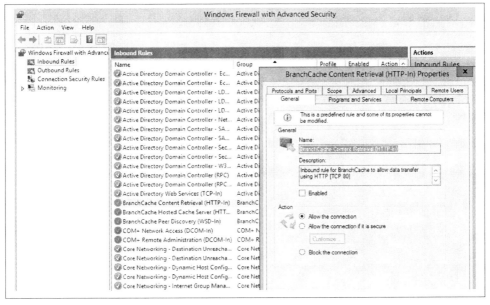

Figure 9-9. Configuring Windows Firewall for BranchCache

Click Apply and then OK. Repeat these steps for the "BranchCache Peer Discovery (WDS-In)" rule.

Deploying the BranchCache Role via Server Manager

You can deploy the BranchCache role, as with other server roles, through Server Manager or PowerShell. To deploy BranchCache through Server Manager as part of a Remote Access deployment:

1. From your Windows Server 2012 machine that will be used as either the Branch-Cache hosted cache server or the content server, click "Add Roles and Features" from Server Manager. Click Next three times to get to the "Select Server roles" window. Choose the Remote Access role and add required features. Click Next. From Select Features, check the box next to BranchCache.

2. Click Next. In the following screen, you must select the DirectAccess and VPN service to install BranchCache; you can also install the routing service. Click Next twice, and the Web Services role is selected for install. Click Next once more and then Install.

Deploying the BranchCache Role with PowerShell

You can also install the BranchCache feature on the machine that will serve as a hosted cache server through PowerShell. I prefer this option, because it allows you to install BranchCache alone, without needing to deploy extra remote access services. This is the way to go if, for example, you want to deploy DirectAccess or VPN on a different box from BranchCache.

To deploy from PowerShell:

1. Launch PowerShell with "Run as Administrator."

2. Execute the cmdlets:

```
Import-Module ServerManager
Add-WindowsFeature -name BranchCache
```

Upon successful execution, you will see the screen shown in Figure 9-10.

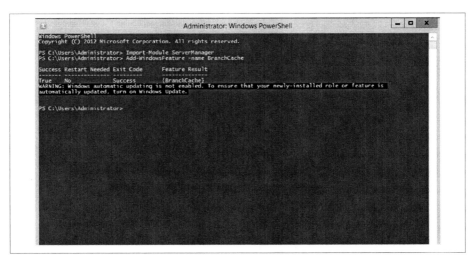

Figure 9-10. Installing BranchCache in PowerShell

 PowerShell will display any warnings or advisements about install at this point, such as the one about turning on Windows Update shown in Figure 9-10.

3. Next, run the command `Import-Module BranchCache`.

4. If setting up a BranchCache server in hosted cache mode and to enable automatic client discovery, execute: `Enable -BCHostedServer -RegisterSCP`.

 If you're installing a BranchCache server on a domain controller and that server will act as a hosted cache, the DC has to be read-only; otherwise, the `Enable-CHostedServer -RegisterSCP` cmdlet will report an error that the DC is writable and cannot be set up as a hosted cache server.

After executing these commands, you can get the status of the newly installed Branch-Cache from PowerShell by running `Get-BCStatus`.

Figure 9-11 shows the results of entering this cmdlet.

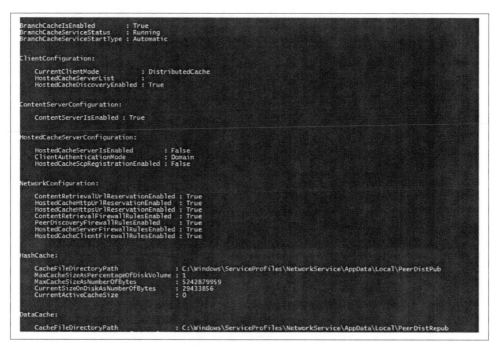

```
BranchCacheIsEnabled         : True
BranchCacheServiceStatus     : Running
BranchCacheServiceStartType  : Automatic

ClientConfiguration:

    CurrentClientMode          : DistributedCache
    HostedCacheServerList      :
    HostedCacheDiscoveryEnabled : True

ContentServerConfiguration:

    ContentServerIsEnabled : True

HostedCacheServerConfiguration:

    HostedCacheServerIsEnabled        : False
    ClientAuthenticationMode          : Domain
    HostedCacheScpRegistrationEnabled : False

NetworkConfiguration:

    ContentRetrievalUrlReservationEnabled   : True
    HostedCacheHttpUrlReservationEnabled    : True
    HostedCacheHttpsUrlReservationEnabled   : True
    ContentRetrievalFirewallRulesEnabled    : True
    PeerDiscoveryFirewallRulesEnabled       : True
    HostedCacheServerFirewallRulesEnabled   : True
    HostedCacheClientFirewallRulesEnabled   : True

HashCache:

    CacheFileDirectoryPath                : C:\Windows\ServiceProfiles\NetworkService\AppData\Local\PeerDistPub
    MaxCacheSizeAsPercentageOfDiskVolume  : 1
    MaxCacheSizeAsNumberOfBytes           : 5242879959
    CurrentSizeOnDiskAsNumberOfBytes      : 29433856
    CurrentActiveCacheSize                : 0

DataCache:

    CacheFileDirectoryPath                : C:\Windows\ServiceProfiles\NetworkService\AppData\Local\PeerDistRepub
```

Figure 9-11. Getting the BranchCache status

Prepping and Testing Client Connectivity

Once you set up BranchCache in either distributed or hosted cache mode, connected network clients should receive the appropriate Group Policy updates needed for connecting. Since Group Policy updates in periodic intervals, you can force a Group Policy update on the client side and check the client's BranchCache status by using the Get-BCStatus cmdlet in the client's PowerShell. In Figure 9-11, the client is configured to connect to a BranchCache server configured in distributed cache mode.

Virtual Desktop Infrastructure

Remote Desktop Services (RDS), the evolution of Terminal Services, was introduced in Server 2008 R2 and is the heart of VDI (Virtual Desktop Infrastructure). Whereas DirectAccess and RRAS provide remote client connectivity on the server side, VDI is about the desktop and user experience on the client side.

Microsoft has made significant improvements with VDI because it really had no choice. With the consumerization of IT, employees, consultants, and other end users of a network are using personal devices to perform work-related tasks. As these devices are increasingly touch-enabled, Windows VDI technologies have been updated to support touch devices and other gadgets that are being introduced into Windows networks. VDI and Remote Desktop are no longer solely about the PC or laptop, but about the tablet and smartphone, too.

VDI is desktop virtualization. Although both technologies achieve the same ends—thinly provisioning desktops—Remote Desktop and VDI are different. Remote Desktop is the later iteration of Terminal Services and uses hosted sessions to remotely connect users to a shared desktop experience. VDI is a customizable virtualized desktop experience and, just like building a virtual machine in Hyper-V, you can create custom VDI images that are tailored to an end user's particular needs.

What Server 2012 improvements strive to accomplish is to enable you to deliver a rich and consistent virtual desktop user experience to any end-user device, be it a hardware-thin client machine or a Windows 8 tablet. This user experience is created through a number of VDI technologies: Hyper-V and Remote Desktop Services are the building blocks of VDI, but there are other components to use with Server 2012 to implement solid VDI for your end users. These include:

UE-V

> User Experience Virtualization was introduced with the beta of Windows Server 2012. UE-V allows users to keep their desktop experience across any device they use. Available as a downloadable public beta (*https://connect.microsoft.com/MDOP TAP/UEV%20Beta*), UE-V will be included with Microsoft Desktop Optimization Pack (MDOP). Combined with Folder Redirection, it allows users to keep all of their custom desktop and application settings across their devices.

App-V 5.0

> Providing application virtualization, App-V 5.0 allows applications to be streamed, stored, and centrally managed.

Microsoft RemoteApp

> RemoteApp is used to publish applications via Remote Desktop or Hyper-V.

System Center

> Although a full discussion is beyond the scope of this book, you should be aware that you can perform additional management over VDI using System Center 2012's Virtual Machine Manager (VMM). Management tasks you can do with VMM include monitoring the health and performance of the VDI environment and generating reports. System Center also provides additional management options in Server 2012, such as for Hyper-V.

Quick deploy is a new way of installing VDI. IT can administer sessions and VMs from a single console. Intelligent patching and scanning means that clients don't get patched all at once, which can negatively impact performance. With Server 2012, VDI has high scalability and improved performance with FairShare—a sort of VDI load-balancing feature that ensures bandwidth is distributed equally among VMs and users.

One of the most important considerations before deploying VDI is to determine how it's going to be deployed. There are three deployment scenarios:

Session

> With a session deployment, you are installing a virtual server operating system and sharing that OS across multiple users. The benefit of a session deployment is you have one standard VDI experience for end users. Session deployment is useful when you want to provision thin desktops to users who need limited desktop customization. Session VDI is also less complex to manage, because you have to worry about only the one OS. The downside is that since you are deploying a server OS, there may be problems with some application compatibility—apps designed to run on client machines may not be able to be installed on a server OS.

Pooled VMs

> With pooled virtual machines, you are assigning one virtual machine to many users. This is a useful deployment option if, for instance, you have groups of users within an organization who require the same desktop experience. Perhaps you would roll out one virtualized desktop to the employees who work in Customer Service, and a different desktop to the Sales team. The benefit of pooled VMs is fewer virtual images to manage, which saves storage space. Because the VM streamed to users is a client OS, there is little potential for issues with compatibility with applications you need to install on the client OS. There are also more customization options for pooled VMs; back to our example, the streamed desktop for the Customer Service group may be configured differently than that for the Sales team.

> The cons with a pooled deployment are that you do have more images to manage than with a session deployment, and because many users can access one virtual desktop, a user may not always have a consistent desktop.

Personal VMs

> A personal deployment provides a highly customizable image for users: it's a one desktop image to one user deployment scenario. A user's customizations stream to any device she uses. The downside is that the more personal VMs you have in an organization, the more storage you need.

Remote Desktop Services (RDS)

The Windows 8 user interface experience is not limited to just the GUI of Server 2012, but it's also incorporated into the interface of the new Remote Desktop client. Like the interface in Windows 8, the interface in Remote Desktop is touch-enabled. Touch capability is offered, of course, to meet the increasing demand from employees who want to use their personal mobile devices for work.

As with most features within Windows Server, Remote Desktop has several improvements. It's easier to enable single sign-on. If users are accessing RemoteApp programs that have been published through Remote Desktop Web Access (RD Web Access), single sign-on is automatically enabled in Windows Server 2012 and Windows 8 virtual machine VDI, and if all clients support Remote Desktop Protocol (RDP) version 8.

Single sign-on can also be enabled for users subscribed to a RemoteApp and Desktop Connections feed subscription. Finally, adding the Remote Desktop Gateway (RD Gateway) role service supports web single sign-on by default.

Remote Desktop also now has a Favorites list that keeps track of all RDP connections. Tabbed viewing in a client instance provides multisession support.

RemoteFX is used to deliver graphics virtualization and multimedia support such as video streaming to remote desktops. In Server 2012, RemoteFX can provide 3D graphics with the use of a DirectX 11 graphics card installed on a Hyper-V host. RemoteFX also supports USB redirection and multitouch in Remote Desktop sessions.

Remote Desktop Services Install

In this example, we'll deploy Remote Desktop services with a session deployment scenario. The example also demonstrates how to publish a remote app.

For the deployment, there are four servers that are set up: a domain controller, two Remote Desktop Session Host servers, and a server configured as a Remote Desktop Connection Broker, a Remote Desktop Management server, and a Remote Desktop Web Access server. The DC is installed with DNS and DHCP, and also configured as an Enterprise Root Certificate Authority.

The Remote Desktop Session Host role is used for hosting Windows apps or Windows desktops for Remote Desktop clients. Clients connect to the RD Session Host and can perform the same functions remotely as they would locally, such as running apps, saving files, and accessing server resources.

To configure your Remote Desktop Session Host:

1. Click "Add Roles and Features" from Server Manager. From Selection Type, choose "Role-based or feature-based installation." Click Next two times to get to "Select Server roles." Check the box next to Remote Desktop Services and click Next in the following three screens.

2. From the "Select role services" window, select Remote Desktop Session Host, as shown in Figure 9-12.

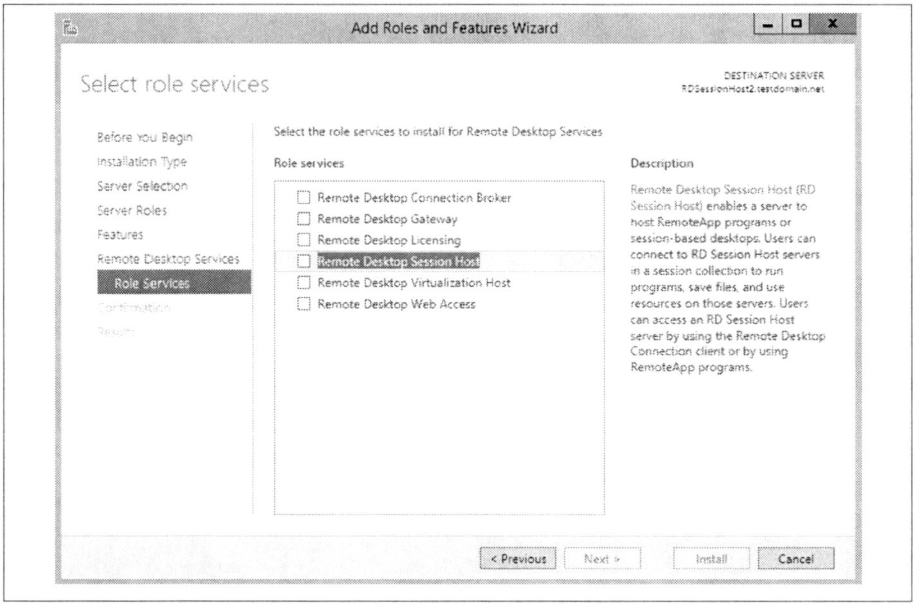

Figure 9-12. Installing the Remote Desktop Session Host role

3. Click to add the other features, and click Next and then Install.

To configure a server with the RD Connection Broker and the RD Web Access server roles, follow the same steps just outlined and select these roles from the "Select Server roles" window.

To install the RD Management server and an RD Services scenario install, from the server the Connection Broker is installed on:

1. In Server Manager, click "Add Roles and Features," click Next, and then select Remote Desktop Services Installation. Click Next.

   In the Select Deployment Type window, the Connection Broker is already detected. (See Figure 9-13.)

Connection Broker does not have to reside on the same server as RD Management and RD Services. The Connection Broker server just has to be installed on a server joined to the domain.

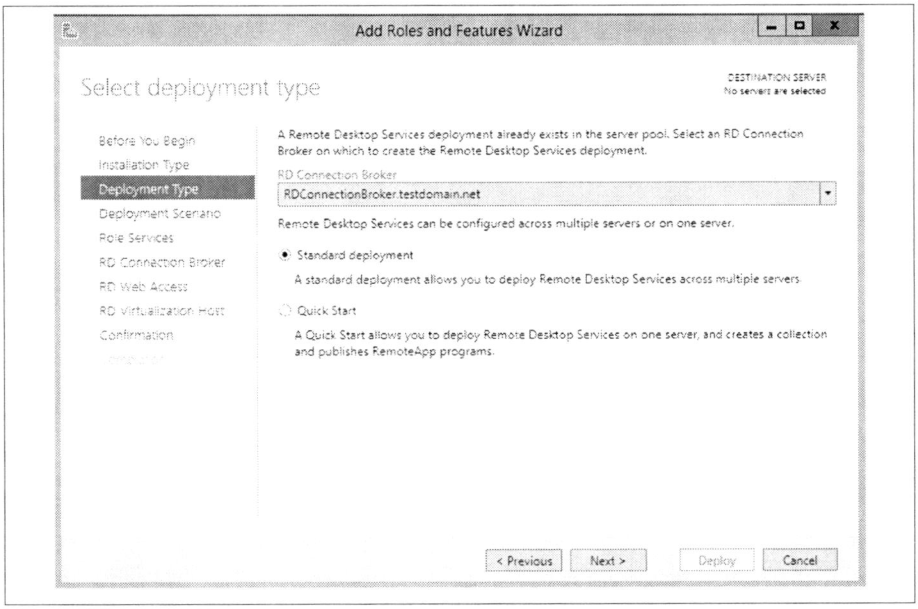

Figure 9-13. Selecting the deployment type

 Notice in Figure 9-13 the choice between a Standard deployment or the new Quick Start option. Quick Start will install all of the Remote Desktop services on one server, and is best used when you're doing a test deployment of RDS.

2. Select "Standard deployment" for most production environments. Click Next. In "Select deployment scenario," the options are to perform a virtual machine–based deployment or session-based desktop deployment. For this example, let's go with a session-based deployment. (See Figure 9-14.)

3. Because you've already installed the Connection Broker role, the install process detects that the Connection Broker server already exists, and all you have to do is click Next. (See Figure 9-15.)

4. Add the RD Web Access role service on the RD Connection Broker server. (See Figure 9-16.)

5. Click Next. In the "Specify RD Session role," add the RD Session Host servers. Click Next and finish the install.

Figure 9-14. Opting for session-based deployment

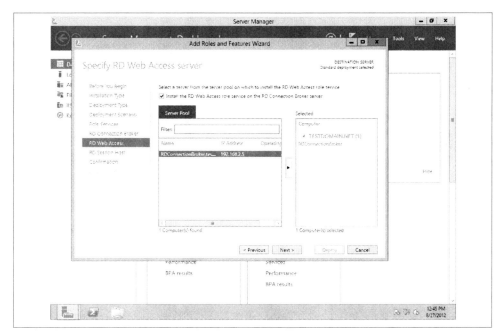

Figure 9-15. Adding the RD Connection Broker

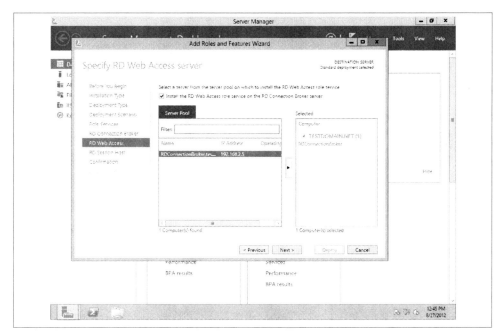

Figure 9-16. Adding the RD Web Server role

Remote Desktop Services Management

After deployment, you can view the Remote Desktop Services Management console from Server Manager on the machine that has the RD Connection Broker role installed. (See Figure 9-17.)

Figure 9-17. Remote Desktop Services Management console

From this interface, you can create a *session collection*—a grouping of apps that can be pushed out to users. AD users or groups who need access to those apps are given access to the collection. For a collection to be created, the RDS environment must include one RD Session Host server that is not added to a collection.

To create a session collection:

1. From the Remote Desktop Services view in Server Manager, click "Create session collection." (See Figure 9-18.)

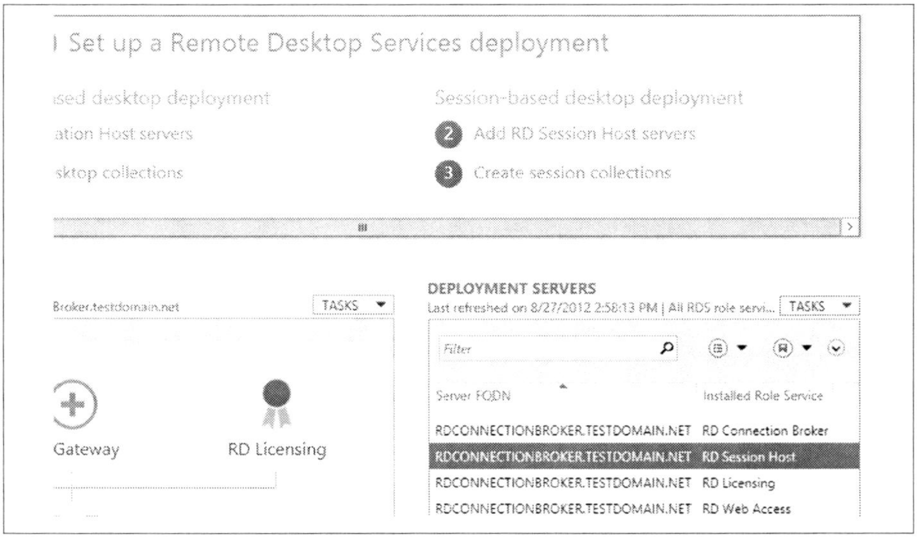

Figure 9-18. Creating a session collection

2. The Create Collection wizard launches. Give the collection a name; you can optionally add a description here as well. (See Figure 9-19.)

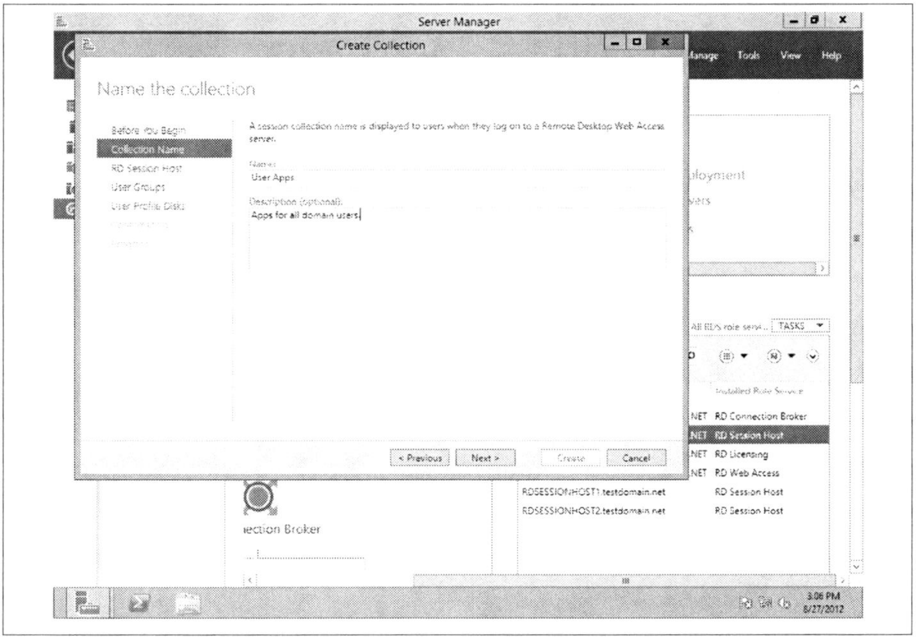

Figure 9-19. Naming the collection

3. Next, select the RD Host Session server to add to the collection. Click Next and then add the AD user or group to be given access to the collection (the default is Domain Users).

4. Click Next. You can then opt to enable user profile disks. Enabling will store user profile settings and data in a central location for the collection.

5. Click Next and then Create. Once created, the new session collection is listed under Collections on the left-side menu in the Remote Desktop Services view.

Associating Apps to a Collection and Publishing Remote Apps

Once you've created a collection, you can add and publish to that collection apps that users need to access remotely. To do so:

1. From Server Manager on the machine running the RD Connection Broker, click Remote Desktop Services, then Collections, and then click on the created collection. In Figure 9-20, the newly created User Apps collection is selected.

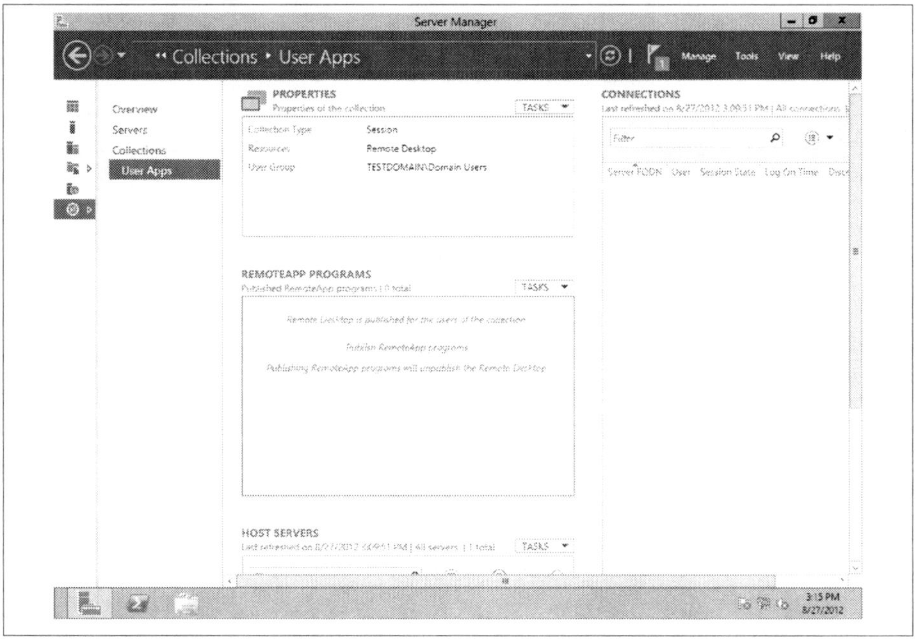

Figure 9-20. A new session collection

2. To select programs to publish, click the link "Publish RemoteApp programs" under the RemoteApp Programs window. You can also add apps that are not listed by clicking the Add button.

3. Select the apps to publish to the collection. (See Figure 9-21.)

Figure 9-21. Selecting RemoteApp programs

4. Click Next. Confirm that the proper apps were selected, and click Publish.

Adding Published Apps to the RD Web Folder

You can add apps as part of the RD Web Access server so that clients can access them via a browser. The app has to be added to the RD Web folder.

To add an app, from Server Manager on the machine running the RD Connection Broker:

1. Click Remote Desktop Services, then Collections, and then click the collection.

2. In the RemoteApp Programs window, right-click the app and select Edit Properties.

3. In the Properties window, the program name, the program's alias, and the RemoteApp program location are displayed. Leave the default option "Show the RemoteApp program in RD Web Access" and give a name to the folder in which the app will reside on the RD Web Access server. In this example, we'll name the folder User Apps. (See Figure 9-22.)

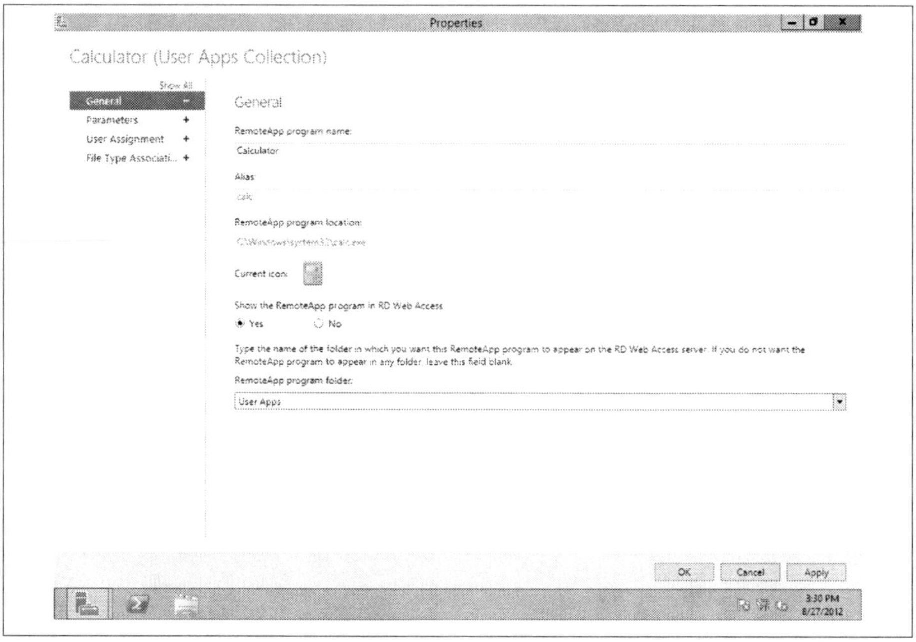

Figure 9-22. Adding an app to the RD Web folder

4. Click Apply and then OK.

Connecting Clients to Remote Apps

After RDS is installed and apps are published to the RD Web Access server, clients can access work resources by entering the URL in the following format: *https://<RD Connection Broker server name>.<domain name>/RDWeb*. (See Figure 9-23.)

Figure 9-23. Client interface for accessing published apps

Figure 9-24 shows the published folder, with apps displayed and ready for the user to access remotely.

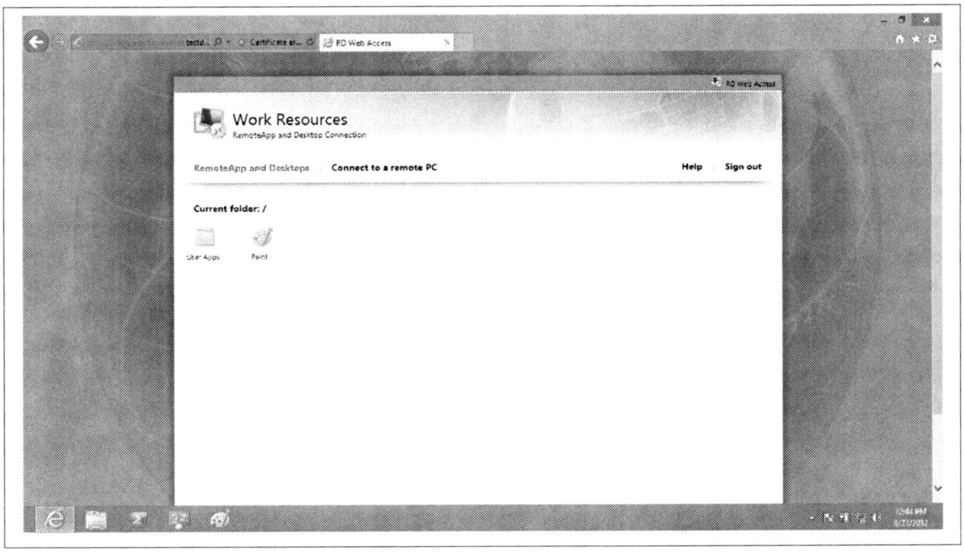

Figure 9-24. Client access to remote apps

Installing RemoteFX

To help you eke out the best graphics and multimedia performance on streamed remote desktops, RemoteFX requires a DirectX 11 graphics card, such as AMD's FirePro series, installed on the RemoteFX server.

RemoteFX clients require a SLAT (second-level address translation)–capable processor. This technology is referred to as EPT (extended page tables) on AMD servers and NPT (nested page tables) on Intel machines.

You install RemoteFX by deploying the Remote Desktop Virtualization role. Here, the role is installed on the same box that serves as the RD Connection Broker:

1. From Server Manager, click "Add roles and features." Under Select Installation Type, choose Remote Desktop Services Installation. Click Next.

2. Select "Standard deployment," click Next, and from "Select deployment scenario," click the radio button for "Virtual machine–based desktop deployment." Click Next until you see the "Specify RD Virtualization Host server" option. Select the server on which to install the RD Virtualization host, and click Next. Click Deploy.

3. Remote FX also has to be enabled in Hyper-V. From Hyper-V settings, select the physical GPU to use for Remote FX and click the checkbox next to "Use this GPU with RemoteFX."

Summary

Server 2012 delivers the ability to connect clients both outside and inside the corporate network to resources on the network through Unified Remote Access. For external connectivity and for connecting remote sites to main offices, technologies such as DirectAccess, RRAS, VPN, and BranchCache fall under the Unified Remote Access umbrella.

To provision virtual desktops and remote desktop sessions and stream apps remotely, Remote Desktop Services incorporates a number of new features and capabilities that provide users with arguably the richest remote desktop experience ever with Windows server, due largely in part to the revamped RemoteFX, the ability to easily publish web apps, and more centralized and easier deployment of a Remote Desktop VDI environment.

CHAPTER 10

Troubleshooting, Securing, and Monitoring

Having tested Windows Server 2012 for quite some time now, I have had two things become abundantly clear to me: this is Microsoft's most evolved server product, and it is still an ongoing project that will most likely not be fully mature until the first Service Pack. On a simple note, I had no driver issues, and not just when installing a simple USB external drive, but even when adding a high-end graphics card with only Windows 7 drivers available.

Windows Server 2012 also feels like the most streamlined Windows Server ever. Installation is quick and peppy, whether you are doing a Core or full GUI install. Performance moving between screens and apps is, to borrow a favorite phrase of Microsoft's, "fast and fluid."

However, there are still some issues that need to be addressed. I find some services slow to load on reboot, with some of them remaining in a suspended state until forced to start. Inexplicable errors crop up periodically in the event viewer, such as one pesky Netlogon error I kept receiving that pointed to a problem in DNS. However, there was no discernible problem with the DNS Server, and that same error would get flushed out with another reboot.

Of course, other issues will surface as more users, system administrators, and organizations deploy Server 2012. Many of these issues will surround specific hardware of certain types or unique configurations that a particular infrastructure may have. We see this all the time with a new operating system; on its initial release to the public, a new OS is akin to fresh-baked bread that's come out of the oven just a bit undercooked. It would be a Herculean task for the developers, engineers, and program managers to foresee every possible deployment scenario with Windows Server 2012.

That impossible level of prognostication on Microsoft's part is why it's critical that Server 2012 is outfitted with diagnostic tools to help you troubleshoot and monitor the server. And indeed, Server 2012 has many management and diagnostics features to tell you when things aren't working the way they should, and features that can warn you about potential problems.

The most central tool for managing and troubleshooting Server 2012 is Server Manager. For me, the revamped Server Manager may be one of the—if not *the*—greatest user interfaces to come out of Redmond. This is rather ironic, because with Server 2012 Microsoft is pushing you to go with a Core install and to use PowerShell for most of the same management tasks that can be performed through Server Manager. At the risk of incurring the wrath of PowerShell aficionados, I still predict that many administrators, particularly those who wear many different IT hats in smaller organizations with not enough IT staff but many IT responsibilities, will largely opt for the Server Manager GUI.

Server Manager

Besides the obvious tile-based UI update that's in line with the new Windows 8 interface, it's hard to discern what's functionally different in the new Server Manager at first glance. As with Server Manager in Windows 2008 R2, you can still perform tasks such as adding roles, running the Best Practices Analyzer, and checking out Event Viewer logs. Server Manager, introduced in Server 2008, delivered unified server management—that is, managing multiple servers and configuration options from one console.

However, there are new capabilities that make the revamped Server Manager a more comprehensive management tool than its counterpart in Server 2008 R2. For starters, the process to add a server is a bit different in the new Server Manager.

Adding a Server

In Server 2008 R2, to add another server to remotely manage another server, you right-click the server name and then click "Connect to another server" (see Figure 10-1).

In Server 2012's Server Manager, however, you perform the server connection process right from the dashboard by clicking the "Add roles and features" link in the "Configure this local server" tile in the dashboard, shown in Figure 10-2.

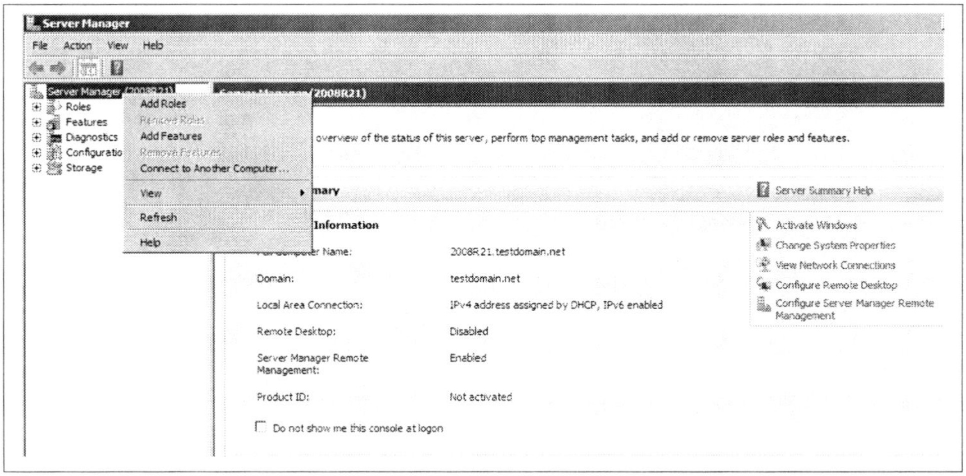

Figure 10-1. Connecting to remote servers in Server 2008 R2

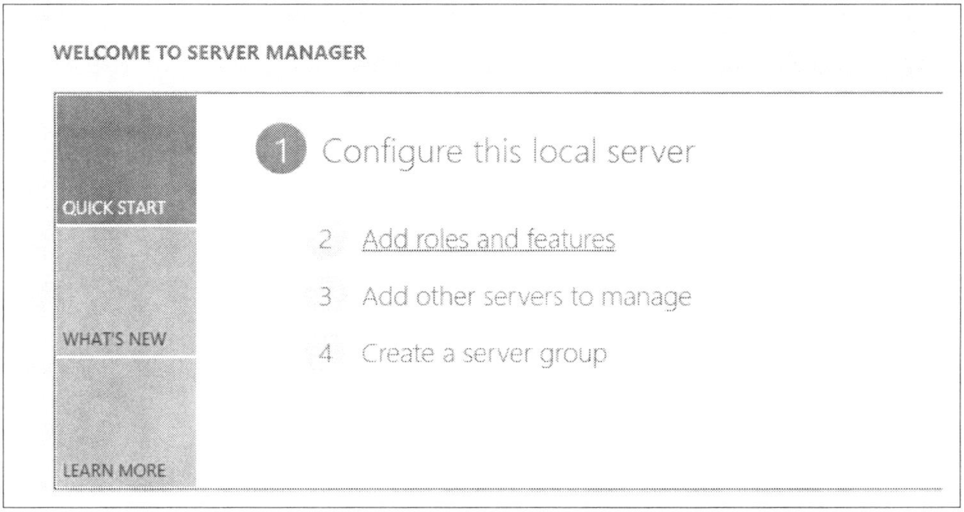

Figure 10-2. Adding other servers to manage in Server 2012

In Figure 10-3, I added a domain-joined Server 2008 R2 virtual machine. A right-click on the VM pulls up a contextual menu that allows you to restart the VM, manage it, connect to it via Remote Desktop, and more.

Figure 10-3. Added Server 2008 R2 VM in Server Manager

Creating Server Groups

Another very handy capability for environments with large numbers of servers to manage is creating server groups. This is a good way to organize servers for expedient management, since tasks are performed on a group rather than on each individual server.

Creating a server group from Server Manager is simple. Click the link for "Create a server group" in the dashboard, add the server to include in the group (see Figure 10-4), and give the group a name. For instance, you can create a group for servers in a main office and another one for servers in a branch office.

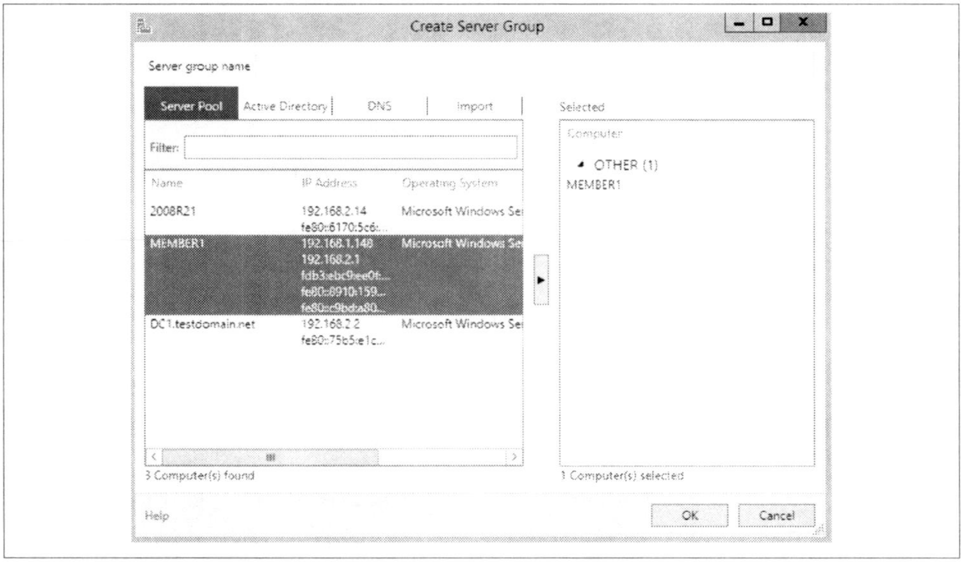

Figure 10-4. Creating a server group

When you've added a group, right-click it to open an extensive menu of management options that you can perform against the servers in that group. See Figure 10-5.

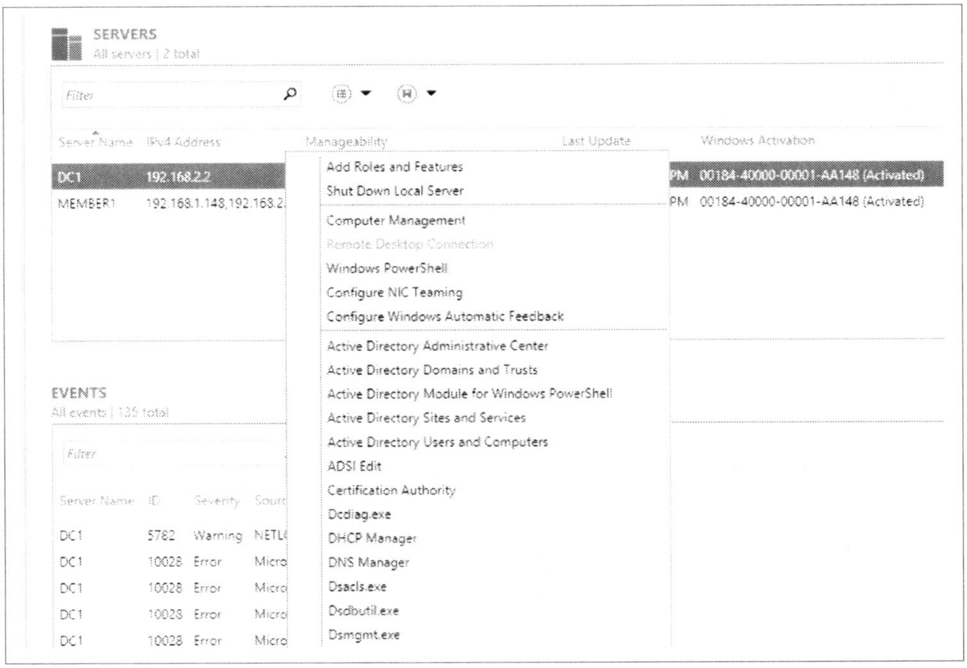

Figure 10-5. Server group management options

Microsoft has claimed that you can manage up to 100 servers using Server Manager. However, once we factor in bandwidth and hardware overhead, as well as roles and services running on those servers that are consuming resources, trying to manage nearly 100 servers in a single Server Manager console may give you more than a few performance headaches. For most organizations that have servers in those amounts, it pays to look into Microsoft's System Center 2012, which is designed specifically to handle the management of large numbers of servers. For a few more recommendations and reminders on using Server Manager appropriately and efficiently, see the sidebar "Keys to Using Server Manager Successfully".

Keys to Using Server Manager Successfully

There are a few important hard-and-fast rules to remember when using Server Manager:

- Adding servers in different domains requires a trust relationship among domains.
- You can manage roles and features on a Core installation of Server 2012 from Server 2012 with a full GUI installation.
- You can add failover clusters to Server Manager, but you will see the name of the cluster rather than individual servers. In addition, you can't install roles and features on clusters.
- You cannot add roles and features to previous Windows Server versions other than Server 2012 remotely through Server Manager.
- You can add roles and features to offline virtual disks that are installed on a Server 2012 server.

The Alert Flag

One of the most useful features in Server Manager is an alert flag that will display upon Server Manager's launch whenever a task is performed or a significant event has occurred on a server. A yellow flag displays whenever a warning event occurs and, as Figure 10-6 shows, a red flag grabs your attention when a critical error has occurred.

Clicking the flag will open up the message details, giving you a better idea of what's going on with the server and allowing for quick attention to the problem or warning.

You can, of course, also use Server Manager to run a client machine by installing the Remote Server Administration Tools (RSAT). You get the full Server Manager experience by installing RSAT on a Windows 8 client. You can also install Server 2012's companion Server Manager RSAT tool on Windows 7, but it gives only limited support—and you can see only if Server 2012 machines are online or offline—so go with a Windows 8 client for full client-based management.

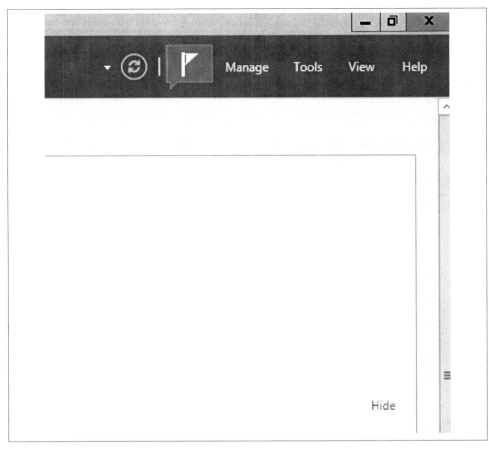

Figure 10-6. Error warning flag in Server Manager

Best Practices Analyzer

Although the Best Practices Analyzer (BPA) is not new in Server 2012, it's more prominently featured in the Server Manager interface and it's a vital tool for system administrators.

You can execute a BPA scan against any server added in Server Manager. (See Figure 10-7.)

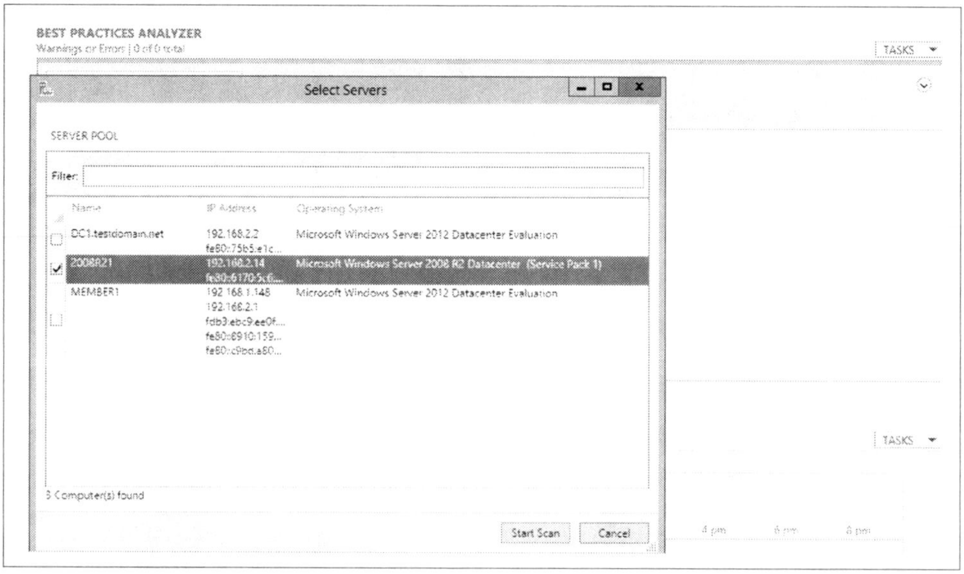

Figure 10-7. Best Practices Analyzer

What is so valuable about BPA is that it is a real-time server troubleshooting tool. It ties in with Event Viewer, but instead of having to independently launch Event Viewer and hunt and filter through logs, you can easily navigate BPA. It is a great example of how Server Manager in Server 2012 allows for robust management through one console.

Windows PowerShell 3.0

We haven't gotten into the ins and outs of PowerShell in this book, because it's simply too vast a subject area and requires a book of its own. While I have mentioned that a large number of administrators in small to midsize organizations will likely use the GUI for many management tasks, it pays to get familiar with PowerShell, particularly because of its new capabilities for management.

PowerShell v3.0 is the version included with Server 2012. A great place for PowerShell newbies to get started is with PowerShell's IntelliSense. This feature will help you learn and create the proper PowerShell. As you type in a PowerShell command, you'll see a list of possible syntaxes to go with the command.

For example, you may want to install a feature through PowerShell, but are unsure of the proper syntax or exact feature name. Features can be installed through PowerShell with the command `Install-`*windowsfeature -name*. If you go into the Windows PowerShell ISE (integrated scripting engine) and start typing **Install-**, you'll see a drop-down menu of all the possible commands that can be used with `Install-` (see Figure 10-8).

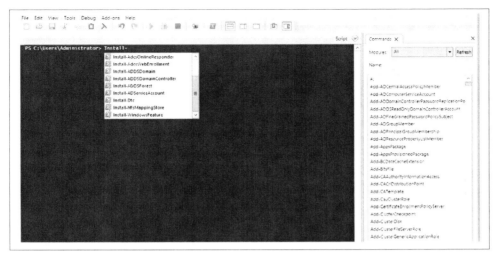

Figure 10-8. PowerShell IntelliSense

Notice in Figure 10-8 that you also have a list of modules to scroll through to find the available cmdlets in PowerShell. PowerShell in Server 2012 provides command-line management, and with IntelliSense, also teaches you how to use correct PowerShell syntax at the same time.

While there are numerous new capabilities in PowerShell, another significant new feature that many of you will want to get acquainted with is Windows PowerShell Web Access. This feature allows you to manage remote machines using PowerShell through a web browser.

To set up this feature, follow these steps:

1. From Server Manager's dashboard, click "Add roles and features." Click Next and select "Role-based or feature-based installation." Click Next. Select the server for installation. Click Next again. In the "Select server roles" window, click Features from the left-side menu. Scroll through the features until you see "Windows PowerShell (Installed)." Expand this feature, and Windows PowerShell Web Access is listed. (See Figure 10-9.)

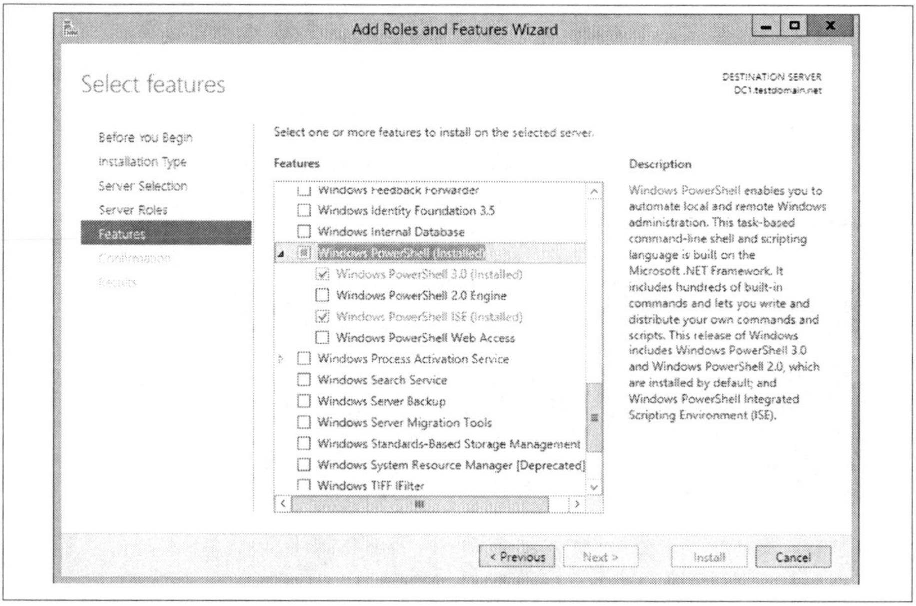

Figure 10-9. Installing the Windows PowerShell Web Access feature

2. Select Windows PowerShell Web Access and click Add Features. Click Next three times and then click Install.

3. To automatically configure Windows PowerShell Web Access to use default settings, run `Install-PswaWebApplication` as an administrator in PowerShell.

   Figure 10-10 shows the results from running the preceding cmdlet.

After installation, you will see IIS listed in the Server Manager dashboard. The next step in setting up PowerShell Web Access is to configure IIS. In this example, you'll set up PowerShell Web Access in an IIS subfolder:

1. From Server Manager, click Tools and then IIS Manager. Now you need to create an application pool, which is done by expanding the IIS server name, right-clicking on Application Pools, and then selecting Add Application Pools.

2. Name the PowerShell Web Access application pool and click OK. (See Figure 10-11.)

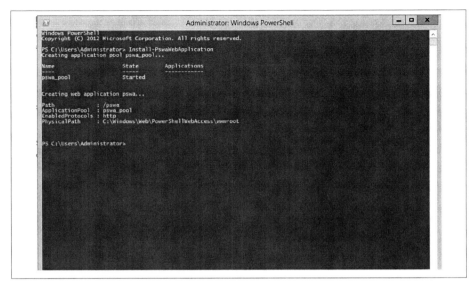

Figure 10-10. Configuring Windows PowerShell Web Access

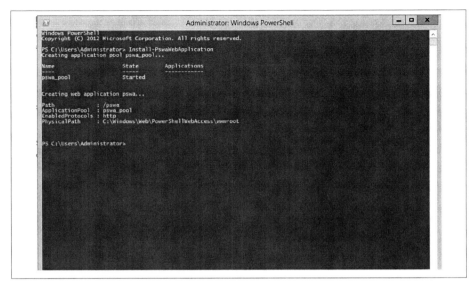

Figure 10-11. Adding an application pool

3. Right-click the *Sites* folder under Default Web Site in the lefthand IIS Manager pane. Select Add Application.

4. Enter an alias for the application and browse to select the application pool created in PowerShell Web Access. Also enter the physical path to PowerShell Web Access, which is *C:\Windows\Web\PowerShellWebAccess\wwwroot*. Configure and check authentication by using the "Connect as" and "Test settings" buttons. Click OK.

You can remotely use PowerShell Web Access through a browser by entering the name of the computer PowerShell Web Access is installed on and the name of the PowerShell Web Access Application as a URL in a browser.

So, for this example, the machine name is DC1 and the PowerShell Web Access Application name is PSWA. After entering the URL *http://DC1/PSWA*, we get the logon screen shown in Figure 10-12.

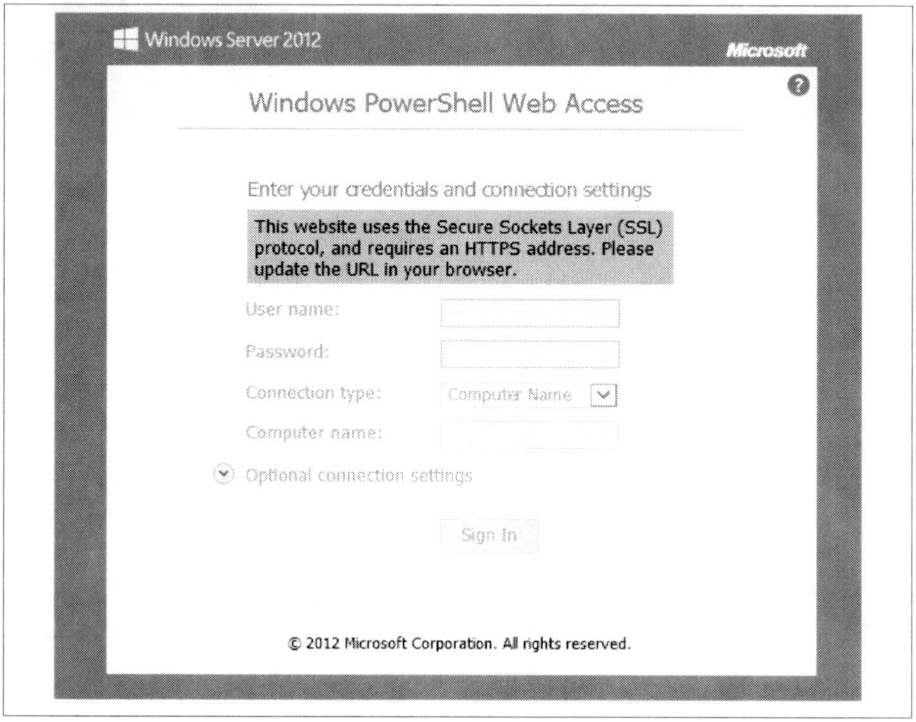

Figure 10-12. Windows PowerShell Web Access logon

5. Log in with the configured credentials, and you can start using PowerShell.

Security

Security in any technology is always challenging, because threats keep coming and they keep evolving. Microsoft has boosted some security features for the Windows Server operating system from Server 2008 R2. Many of the new security enhancements are designed to work with Windows 8 clients and in Windows domains, such as Dynamic Access Control (covered in Chapter 5).

For domain security, there are five new Group Policy settings available in Server 2012 that can be used for extra security:

Accounts: Block Microsoft accounts
> This option prevents a new Microsoft account from being added to a computer. In Group Policy, you can configure this feature by going to Windows Settings→Security Settings→Local Policies→Security Options.

Interactive logon: Machine account threshold
> This option can be configured to enable a computer lockout policy on system volumes that use BitLocker encryption. Enter a value between 1 and 999 to specify the number of failed logon attempts before the system is locked. This option is also found in Windows Settings→Security Settings→Local Policies→Security Options.

Interactive logon: Machine inactivity limit
> This option locks a session after a specified number of seconds of inactivity. The setting is located in Windows Settings→Security Settings→Local Policies→Security Options.

Microsoft network server: Attempt Service for user to self (S4U2Self) to obtain claim information
> Enable this setting to allow legacy Windows clients access to file shares on Server 2012 file servers that are configured with user claims as part of Dynamic Access Control. The setting is also found in Windows Settings→Security Settings→Local Policies→Security Options.

Packaged app rules
> This setting applies AppLocker rules to files that share attributes such as package name or version. AppLocker, introduced in Windows Server 2008 R2, allows you to set permissions on applications to define which users and groups can run those apps. Find this setting in Group Policy by clicking through Windows Settings→Security Settings→Application Control Policies→AppLocker.

BitLocker

BitLocker, which debuted in Windows 7 and Windows Server 2008 R2, also has new capabilities in Server 2012 that can be used with the Windows 8 client. BitLocker encrypts drive volumes using very strong AES (advanced encryption standard).

In Server 2012, you can install the BitLocker Drive Encryption feature through Server Manager. Once installed, BitLocker can be managed through the server's Control Panel. (See Figure 10-13.)

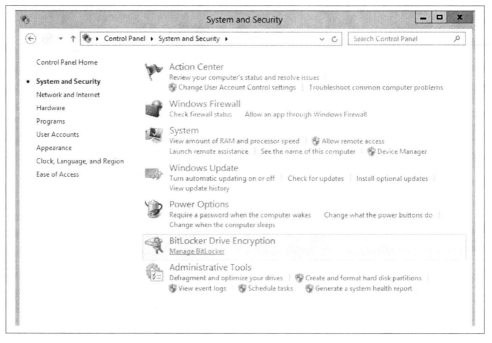

Figure 10-13. BitLocker Drive Encryption in Server 2012

You can use either a password or a smart card to unlock a drive. Once you select an option, you have to choose how to back up a recovery key. The choices are to save the key to a USB drive, save to a file, or print the recovery key.

As you go through the BitLocker Manager wizard in Server 2012, there's a new option. Before, you could encrypt only the entire volume. Now you can opt to encrypt only used space, which means faster encryption time. (See Figure 10-14.)

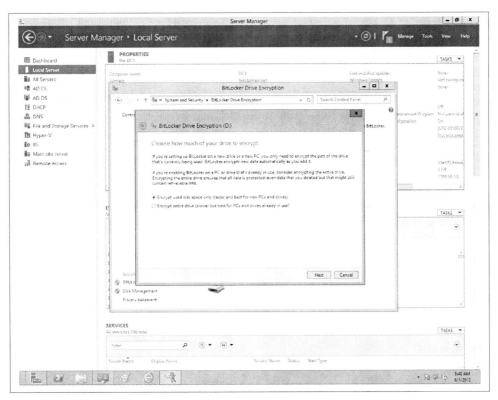

Figure 10-14. Encrypting only used disk space

Another new BitLocker feature is the ability to grant users permission to change their BitLocker PINs and passwords. This can cut down on a significant amount of calls to the helpdesk. To enable this feature, go to Group Policy and click through to Computer Configuration→Administrative Templates→Windows Components→BitLocker Drive Encryption→Operating System Drives. Disable the option for "Disallow standard users from changing the PIN or passwords."

Network Unlock is a new feature that automatically unlocks system volumes at reboot when they are connected to the corporate network. You can install this feature through "Add roles and features" in Server Manager.

Other Security Enhancements

Be aware that Server 2012 also has several under-the-hood security enhancements such as those with Kerberos, the protocol used for authentication, as well as additional security support for third-party security devices such as smart cards and biometric technology. If your organization has specific needs related to Kerberos or any third-party devices, there is information available in Microsoft's TechNet website that specifically addresses these capabilities in Server 2012.

There are also several add-ins Microsoft provides for administrators to assess the security of an infrastructure. Some of these tools include:

- Microsoft Security Assessment Tool 4.0 (*http://www.microsoft.com/en-us/down load/details.aspx?displaylang=en&id=12273*)
- Microsoft Baseline Security Analyzer 2.2 (*http://www.microsoft.com/en-us/down load/details.aspx?displaylang=en&id=7558*)
- Microsoft Security Compliance Manager (*http://www.microsoft.com/en-us/down load/details.aspx?displayLang=en&id=16776*)

Summary

Server 2012 is designed to scale far beyond the typical client/server infrastructure model that has been prevalent in datacenters for years, and to embrace newer technology trends such as cloud computing, the influx of mobile devices in corporate networks, and virtualization; thus, security and monitoring are vital to keep systems operational.

With the new Server Manager, a single console provides unified management of not just the physical servers deployed in an infrastructure, but other objects such as virtual machines and clusters. Server Manager's seamless integration with Event Viewer and its alerting capabilities enable you to perform quick and efficient troubleshooting and monitoring.

Besides the new security features that are readily apparent in Group Policy and BitLocker, Server 2012 as a platform has security enhancements that include authentication, managing users and files with Dynamic Access Control, and support for additional security hardware such as smart cards and fingerprint readers.

Index

We'd like to hear your suggestions for improving our indexes. Send email to index@oreilly.com.

CMAK (Connection Manager Administration Kit), 188
cmdlets (PowerShell), 4, 224
collections
    associating apps to, 212
    session, 210
Command Prompt icon, 45
Computer tile (Start screen), 42
Configure Cluster Quorum Wizard, 124
Configure Disk window, 139
Configure Networking screen, 140
Configure Self-Updating Options Wizard, 126
Configure Server Discovery window, 160
Connection Manager Administration Kit (CMAK), 188
consumerization of IT, 2, 202
content classification rules, 109–110
Control Panel
    accessing, 42, 45
    adding as shortcut to desktop, 47
    System Properties window, 74
copying virtual machines, 148
CPU throttling, 8
Create Cluster Wizard, 120
Create Group screen, 81
CredSSP authentication, 135
CSV (Cluster Shared Volume), 8, 118
CSV file format, 163, 170

D

DAC (Dynamic Access Control)
    about, 2, 93
    Access Denied Remediation feature, 94, 105–107
    auditing support, 107
    automatic file classification, 109–110
    building blocks of, 94
    creating central access rules, 99
    deploying, 96–105
    NTFS permissions and, 95
    predeployment pointers, 95
    requirements, 95
    security management, 4, 229
    server management, 4
    validating configuration, 102
    viewing effective permissions, 102
data center bridging (DCS), 180
Data Classification Toolkit, 95
data deduplication, 5

data execution prevention (DEP), 133
Datacenter edition (Windows Server 2012), 12, 133
date and time display, 43
dcpromo command
    about, 70
    Server Manager support, 3
DCS (data center bridging), 180
denial of service (DoS) attacks, 8, 186
DEP (data execution prevention), 133
Deployment Image Servicing and Management tool, 31
desktop
    accessing from Start screen, 42
    adding apps as shortcuts, 47
    customizing, 46–48
    Start menu distinction, 40, 44
Desktop Connections, 205
Desktop Experience feature, 25, 47
DHCP (Dynamic Host Configuration Protocol)
    about, 17
    IPAM and, 157–175
    server management, 3
differencing virtual disks, 138
differentiated services code point (DSCP), 180
DirectAccess
    about, 5, 185
    combining with RRAS, 185
    configuring, 189–195
    deploying, 188
    hardware requirements, 187
    installing, 189–195
Directory Services Restore Mode (DSRM), 72
Dism command, 29
Display window, 46
DNS (Domain Name System)
    about, 17
    DNSSEC support, 6
    IPAM and, 157–175
    server management, 3
DNSSEC (Domain Name System Security Extensions), 6
domain controllers (DCs)
    adding servers, 70
    adding to domains, 71
    changing, 84
    cloning virtual, 146–148
    configuring file servers, 102
    as global catalog servers, 72

About the Author

Samara Lynn has over fifteen years of experience in information technology, most recently as IT director at a major New York City healthcare facility. She is a lead networking and business analyst at *PCMag.com*. She has several technology certifications, a bachelor's degree from Brooklyn College, and was a technology editor for the CRN Test Center.

Colophon

The animal on the cover of *Windows Server 2012: Up and Running* is the Dorcas gazelle (*Gazella dorcas*), also known as the Ariel gazelle. This animal survives on vegetation in grassland, steppe, wadis, mountain desert, and semidesert climates of Africa and Arabia, and about 35,000 to 40,000 exist in the wild. The Dorcas gazelle is similar in appearance to, yet smaller than, the closely related mountain gazelle, although Dorcas have longer ears and more strongly curved horns.

Dorcas gazelles are highly adapted to the desert; they can go their entire lives without drinking, as they can get all the moisture they need from the plants in their diets, though they do drink when water is available. They feed on the flowers, leaves, and pods of Acacia trees in many of the areas they inhabit and are able to withstand high temperatures, but when it is very hot, they are active mainly at dawn, dusk, and during the night. When they feel threatened, they sound their alarm call, which sounds like barking. When chased, these gazelles use "stotting" (leaping straight up during pursuit by a predator) as a method to signal their fitness to the predator and warn other gazelles a predator is present. Dorcas gazelles are also able to run at speeds up to 50 to 60 miles per hour to escape danger.

The cover image is from Wood's *Animate Creations*. The cover font is Adobe ITC Garamond. The text font is Minion Pro by Robert Slimbach; the heading font is Myriad Pro by Robert Slimbach and Carol Twombly; and the code font is UbuntuMono by Dalton Maag.

Get even more for your money.

Join the O'Reilly Community, and register the O'Reilly books you own. It's free, and you'll get:

- $4.99 ebook upgrade offer
- 40% upgrade offer on O'Reilly print books
- Membership discounts on books and events
- Free lifetime updates to ebooks and videos
- Multiple ebook formats, DRM FREE
- Participation in the O'Reilly community
- Newsletters
- Account management
- 100% Satisfaction Guarantee

Signing up is easy:

1. **Go to: oreilly.com/go/register**
2. **Create an O'Reilly login.**
3. **Provide your address.**
4. **Register your books.**

Note: English-language books only

To order books online:
oreilly.com/store

For questions about products or an order:
orders@oreilly.com

To sign up to get topic-specific email announcements and/or news about upcoming books, conferences, special offers, and new technologies:
elists@oreilly.com

For technical questions about book content:
booktech@oreilly.com

To submit new book proposals to our editors:
proposals@oreilly.com

O'Reilly books are available in multiple DRM-free ebook formats. For more information:
oreilly.com/ebooks

Spreading the knowledge of innovators   **oreilly.com**

CPSIA information can be obtained at www.ICGtesting.com
Printed in the USA
BVOW051126111212

307885BV00002B/2/P